Children at War

Contemporary Classics of Children's Literature

Series Editor: Morag Styles

This exciting new series provides critical discussion of a range of contemporary classics of children's literature. The contributors are distinguished educationalists and academics from Britain, North America, Australia and elsewhere, as well as some of the foremost booksellers, literary journalists and librarians in the field. The work of leading authors and outstanding fictional texts for young people (popular as well as literary) are considered on a genre or thematic basis. The format for each book includes an in-depth introduction to the key characteristics of the genre, where major works and great precursors are examined, and significant issues and ideas raised by the genre are explored. The series will provide essential reading for those working on undergraduate and higher degrees in children's literature. It avoids jargon and is accessible to interested readers from parents, teachers and other professionals, to students and specialists in the field. Contemporary Classics of Children's Literature is a pioneering series, the first of its kind in Britain to give serious attention to the excellent writing produced for children in recent years.

Also available in the series:
Julia Eccleshare: *A Guide to the Harry Potter Novels*
Nikki Gamble and Nicholas Tucker: *Family Fictions*
Peter Hunt and Millicent Lenz: *Alternative Worlds in Fantasy Fiction*
Kimberley Reynolds, Geraldine Brennan and Kevin McCarron: *Frightening Fiction*

CHILDREN AT WAR

From the First World War to the Gulf

Kate Agnew and Geoff Fox

CONTINUUM
London and New York

Continuum

The Tower Building
11 York Road
London SE1 7NX

370 Lexington Avenue
New York
NY 10017–6503

www.continuumbooks.com

First published 2001

British Library Cataloguing-in-Publication Data

A catalogue record for this book is available from the British Library.

ISBN 0–8264–4849–6 (hardback)
      0–8264–4848–8 (paperback)

Typeset by YHT Ltd, London
Printed and bound in Great Britain by Creative Print and Design, Ebbw Vale, Wales

Contents

Introduction

This book is concerned with a fascinating and rapidly increasing body of literature for young readers: texts about the two world wars and their impact upon the United Kingdom, continental Europe and North America. We have not confined ourselves to novels written for children and young people, for it seemed to us that we should also consider autobiographies, popular fiction, comics, storypapers and picture books.

Chapter 1 provides an account of the treatment of war by writers and artists from the outbreak of World War I to the end of the century. We do not claim to offer an exhaustive survey but, through our discussion of selected literature produced in different periods, we trace the gradual shift – especially in the United Kingdom – from the cultural certainties of 1914 to the pluralism and ambiguities of 2000.

The remaining chapters focus more closely upon individual texts. Chapter 2 looks at literature about the First World War; Chapter 3 concentrates on the Second World War as experienced in the United Kingdom and North America; while Chapter 4 explores texts about the Second World War set on the European mainland. The books examined in these three chapters have, in some instances, remained in print for many years and achieved the status of modern classics, but most of the titles we have selected have been published in the last three decades of the twentieth century. Our purpose is to bring into closer focus books which we believe evoke a range of positive reactions among young readers; we have not been interested in using our space to point out the limitations of other books about war. Some of our chosen texts may intrigue or excite, some will inform, others may, in a productive sense, disturb.

Many of our texts draw upon an author's own memories, others are rooted in historical fact. The impact of these books frequently lies in the power of the events they describe, rather than in the manner of the telling; the experience of Auschwitz needs little elaboration. Consequently, we have quite often given some account of the narrative itself and allowed the texts to speak for themselves through quotation, since this seemed most useful for students, teachers, academics and parents who want to introduce this powerful field of literature to young readers.

KA & GF

CHAPTER 1

From the Great War to the Gulf: 1914–2000

A hoarse cheer came down from the relieving force on the hill, and the Germans, like the cowards that they were, turned to run. It was only a matter of two hundred British troops who had come to the relief of their comrades, but that was at least double what the gallant soldiers of the Kaiser would have faced. Five to one in their favour was about their mark.

The battle is not over yet, for the unscrupulous Germans hoist wounded Tommies onto their shoulders, forcing the pursuing British to hold their fire for fear of hitting the human shields. A corporal's bravery wins the day for our side. Racing after the Huns 'like a greyhound', ignoring a storm of bullets, he resorts to cold steel:

> On went the man with the corporal's stripes, then suddenly he turned, and his bayonet went neatly into the chest of the German who was carrying Bill Stubbs. The man's knees crumpled under him as if the bones had suddenly been removed from his legs, and the cockney ex-'bus-driver sat up, quite conscious now – sat up and laughed shrilly.

Bill Stubbs – 'the little cockney' as he is repeatedly called – is the hero of Claude Custer's complete story 'The Human Shields' from *The Dreadnought and War Pictorial*, 24 October 1914. Followers of the irrepressible Bill's exploits in this issue's adventure – he would be back next week in 'The Town of Trenches' – have seen him arrest and reform a burglar (none other than the corporal who saves his life), carry out running repairs on the propeller of an airship in mid-air under heavy fire, engage in some brisk hand-to-hand fighting, and fit in a spot of courting with his beloved Lil back home in Lewisham.

This is a story of certainties: the down-to-earth decencies of Britishers of all social classes; the patent cowardice of the wicked enemy; and a just cause – the defence of Britain and her Empire, its King and Queen, and especially its women and children. At the end of his adventures in this episode, there is talk of Bill being recommended for the Victoria Cross. ' "I don't want the blessed thing, only did my bit," the cockney ex-'bus-driver growled; then he grinned broadly. "Perhaps it might please Lil, though, if it ain't too big ter make into a brooch." ' Bill Stubbs exemplifies the courage of ordinary men in danger, their unwavering loyalty to their mates, and their unquestion-ing obedience to their all-wise officers, from dashing ex-public school subalterns to the battle-hardened Lord Kitchener. When Lil 'plaintively' asks ' "Why can't some of the other chaps go out instead of you?" ' since Bill has already 'done his bit', her fiancé replies:

> 'It ain't no good talkin' ole girl. You ain't been out there, or you'd know as Kitch. wants all the chaps 'e can get, even mugs like meself, what's only good for shovin' the ole transport 'buses along.'

The moral convictions of this story, typical of the many available to young readers during the 1914–1918 war, could hardly stand in greater contrast to the complex ambiguities of, say, Robert Westall's *Gulf* (1992) or Bernard Ashley's *Little Soldier* (1999). Between *The Dreadnought* and these titles lies almost a century of erosion of the moral high ground on which Bill Stubbs planted his cockney boots: the disenchantment and economic hardship which followed the war to end all wars; the growth of the Third Reich; a second, less jingoistic, world conflict with its subsequent revelations of genocide; and Hiroshima, Korea, Vietnam, the Falklands, the Gulf and the Balkans. And, scarcely more than rumours of war to North Americans and Europeans, the atrocities and struggles for freedom in Rwanda and East Timor.

The Great War, 1914–1918

Young readers of the boys' papers published before World War I by Lord Northciffe (the former Alfred Harmsworth) should not have been caught by surprise when hostilities broke out in the summer of 1914.

The Dreadnought had first been issued in 1912. Well before that, stories of the invasion of the British Isles were popular in adult as well as juvenile fiction – and in the early years of the century, distinctions between adult and juvenile literature were far less clear cut than today. No doubt young readers might well have borrowed their father's latest John Buchan, while the correspondence columns of *The Boy's Own Paper* demonstrate that some fathers remained avid readers of the magazine. Erskine Childers' *The Riddle of the Sands* suggested the likelihood of a German invasion upon an ill-prepared Britain as early as 1903, while William Le Queux's *The Invasion of 1910* was serialized in Lord Northcliffe's *Daily Mail* in 1906 prior to publication as a book. Stories of invasion and espionage regularly appeared between 1906 and 1914 in Northcliffe's weeklies – *Boys' Friend, Boys' Herald, Marvel, Magnet* and *Gem*. Sexton Blake himself was involved in the capture of several spies; on one adventure in France, he and his assistant Tinker pursued a French traitor escaping in a get-away plane. The spy opens fire on the unarmed Blake, who is forced to ram his opponent in mid-air. On another occasion, as Cadogan and Craig note, Blake prevented the escape of the Kaiser, who clambers onto the roof of a train travelling from Liverpool to London ('"Hardly a comfortable way of travelling, sire!" calls out Sexton Blake, nonchalant as ever').[1]

Young readers were also warned by the immensely popular 'Herbert Strang' (the pen name of G. Herbert Ely and C. J. L'Estrange):

> The race will still be to the swift and the battle to the strong ... but the speed and strength that will win the great struggles of the future must be the fruit of long and patient training. Our natural genius for making good lost ground by spasmodic effort is likely to avail us less and less as time goes on. Organisation must be our watchword.
> (from *The Air Scout: A Story of National Defence*, 1912)[2]

Despite such warnings to both adults and children of the unpreparedness of Britain and the malign intent of the Germans, literature for young readers was pervaded by a sense of confident aggression, especially in stories for boys. The best-known proponent of the invincible Empire is G. A. Henty (1832–1902); he wrote some 100 books, regularly achieving sales of 150,000 copies for each edition. Many of his titles were still on the shelves of public libraries long after the Second World War; and, as late as 1977, Foulsham thought it worth republishing four of his adventure stories, noting that 'This book has been carefully edited and slightly abridged to meet the reading tastes of the Modern Boy'. W. H. G. Kingston (1814–1880) wrote 130 books, including a series of nautical adventures involving 'The Three Midshipmen'. Like Henty and Kingston, Gordon Stables (1840–1910) serialized his novels in popular magazines such as *The Boy's Own Paper* and *The Captain*. For nine years, Stables served as a surgeon in the Royal Navy, and titles such as *How Jack Mackenzie Won His Epaulettes: A Story of the Crimean War* (1896) or *From Slum to Quarterdeck* (1909) imply the tenor of his work.

Tales of derring-do in remote corners of the Empire, where British decency, pluck and integrity triumphed over all opposition, proliferated in novels and storypapers. Their only rivals in popularity were stories set in fictional or actual public schools, which in their way also contributed to a confident stance towards any possibility of war.[3] From epic encounters on the playing fields of Eton or Greyfriars, it was a natural progression to exchange cricket flannels or footer kit for army or naval uniform. In one of the most enduring of those stories, H. A. Vachell's *The Hill* (1905), the golden youth 'Caesar' Desmond, on the eve of the assault on 'a small hill' in the Boer War, writes to his friend John Verney back in England. Desmond rests secure in the knowledge that all he has learned at Harrow (standing proud on the top of 'The Hill') has equipped him fully for the fight.

> Tomorrow, I shall get up the hill here faster and easier than the other fellows because you and I have so often run up our Hill together – God bless it!

Desmond dies in the battle, racing ahead of his men. Service to School, to Empire and to God are indivisible and beyond questioning; a death in such a cause is a glorious consummation. In chapel, the Head Master celebrates the death of the young officer:

> 'To die young, clean, ardent; to die swiftly, in perfect health; to die saving others from death or, worse, disgrace; to die scaling heights … It stands for all we venerate and slave for: loyalty, honour, purity, strenuousness, faithfulness in friendship.'

The Hill remained in print until 1985, and its influence was widespread. The archives of its publisher, John Murray, show that large numbers were sold in Australia, where the book was on the prescribed reading list for all 15-year-olds in New South Wales in the early 1920s.

One of the best-known expressions of the link between the disciplines of sport and soldiering is Sir Henry Newbolt's 'Vitaï Lampada' (1893). From the 'breathless hush in the Close tonight' where the resolve of the last man in is stiffened by his Captain's hand on his shoulder, it is only a short military step to,

> The sand of the desert is sodden red, –
> Red with the wreck of a square that broke;–
> The Gatling's jammed and the Colonel dead,
> And the Regiment blind with dust and smoke.

But 'the voice of a schoolboy rallies the ranks' echoing the words of his cricket captain that evening in the Close, 'Play up! play up! and play the game!' Cricketing metaphors remain embedded in the language of the English facing difficult odds: ('keeping a straight bat', 'on a sticky wicket'). Jessie Pope, whose patriotic verses were regularly published in *The Daily Mail*, saw the war in mainland Europe as a testing Away Fixture:

> Where are those hefty sporting lads
> Who donned the flannels, gloves and pads?
> They play a new and deadly game
> Where thunder bursts in crash and flame.
> Our cricketers have gone 'on tour',
> To make their country's triumph sure.
> They'll take the Kaiser's middle wicket
> And smash it by clean British cricket.[4]

The early drafts of Wilfred Owen's 'Dulce et Decorum Est . . . ' with its agonized reality of a gas attack set against the supposed glory of dying for one's country, were headed, 'To Jessie Pope'.

In 1915, W. T. A. Beare, a prominent Rugby Football administrator, told the readers of *The Boy's Own Paper*:

> War is the serious, vital thing of which all our games of antagonistics are but imitations: imitations designed in part by way of amusement and recreation, but also essentially as part of the process for preparing the individual as a mode of training and hardening him, for the real, grim business of warfare.[5]

Public school stories were read not only by boys attending such schools themselves. In *The Classic Slum* (1971), Robert Roberts records the excitement with which he and his friends in Salford devoured *The Gem* each week, even modelling their behaviour on Frank Richards' Famous Five. Fellows' sisters were invited by editors to share such adventures, although girls often appeared in the stories merely to decorate the boundaries at cricket matches. The shelves of second-hand bookshops in the present day may well contain boys' school stories or tales of

Empire inscribed to girls (often from their mothers), or highly coloured prize bookplates commending the recipient for regular attendance at Sunday Schools, often in the poorer districts of industrial cities.

Once hostilities began, it was not long before the editors of storypapers and novels encouraged boys to fight the good fight on foreign fields when their time came. For their part, girls were exhorted to challenge boys to do their duty by enlisting (conscription did not begin until 1916). Jessie Pope blithely writes of Rose, a girl who finds she can respect only those willing to serve King and Country:

> The lad whose troth with Rose would plight,
> Nor apprehend rejection,
> Must be in shabby khaki dight,
> To compass her affection.
> Who buys her an engagement ring
> And finds her kind and kissing,
> Must have one member in a sling
> Or, preferably, missing.
>
> (from 'The Beau Ideal' in *The Daily Mail* 1915)[6]

Equally inspiriting verses were regularly to be found in the storypapers and magazines for young readers. Poems which explored the notion that British and German soldiers shared a common humanity, such as those by Sassoon and Owen, were either not published until after the war or not introduced to children through their books and magazines.

Readers of *The Boy's Own Paper*, distributed wherever the map of the world was coloured pink, would have met John Lea's 'The Drum' in 1915:

> Mother of Nations, east and west,
> We gladly, proudly, give our best
> To follow afar through pain and woe
> The freest flag the world can show.
> We hear the call of the Empire's Drum!
> Mother of Nations, see! – we come!

Or, in 1917, they could share the sentiments of GRS's poem, 'Jimmy',

> Jimmy's just the jolliest sport
> One could wish to see!
> Golden conquests lie before him
> Where's the Hun that dare ignore him?
> Here's his health! for we adore him,
> Jimmy – RFC!

At the time, the life expectancy of a Royal Flying Corps pilot at the front was no more than three weeks.

Among the novelists, Captain (later Lieutenant-Colonel) F. S. Brereton was probably the most prolific and the most popular. Brereton was already a very successful writer for boys. He was a veteran of the Boer War and his accounts of the Great War may have been coloured more by an old soldier's memories than the realities of the trenches. He took his young readers into battle in *Under Haig in Flanders, With Joffre at Verdun, With Allenby in Palestine* ('A Story of the Latest Crusade'), *With French at the Front, Under Foch's Command*, and on several other expeditions in handsome volumes with decorated pictorial cloth covers and full plate illustrations. He put those readers ashore on the beaches of Gallipoli in *At Grips with the Turk*, providing a map for their better appreciation of tactics. Brereton had no doubts about maintaining the social order under fire. When Midshipman Derek Smallweed, fresh from 'a couple of terms at Dartmouth', steers his pinnace ashore, he is devotedly supported by Jack Barnsby, an old tar who had sailed under Admiral Smallweed, Derek's father:

> ''Cos I knew 'is dad,' [Jack] would whisper hoarsely to his messmates. ''Im – that's Mr Smallweed – 'is father, the Admiral, you know, and me sailed along in company many a time; that we did.'

Derek's pinnace lands many of the Australian and New Zealand troops ('a magnificent set of men they looked, well set-up and sturdy to a degree') and no doubt Brereton sold well throughout the Empire. Bullets may 'bizz' by, but they will not find our heroes' hearts in this novel:

> 'Ah! Hurt, Barnsby?'
> 'Not me, sir, thank 'ee. Just a rap over the head from one of their shrapnel bullets.'

Brereton was not the only serving officer to write for young readers during the war. Captain Charles Gilson fought in the Boer War and served in the Naval Division at Antwerp in the Great War, being mentioned in despatches, though Lofts and Adley tell us 'much of his work was done in bed, as he was more or less an invalid through ill health and war experiences'.[7] A sample of the captions to the illustrations in *A Motor Scout in Flanders* (undated) catches the spirit of his work: '"Mate," said Sharp, "Kombiang de kilomeat a Paree?"'; 'The young Englishman drew back his fist and struck'; and '"Mademoiselle, I give you fair warning. If you ring that bell, though I love you – I will shoot."' In the last instance, wasp-waisted Desirée

D'Avignon, confronted by the levelled revolver of a German spy in Belgian uniform, observes with admirable *sang-froid*: ' "You must admit that the present time is not very suitable for love-making. Our nations, monsieur, are at war." '

Captain Frank H. Shaw traded on his pre-war popularity as a novelist with the readers of *Chums* to urge them to enlist. His tone is that of the quietly persuasive clergyman looking for help in running a table-tennis evening:

> So I wondered tonight if there were any old-time Chums, men of eighteen and upwards, who hadn't yet answered the call for men; and thinking of this made me decide to ask any who hadn't yet volunteered – not many I'll wager, of the old CHUMS breed – if they would come along and help me make the Kite-Balloon Section of the Royal Flying Corps the most loyal and forthright part of the Army.[8]

Loyalty and forthrightness were also the watchwords of Percy F. Westerman, whose first novel appeared in 1909 (he published his last in 1958). He was perhaps the most blatantly chauvinistic of the novelists for boys. He made few distinctions between foreigners: 'What else would you expect from Belgians ... didn't they skedaddle at Waterloo and almost let our fellows down?'; 'the South American habit of procrastination ... '; 'a general, swarthy and heavy jowled, who scowled under his heavy eyebrows at the crowd as he rode by. He was the personification of German brute force, a stiffly rigid figure in grey.'[9]

Novels and storypapers alike had no compunction about whipping up hatred against the Germans, most famously in suggesting that German troops habitually supplemented their rations by eating babies. *The Boys' Friend*, 19 September 1914, is packed with war stories. After the opening episode of 'The Mailed Fist or A World At War' by John Tregellis (the author is pictured in a minute grainy photograph 'on his Hunter'), readers could enjoy 'The Prussian Butchers, A Complete Tale Telling How a Britisher Fell a Victim to the German Atrocities and Was Avenged by His Brother'. The illustration depicts Steel, a cool Britisher in plus-fours facing a firing squad of pickel-helmeted Germans. The officer in charge, the evil Colonel von Taal, is a Uhlan – one of the Prussian Cavalry whose sadism was portrayed in British literature as the most vile of all. Von Taal meets a well-deserved fate in the closing paragraphs, the sword of Steel's brother through his heart.

John Buchan's *Greenmantle* (1916) is a tale which must have offered many pleasures to those with an appetite for British daring. Buchan's hero of *The Thirty Nine Steps* (1915), Richard Hannay, now finds himself despatched on a spying mission to put a stop to a dangerous Islamic Jehad in Turkey, led by a mysterious prophet, Greenmantle. Without hesitation he travels by the direct route – through enemy Germany, meeting a sinister opponent in the Prussian Stumm, 'a man who had a fashion for frippery, who had a perverted taste for soft, delicate things ... I began to see the queer other side to my host, that evil side which gossip had spoken of as not unknown in the German army. The room seemed a horribly unwholesome place'. As if that were not enough, Hannay is also up against the seductively dangerous Hilda von Einem. At one point Hannay finds himself sharing a car with her. Hannay is petrified: 'Women had never come much my way, and I knew about as much of their ways as I knew about the Chinese language ... I had never been in a motor car with a lady before, and I felt like a fish on a dry sandbank.'

Only Sandy Arbuthnot, Hannay's staunch friend, is a match for Frau von Einem. Sandy is one of a long line of fictional British adventurers who, given a moment or two, can disguise themselves impenetrably as anyone from an Afghan beggar to a Russian aristocrat, and are fluent in numerous languages (no doubt including Chinese). In a splendidly theatrical climax to the novel, Hilda bids Sandy join her in her misguided crusade: ' "You are my household in spirit, and you alone of all men I have seen are fit to ride with me on my mission." ' Hannay's cheeks turn scarlet with embarrassment at this show of emotion, and he has to turn aside. Sandy does not flinch, despite the fascination the woman exerts over him: ' "You can offer me nothing that I desire," he said, "I am the servant of my country, and her enemies are mine." '

The novel concludes with a thunderous battle on a Turkish hillside ending, to the surprise of no one, in the successful accomplishment of Hannay's task and the deaths of Britain's enemies.

Many of the stories for girls produced during the war were conservative in tone, urging girls and women to support their menfolk, to set aside the talk of independence and feminism of pre-war days. *The Girl's Own Paper* (which aimed at a rather older age group than its male counterpart) offered the following advice from the Duchess of Albany: 'We must learn to be heroic, to be calm, and of good courage and to remain in the place where God has placed us, and to do our duty there.'[10]

However, not all of the heroines of fiction adopted such passive attitudes. Brenda Girvin's *Munition Mary* (1918) unmasked no fewer than four enemy agents (a hotel matron, a factory canteen manageress, a bench hand and a maid). In the end, though, Mary cannot quite keep things up: 'Suddenly, she felt she was just a weak girl with no self-control or courage left. She sank down in a chair and burst into a flood of tears.'[11] Bessie Marchant (1862–1941) author of some 150 books in a writing career of 48 years[12] wrote stories set in exotic locations, often featuring independent and active heroines. Her books with wartime settings, all published during the war years, featured a munitions worker, a nurse in the Voluntary Aid Detachment (VAD), and a Transport Girl. Adventurous though her characters were, they sometimes subsided into more traditional behaviour. '"My word, I'd be grateful for the privilege of blacking his boots!" says Gwen in *A Transport Girl in France* (1918). "Oh, I know it sounds silly, but girls are made that way! Hero worship is just a necessity to us."'[13]

Girls play more resolute parts in a book with many full colour plates and black and white illustrations for younger children, *Brave Boys and Girls in Wartime* (1918) by John Lea, whom we have met previously (p 8) as one of the patriotic poets of *The Boy's Own Paper*. The illustrations are by the eminent artists, H. M. Brock and G. Browne. Madeleine, 'a little French peasant girl', takes coffee to the English soldiers each morning in the trenches, chattering 'in a friendly way, though only a few could understand what she said'. Marusia Charushina, a young Russian girl, travels 1000 miles to work for the Red Cross close to the front line. Doris Walton, dying from a shrapnel wound, sees that the two Canadian soldiers who have carried her to the hospital have also been wounded: '"I must kiss you both, because I see you have both suffered."' A Belgian girl secretly aids a party of wounded soldiers, caught behind enemy lines. A girl at a London railway terminal leaves her elegant mother's side to carry an exhausted soldier's kit, while another rescues her baby sister from a burning home. Other stories tell of boys in action with the troops as messengers, scouts and buglers. A French Boy Scout, tied to a tree, faces a firing squad, still refusing to give information that would betray his regiment; 'He died, faithful unto Death.'

Surprisingly, this text for younger readers is more direct in its account of death and injury than the tight-lipped prose of Brereton or Westerman, even if the author's dialogue is less than convincing. A young boy attached to the Connaught Rangers determines to bring refreshment to a wounded infantryman. Out in No Man's Land, between the lines, there is an apple-tree, laden with fruit:

'I will go!' cried the boy. 'I will make a dash across the open ground, and do my best to get back safely.'

But when less than 50 steps from safety, he fell dead to the ground his brave heart pierced by more than one German bullet.

One of his adult comrades, inspired by the boy's example, goes out for the apple still grasped in the boy's hand. 'Though wounded in turn, [he] brought to the suffering man the apple for which the boy had paid with his life.'

Another picture book for the very young concentrated on the part played by *Animals at War* (Frank Hart, undated). Here the creatures facing frightening experiences in battle are usually personified – 'a good sheep dog is a trusted and responsible person'. This description of mules and their masters transporting ammunition is typical:

> Covered often to the ears with mud, maddened by noise and fumes from gas and shell, whipped and stung by driving rain and icy sleet, it is one long aching toil for man and beast, quite apart from the danger of being killed or wounded.

Walter A. Dyer also wrote about an animal caught up in the war in his short novel, *Pierrot, Dog of Belgium* (1915). Pierrot is descended from the boarhounds of the Dukes of Brabant, but his breed was used in Belgium in the early years of the century as working dogs and Pierrot's task is to pull a small milk-cart. When war comes, he is appropriated by the army to pull a machine-gun mounted on two bicycle wheels, in harness with a second dog.

The novel is detailed in its account of Pierrot's frightening experiences as he races about the battlefields, then stands quietly in the traces while his master fires the gun. Eventually, when Pierrot sees his team-mate bayoneted, he attacks the German killer:

> Unreasoning rage seized Pierrot, and with what remained of his once agile strength he leaped at the man's throat and sank his fangs into the flesh. The soldier dropped his rifle, and grasping Pierrot in his strong hands sought to choke him and force him off. But the dog was crazed and blind with rage and insensible to pain. He felt the tearing of the man's neck muscles between his jaws and he tasted the hot blood. Then the man's grip relaxed and he fell backward.

For all the detail of the carnage, Dyer's foreword to the book is sententious:

> Belgium lies bleeding.
> Across her level, lush meadows the harsh-shod hosts of war have marched. Beside her peaceful waters the sons of God have spilled each other's blood. Beneath her noble trees have raged the fires of human hate ...

Belgium lies moaning . . .

And amid the cries of anguish and despair there have come to me the weeping of a little girl named Lisa and the voice of a faithful dog whining for his master.

In the texts of these three books for younger readers, however, there is a recognition of the physical misery and peril of those embroiled in the war not found in books for older readers. As Chapter 2 illustrates, a less romanticized and more ambivalent treatment of the war was not to be provided for younger readers until the last three decades of the century.

1919–1939

In the years following the Armistice of 11 November 1918, novels and storypapers for boys refought old battles by land, sea and air. Only four years later, the Amalgamated Press's *Champion* even ran a serial in which World War II was declared in 1962. Once again, the frightful Boches were the aggressors, hurling radio-controlled aerial torpedoes at major British cities as a prelude to an invasion in which they mercilessly deployed lethal inventions such as a green ray and a red gas.

But there was plenty of material to be mined from the immediate past without venturing into fantasy, and writers such as Percy F. Westerman, Charles Gilson and Rowland Walker kept an eager market well supplied. It was the war in the air which had a particularly glamorous appeal to readers. As early as 1915, the rather pedestrian *Heroes of the Flying Corps* had appeared. Its authors were C. Grahame-White and Harry Harper, who produced at least six further books about aerial warfare. Here they collected accounts of the 'exploits of individual aviators, using official and unofficial evidence' – evenhandedly including the courageous deeds of German airmen as well as those of our own side, for aviators were seen as sportsmen, chivalric knights of the air, never stooping to the beastliness of the Uhlan. This 350-page volume is most notable for three dramatic colour plates by the well-known artist Cyrus Cuneo, showing daring attacks by aircraft on a German armoured car whose terrified occupants are leaping out of the doomed vehicle; a raid on an airship shed guarded by a balloon carrying German riflemen; and a zeppelin caught in the crossed rays of searchlights.

In 1919, Westerman published *Winning His Wings: A Story of the RAF*, in which his hero Derek Daventry progresses from being a cadet at Training School to aerial combat and an eventual DSO in the war. Rowland Walker had served in the RFC and in the newly established

RAF. His *Deville McKeene: The Exploits of the Mystery Airman* is prefaced with a poem in praise of the eponymous hero, a veritable Scarlet Pimpernel of the Western Front:

'And what did ye do,
　　Deville McKeene,
　　What did ye to the Hun?'
'I bombed his bridges, his billets, and dumps,
　　I showed him that Britain
　　Held the Ace and the Trumps.'
And he laughed, I ween, did
　　Deville McKeene,
As he spiralled down from the azure blue
　　And taxied home in the old B.2.

McKeene is a perpetual thorn in the side of Von Richthofen, the real life German pilot known as the Red Baron, and his 'circus' of aviators:

'Deville McKeene,' whispered the [pilot], mentioning for the first time that evening the hated name of the British ace, the man of mystery – the super-airman of the Western front. He it was who went hither and thither, reading the riddle of the Western front, just as Oedipus read the riddle of the Sphinx four thousand years ago.

McKeene is everywhere – a blood brother to John Buchan's Sandy Arbuthnot, 'capable of carrying out half a score of disguises successfully, speaking half a dozen languages fluently'. He has escaped detection while serving 'in the ranks of the Kaiser's legions', working under Von Richthofen's aristocratic nose as an air mechanic in the German Flying Corps. 'The true Briton is still a hero-worshipper,' comments the author in mid-text, 'but he loves his hero to be a man of mystery, seldom mixing with his fellows, passing like a meteor in their midst, always cool and collected, but capable of the most daring and thrilling deeds.' McKeene even maintains his anonymity when on home soil, posing, like some parody of T. E. Lawrence, as the imbecilic Third-Class Air Mechanic, Winckles.

In a collection of *Stories of the Great War*, published in 1929 and immediately reprinted, Walker wrote to a similar recipe in a tale entitled *The Mystery Airman*. Our hero Jake Langford shoots down the Hun after a desperate dogfight, lands and 'races to the help of the German Ace'. ' "You fought magnificently, Red Devil!" shouted Jake as he dashed with outstretched hand towards the German.' Only then does Jake realize that his dying opponent is none other than Carl, his greatest chum at his public school.

Dennis Butts writes of the development of flying stories as 'a minor literary genre' which perhaps reached its zenith in the 1930s with the emergence of a hero who dominated war fiction for young readers for more than thirty years and is still flying today.[14] James Bigglesworth, known to generations of young readers as 'Biggles', flew and fought in both world wars and in countless skirmishes around the globe between and after those wars.

Before Biggles first took to the air in 1932, however, there were two notable fictional returns to the battlefields of World War I. Among enthusiasts for the period, Ernest Raymond's *Tell England* (1922) has received considerable critical attention;[15] the second book, Rudolf Frank's *No Hero for the Kaiser*, has endured such a turbulent publishing history since it first appeared in 1931 that it seems to be little known and less discussed by commentators writing in English.

It is safe to assume that *Tell England* was one of those books which young readers, of both genders, claimed, even though it was not published on children's lists and would not sit comfortably on the shelf alongside Brereton or Westerman, or even among the school stories which developed so strongly during the 1920s. However, it is both school story and war story – a distinguished descendant in the Newbolt tradition of 'Vitaï Lampada' where a school uniform is exchanged for that of a soldier. Its success was immediate. The novel had reprinted fourteen times before the end of 1922. By 1939, it had sold 300,000 copies and been made into a film (in 1931) directed by Anthony Asquith and Geoffrey Barkas. In 1965, it went into its fortieth edition.

A brief account of the book must suffice. The first half describes the growth of a powerful friendship between two boys, Doe and Ray at Kensingtowe School ('of course, the finest school in England'). During the final cricket match in which the boys are playing, news comes through of the assassination of the Archduke Franz Ferdinand in Sarajevo. The boys are swiftly kitted out in their subalterns' uniforms and on their way to the Gallipoli beaches. Here they are both to die, but Edgar Doe's attitude to death is one that most boys' writers, and indeed most boys, would never have dreamed of:

> 'If I'd never known the shock of seeing sudden death at my side, I'd have missed a terribly wonderful thing ... I'd never have known what it is to have my soul drawn out of me by the maddening excitement of an intensive bombardment. And – and, *que voulez-vous*, I have *killed*!'

This is too much for the more earthbound Ray, who is the narrator of the plot until the closing chapters:

'Hm!' muttered I. He was too clever for me, but I loved him in his scintillating moments.

'*Tiens*, if I'm knocked out, it's at least the most wonderful death. It's the *deepest* death.'

Doe dies in a single-handed assault on a whizz-bang emplacement. As Ray grieves for his friend, the lugubrious (and tedious) Padre Monty tells him:

'And your friendship is a more beautiful whole, as things are ... the war has held you in a deepening intimacy till – till the end. It's – it's perfect.'

Wilfred Owen also wrote, with less sentimentality, of the bonds between comrades-in-arms:

I have made fellowships,
Untold of happy lovers in old song.

For him, this love was bound 'with war's hard wire'.

The love between Ray and Doe is charged with a powerful sexuality. *Tell England* is perhaps the most notable expression of the 'David and Jonathan' relationships which occur in both school and war stories in the first quarter of the century – a love between comrades-in-arms which, since it cannot be consummated, reaches its perfection only in death. This is not so much the love which dare not speak its name as the love described in 2 Samuel 1 as passing the love of women (though love for one's mother runs it close in this novel). Some 46 years later, in the first volume of his autobiography (*The Story of My Days*, 1968) Ernest Raymond wrote of the book's 'indubitable but wholly unconscious homosexuality ... a word which – absurd as this may seem now – I had never heard'.

Raymond wrote the early drafts of his book in army notebooks while on active service in Gallipoli, where he served as a chaplain. Padre Monty must be something of Raymond's persona, given the coy fusion of the two narrators' names, Ray and Monty (who completes the story after Ray's death). Ray's description is graphic as he leads his men over the top:

With an agony in my wrist, I snatched at his rifle and, wrenching the bayonet free, stabbed him savagely with his own weapon, tearing it away as he dropped ... My fist shot out towards [the Turkish officer's] chin as an automatic action of self-defence, and the bayonet ... passed like a pin right through the man's throat. His blood spurted over my hand and ran up my arm, as he dropped forward, bearing me down under him.

'Hurt, sir?' asked the sergeant-major, kindly.

The clipped sentences capture the speed and the confusion, the sense that actions race ahead of thought, until Ray is borne down by the weight of his enemy.

For all the blood, it is the perfection of the heroes' deaths which Raymond thought fascinating; perhaps his thousands of readers in the 1920s found a rationalization here for the slaughter of a generation. In meeting their deaths in battle, Raymond seems to say, these young men are translated beyond the mud of the trenches – they are for ever the golden youths of the sports field.

Despite its huge and enduring popularity, Raymond's novel was dismissed by some of the critics of its time. '*Tell England* is apparently by a rather illiterate and commonplace sentimentalist – the book has no beauty, and its silliness and bad taste are not the work of a writer,' wrote Rose Macauley; while in a radio broadcast, Frances Birrell called the novel, 'the most nauseating book to come out of the war'.

Rudolf Frank's *No Hero for the Kaiser* tells a different story. Frank was born in Mainz in 1886. He served in the German Artillery in 1914 and subsequently became a military correspondent. Frank described his novel, much acclaimed on its publication in Germany in 1931, as 'an anti-war novel to warn young people'. Two years later, on 10 May 1933, it was banned and publicly burned by the Third Reich, and its author was arrested. When released from prison, he fled to Switzerland where he lived until his death in 1979. In the late 1970s, the book was republished in Germany where it was awarded three prizes within two years. Patricia Crampton's admirable English translation was not published in New York until 1986. It seems incredible that the book has not made a greater impression in schools, for it is a powerfully moving story in its universality and its bitter complaint against the cruel impact of war upon ordinary people.

Fourteen-year-old Jan Kubitzky lives in the Polish village of Kopchovka. His country is yet again reduced to a battlefield, fought over by the Russian and German armies. As the Russians are driven eastwards, and Jan's village is razed to rubble and his parents killed, the boy and his dog are taken along by a unit of German soldiers.

These men have no sense of their superiors' objectives in the war – if indeed there are any. Their goal is simply to survive the war, the weather, the lack of food, the pain of absence from their homes, the idiocy of their orders, the stupidity and corruption of most of their upper-caste officers.

Neither side is in the right, neither side is in the wrong. The deaths of their enemies are a cause for horrified grief just as much as the deaths of their comrades:

> everything was still there: weapons, helmets, caps, sabres lay in wild confusion on the edges of the ditch; eating implements, clothing, boots, spades, and bloodstained dressings. And in the ditch and in the holes made by the grenades, great God, there they all were. The men were there, brown and grey like the earth and rubble, crumpled or stretched out in dust, blood, and dirt. Men's faces gaped, human trunks stuck out of the ground like tree stumps, human arms and legs lay like hacked branches, human hands and fingers grew out of the earth like plants. This was the field they had dug and planted; this was the harvest that had sprung from the seed of their bullets, filling the whole ditch.

An advance is no more significant than a retreat. Promotion and honours are meaningless to the men, and far too important to the officers.

> [Jan] ... heard the general's speech, but although he was standing quite near the front and von der Aue spoke very loudly, he did not understand much of the long discourse. The powerful voice spoke of laurels, fame, the flag, the fatherland. And the importance of holding out.
> 'Holding out. How do you do that?' Jan whispered to Lance Corporal Cordes, standing beside him.
> 'Holding tight, holding you tongue, and holding the fort, that's holding out,' said Cordes.

Frequently, the author interposes a brief comment about the self-deluding arrogance of the Kaiser or the folly of military life in general:

> In the Army everyone wears a uniform – everyone, from simple gunners and infantrymen to generals and field marshals. The word *uniform* means equal, alike all over, but like so many military words this word, too, is something of a deception. Speaking plainly: it is a lie.

Jan proves invaluable to the battery. He has an extraordinary skill as a guide, a warning nose for danger, so that even the officers value him highly. In the end, after the soldiers have slogged aimlessly this way and that across Poland through all weathers, the Army decides to turn Jan into an icon, 'a German Maid of Orleans'. A grand parade is organized to be inspected by the Kaiser himself. Questions are rehearsed ('Have you any children? What are their names?'), cheers are practised. Jan is to be made a German national and formally enrolled in the army. On the morning of the parade, men and officers, cameramen and war artists await His Imperial Majesty the Supreme Commander. Jan fails to turn up. With his dog, he has 'disappeared into the darkness', to become a figure of myth, never to be heard of again. The officers are outraged, but one of the men says,

> 'He always showed us the right way, always the right way ... I believe he's done the same thing this time ... Not only us, them over there too, the *poilus* and the Tommies ... everyone, the whole world.'

'I don't get it,' said Hottenrot, pulling off his uniform.

No Hero for the Kaiser appeared two years after Erich Maria Remarque's *All Quiet on the Western Front*; it makes as poignant a statement about the destructiveness of war from a German perspective. It has the economy of a ballad, and in its episodic narrative and its satire, which is both comic and sharp-edged, it has much in common with Bertolt Brecht's *Mother Courage* (1938/39). (Frank had met Brecht in the 1920s and worked in theatre as a director.) Characters come and go – no sooner do we know them, than the war takes them. There is also, in the comic creation of a wandering hero with a clear-sighted sanity among so much folly, a kinship with Jaroslav Hasek's *Good Soldier Schweik* (1921), which was translated into German from Czech in 1926 and which Brecht helped to stage as a musical drama in 1928.

No Hero for the Kaiser could make a powerful impression upon some young readers – not only for its message, but because it is quite particularly *not* a British book. The authorial stance, the humour, the pace and the scope of the book belong to a landscape which knows what it is to be occupied and fought over.

On the other side of the North Sea, British writers for young readers were making no similar protests. Such was the interest in the war in the air that periodicals such as *Popular Flying* and *Flying* (both edited by W. E. Johns) and *Modern Boy* were packed with fiction and information to satisfy an eager interest in anything to do with civil or military flying. Only just before the Second World War broke out, George E. Rochester was spinning another yarn about the Great War in 'The Poison Train' in *Modern Boy*: 'With its deadly load of poison gas, the German ammunition train thunders towards the Front Line. Can SCOTTY of the SECRET SQUADRON stop it?' He certainly can, and in the accompanying illustration, Scotty pits his black-winged

DH9 biplane in aerial combat against a hurtling Fokker only feet above the gaping infantrymen in the trenches below.

Earlier in the decade, in the same storypaper, Captain W. E. Johns (then claiming only the rank of Flying Officer) was thrilling his readers with the exploits of Biggles. In his earliest adventures, Biggles was a young RFC pilot, as Johns himself had been after service as a soldier at Gallipoli. Having been shot down, Johns ended the war in a prisoner-of-war camp, but he returned to serve in the post-war RAF until 1927.

Close readers of the Biggles canon (usually reckoned at some 96 titles) agree that the early incarnations of the hero were the most interesting. The 17-year-old Biggles arrives at Flying Training School in Norfolk in 1916:

> There was nothing remarkable, or even martial about his physique: on the contrary, he was slim, rather below average height, and delicate-looking. A wisp of fair hair protruded from one side of his rakishly tilted RFC cap; his eyes, now sparkling with pleasurable anticipation, were what is usually called hazel. His features were finely cut, but the squareness of his chin and the firm line of his mouth revealed a certain doggedness, a tenacity of purpose, that denied any suggestion of weakness. Only his hands were small and white, and might have been those of a girl.
>
> (from *Biggles Learns to Fly*, 1935)

In later years, those girlish hands were to prove more than a match for any number of (invariably foreign) opponents: Biggles preferred the straight right to the revolver. The mature Biggles was always obedient to his superiors (Air Commodore Raymond's word was law) and unquestioning in his antagonism to the enemies of his country. In his early days, however, he is so disturbed by his experience of a dogfight that he is sent home on leave to avoid a breakdown. In a story entitled 'Affaire de Coeur' (1932) when his Camel is forced down behind enemy lines, Biggles falls headlong for 'a vision of blonde loveliness wrapped up in blue silk' called Marie Janis. ('"Good Lord," Biggles ejaculated.') Devastatingly, Marie turns out to be something of a Mata Hari, and Biggles is about as well-equipped to deal with that kind of problem as Buchan's Richard Hannay. World War II and dozens of novels were to intervene before Biggles meets Marie again in *Biggles Looks Back* (1960) where he finds her, frail and ageing, in Communist Czechoslovakia. He rescues her with the help of his erstwhile enemy, Erich von Stalhein, who also was once under Marie's spell. When she is established in a little cottage in Hampshire, Biggles and von Stalhein drop in from time to time to chat over old times together.[16]

Biggles' popularity was well established then, in storypapers and hardback fiction, several years before the Second World War. His creator was among those who argued against the government's policy of appeasement; indeed, Johns spoke out so forcefully in his editorials, that he was replaced at both *Popular Flying* and *Flying*. Though Britain may not have been ready for war, Biggles fortunately was. His exploits, and those of fellow fictional flyers such as Hal Wilton's Rockfist Rogan in *The Champion*, were to satisfy a generation of young readers undergoing the rigours of rationing and the loss to the armed forces of a father, brother or sister, or perhaps a mother to work in a factory or hospital. Many children were evacuated, heard the drone of bombers as they hurried to the air-raid shelters, saw dogfights in the air above them or watched their cities and homes burn. For them the weekly storypaper and the occasional novel produced in wartime editions on cheap paper were to be an important distraction – or even a means of coming to terms with the war itself.

The Second World War 1939–1945

For Younger Readers
'Who is this Man?' demanded an advertisement for the penny weekly comic, *Jester*, in late 1939, alongside a cartoon of a furious Hitler.[17] 'Read the comical adventures of Basil and Bert, the secret-servicemen, on the trail of 'Ateful Adolf! See the screamingly funny pictures which made Adolf so angry he chewed half his moustache off!' Basil and Bert are engaged in 'a spot of work' in Dictatorland, spying on the 'Nasty Dictator' and his cronies, General Snoring, Dr Gobbles and Herr von Drippingtop. 'Ateful Adolf is wont to yell 'Heil Me!' and here, as in most of the other picture comics ('for children of all ages'), ridicule was the order of the day. In *Beano* (August 1942), Hitler plans to attack Lord Snooty and his pals ('Your orders are to bomb der garten fete at Bunkerton Castle, Herr Squadron Leader Fitz-Stink, and you'd better not miss!'). Adolf invades ('Follow me, mine brave comrades! Soon I will be der King of England!') but is ambushed in the sand dunes by the pals and ends up, trussed hand and foot, as an Aunt Sally at the fete. Snooty and his pals are rewarded with bumper takings for the war effort, and a commendation from a genial Churchill himself in the last frame ('Never was so much collected so quickly by so few'). In another strip, Mussolini was dismissed as 'Musso the Wop – he's a Big-a-da Flop!'

As in the Great War, the Britain of the comics is overrun by spies. Big Eggo the Ostrich (*Beano*, 4 December 1943) catches a Chinese sword-swallower and fire-eater who has cunningly tattooed a map of secret aerodromes on his chest ('Here's the spy! He's no Chink. He's a Jap!'). *Radio Fun* (March 1940) featured a strip about Lord Haw-Haw (William Joyce, the Irishman who broadcast propaganda from Germany). Dad is so incensed by the broadcast that he punches the wireless set, and his beefy fist emerges in the Berlin studio to clump Haw-Haw on the nose, smashing the microphone. 'Dat'll cost you six weeks' wages! Eeeeek!' screams Hitler, several feet off the ground in his fury. In similar vein, in a strip derived from the classic radio series ITMA, much valued by the government for its contribution to British morale throughout the war, Tommy Handley searches the airwaves for 'a drop of sweet swing or a chunk of chamber music'. He tunes in to Funf, ITMA's cross between Haw-Haw and a super spy, well-known for his catch-phrase, 'Dis is Funf Speaking'. 'Well, I'll twiddle the dials with my eyebrow-tweezers,' quips Tommy. Funf is actually hiding inside the wireless cabinet and tries to make his getaway, only for Tommy to 'turn the tables' on him by switching on the gramophone and whizzing Funf through the window into the fishpond.

Most of the comic paper heroes 'did their bit' at one time or another; Desperate Dan in *Dandy*, Our Ernie in *Knockout*, Pansy Potter in *Beano*. Even Tiger Tim and the Bruin Boys joined the Dig for Victory Campaign in *Tiger Tim's Weekly*. In *Knockout* there was a brief series about 'Our Happy Vakkies' as cheerful, high-spirited kids from the cities invaded the countryside to the astonishment of assorted bumpkins.

Even the Christmas annuals acknowledged the war. *The First War-Time Christmas Book* (1939) shows Father Christmas looking down over darkened roofs, stroking his beard pensively. He wears a tin helmet and carries a gas mask slung over his shoulder. The illustration is by Stead, famous among children as the illustrator of the Biggles series; the annual also included work by such eminent artists as A. E. Bestall (the illustrator of Rupert) and a story by a favourite contributor to BBC Radio Children's Hour, L. du Garde Peach.

A number of illustrated books for young children were produced, although paper shortages limited both quantity and quality. The bulbous protective shape of the barrage balloon seems to have been a particular favourite with titles such as *Boo-Boo the Barrage Balloon* (1943) and even *Bulgy the Barrage Balloon* and *Blossom the Barrage Balloon*. In *Boo-Boo*, the almost full-page coloured pictures have a brief narrative running beneath. A brave barrage balloon marries another barrage balloon and they produce twin baby barrage balloons. Together, they guard the skies of Britain.

Evacuation and the Home Guard were combined in Edith M. Bell's *Chippity Cuckoo*, which begins:

> Some time ago I told you the story of how Mrs Jenny Wren brought an evacuee to stay with Chippity Cuckoo. The evacuee, you will remember, was none other than the Fairy Zeta who had been bombed out of her London home.

Chippity has been rather ostracized by the other birds since he is normally the carved occupant of a cuckoo clock. Now, riding on the back of Zeta's popularity as a storyteller, he is allowed to join the local Birds' Home Guard. Zeta is also handy with a needle and swiftly runs him up a uniform. Chippity is sent on fire watch on the church steeple with Walter Weathercock, allowing a useful narrative framework since each night Chippity can tell Walter, and us, the latest stories he has heard from his lodger. The closest the war comes is when the firewatchers have to tell Gladys Glow-worm, somewhat abruptly, to 'Dim that tail lamp of yours.'

Where very young readers during the First World War were provided with stories about animals, children and soldiers in stirring and even dangerous action, children of a similar age during the Second World War seem to have been protected by either the bravado and ridicule of the comics, or by a gentle insistence that they really shouldn't bother too much about what was going on across the English Channel or in the skies above them. Dorothy Burroughs, who wrote and illustrated *Teddy, the Little Refugee Mouse*, dedicates the book to 'Dear Wendy and Jill'. She tells the two girls that the story 'is all about a little grey mouse who went away from London because of that THING called WAR; and, I think, as you came away too, and for the same reason, you may be interested in his story.'

> I have to hurry this dedication off to the Publisher Man, who may be waiting with the Printer Man, who might be getting Impatient to print it before another message from Mr. Hitler might blow it into the air – and so, you see, WAR is a thing that won't wait, or let us wait for things like poems and such – and so, Good-bye.
>
> With love, from your loving Friend

Teddy has to go to the country because his human 'family' decides to leave their town environment until the war is over. ('"War?" said Teddy Mouse, "What's that?"') And off he goes for a series of carefree adventures with his new rural mouse-friends.

The pressures on paper supplies during the war years helped to produce one particularly intriguing publishing phenomenon. Noel Carrington's Puffin Picture Books, planned before the war, made their first appearance in 1940. Using similar printing techniques, several publishers introduced series of small illustrated stories. The preface to the later books in Raphael Tuck's 'Better Little Books' series links the books directly to the circumstance of war:

> This series, now famous, had its origin in the early days of the war, and was intended to provide a suitable diversion during air-raid alerts. Handy little books like these could be easily carried in the pocket, and handed on from one reader to another in the shelters. At the same time, by their small size, the books made the most of the very limited quantities of paper then available.

Some of the books, especially in W. Barton's 'Mighty Midget' series (measuring $3\frac{7}{8}$th inches by $2\frac{1}{2}$ inches) took war directly as their topic, rather unusually describing children in action alongside servicemen in such titles as *U-Boats Defied* and *Spitfire Sabotage*. In *Missing Death by Inches*, a fair-haired lad, sleeves rolled up, holds a pistol to the head of a scowling German helmsman, while in *Revenge in the Fiord*, a boy in a Fair Isle sweater brains another German mariner with a boathook. Raphael Tuck's series included more factual material in *Life in the W.A.A.F.* and *With the Commandos*.[18]

Storypapers for Older Readers
Rather older readers eager for stories of the war itself were best served by the storypapers – called 'comics' by children of the time, although a typical issue was packed with three columns of print sparsely illustrated, usually containing episodes of four or five serials per issue. Each copy ran to some 20,000 words, even though the papers had been forced to cut down from their pre-war size because of limited paper supplies.

Some of the long-running favourites did not survive the early years of the war. *Magnet* and *Gem*, largely written by the prolific Charles Hamilton (who wrote as Frank Richards, Martin Clifford, Owen Conquest and under several other *noms de plume*), had been declining in popularity; paper shortages finished them off in 1940. The front page of the penultimate issue of the *Magnet* (11 May 1940) nevertheless showed a thrilling moment from 'The Nazi Spy's Secret!' by Frank Richards. The intrigue involved Harry Wharton and the Famous Five, a Gestapo agent, an enigmatic butler of dubious loyalty, several disguises and much improbable comedy involving Billy Bunter which, in spirit, might well have belonged to an entirely different story.

D. C. Thomson's four papers, *Rover*, *Wizard*, *Hotspur* and *Adventure* (the last of 'The Big Five', *Skipper*, was another casualty of paper shortages after Germany invaded Norway in 1940) regularly carried exciting stories about the war. In contrast to the storypapers of the Great War, they did not tie themselves closely to actual events. These were tales of individuals rather than campaigns. The Thomson papers had always had a taste for high drama (or sensationalism, as Orwell saw it).[19] A typical story was 'V for Vengeance' in the *Wizard* about a squad of escaped prisoners of war dressed from head to toe in grey, who pass like ghosts into the cars or private apartments of Nazi staff officers. Having stabbed the victim with a dagger, the men in grey leave a list of future targets pinned to the corpse. Those already killed are neatly crossed off the list. Much like Dickens' stealthy assassins in *A Tale of Two Cities*, these men refer to themselves chillingly as 'Jack Four' or 'Jack Twelve'. Their leader is the British Secret Service man Aylmer Gregson, who has been so successful in insinuating himself into the Nazi regime before the war that, calling himself Von Reich, he now ranks second only to Himmler in the dreaded Black Guards.

Perhaps Thomson's most famous recruit to the armed services was none other than Wilson, the Wonder Athlete, a huge favourite in pre-war days. Born in the late eighteenth century but, thanks to an abnormally slow heartbeat, still breaking Olympic records almost 200 years later, Wilson played his part in the Royal Air Force. Also in the *Wizard*, Bill Samson, 'The Wolf of Kabul', yet another agent whose mastery of disguise was matched only by his fluency in languages, pitted his wits and fists against Nazi agents on the Afghan borders, ably abetted by his native servant Chung wielding his favourite weapon, the much used cricket bat 'Clicky-Ba'.

Other stories were even more fantastic, as Thomson's writers deployed metal robots, parachuting lions, or a squadron of blind airmen (brilliantly effective as night flyers) against their understandably bemused enemies. Thomson's heroes are intelligent and fearless, but not reckless. Their commitment is *against* the evils of the Third Reich rather than *for* an ideal of Empire, or some nostalgic vision of a British way of life or, for that matter, a sentimental vision of death. They are marked by the kind of grim resolve Churchill called for in his speeches after Dunkirk. In the middle of a war, the storypapers could hardly be faulted for adopting a view of the enemy which came close to caricature. The Germans were portrayed as cold, mechanical and cruel, though there was none of the talk of 'frightfulness', baby-eating or sadism which permeated the storypapers of the First World War.

Ironically, the detail of the atrocities of the concentration camps were little more than rumours to writers and readers at this time. The full exposure of the horrors of Auschwitz and Bergen-Belsen were not to be explored in children's literature until the novels of the last thirty years of the century.

Although they lost *Magnet* and *Gem*, Thomson's rivals, Amalgamated Press, were quickly in action behind enemy lines in 1940 in the *Champion* with a story of 'Q.9, The Boxing Spy'. At the outbreak of war, Rockfist Rogan was still patrolling the skies over Flanders. Ever resourceful, he ditched his Tiger Moth for a Spitfire between issues and fought on to victory in 1945, breaking bureaucratic rules with the high spirits of a schoolboy, but always playing the sportsman to his opponents in the ring or in the air. Meanwhile another *Champion* favourite, Fireworks Flynn, sports master at a boarding school in the Canadian forests in the 1930s, spent much of his war keeping up morale among his fellow prisoners in a concentration camp with an ingenious programme of sporting high jinks to the amazement of the slow-witted German guards.

Orwell's main target had been *Magnet* and *Gem*, but he was also dismissive of the storypapers produced by Thomson and the Amalgamated Press. His criticism was over severe. During the wartime period, for all their rapid and colourful excitements, the stories are economically told, fairly demanding in vocabulary and accurate in syntax. These storypapers had an immensely wide readership among all social classes and, in a period when far less reading matter was available, provided readers with a kind of community of their own.

Novels and Series Books for Older Readers
The shortage of paper severely limited the production of hardback novels and few of those published took their readers into battle or behind enemy lines. There were stories of evacuees such as Kitty Barne's *Visitors from London* (1940), in which London children enjoyed their first glimpses of the countryside in the company of a middle-class family in Sussex.[20] Of more interest, if only because the fame of its author was already well established, is *I go by Sea, I go by Land* (1941) by P. L. Travers, whose first two Mary Poppins titles had appeared in 1934 and 1935. The story is told by 11-year-old Sabrina Lind. Her parents decide that Sabrina and her 9-year old brother James should go to America for the duration of the war, for even in rural Sussex the bombs are falling. ('Father said quietly, "Meg, they must go!" and Mother said, "Oh, John!" and James and I lay very still and pretended to be asleep when they came up again.'). Sabrina's shaky spelling and

naive style are simulated to lend authenticity ('Evvaccuee', 'crayter', 'priviledges' and 'Miss Minnett smells of rubber and tooth-paste. Mother smells of walnuts and Floris Sweetbriar'). The children set off by ocean liner for the States, accompanied by the family's closest friend, Pel, who is taking her baby Romulus to safety across the Atlantic. Pel is just the kind of magical adult who appeared in children's books of the period and is perhaps a mixture of P. L. Travers herself and Mary Poppins. She writes books and beguiles the time on the crossing with tales of desert islands, friendly natives and hornpipe-dancing sailors.

> She makes you laugh and dance inside yourself and at the same time you feel she is somebody who will always be there and that is a very safe feeling. Father calls her Glorious Pel and Lovely Woman and Angel One, but you know that *she* knows he doesn't seriously mean it and that he only thinks she's glorious because she thinks *we* are.

For all its middle-class, Home Counties coziness, the novel acknowledges that U-boats might threaten the convoy, though in the end, they don't. The painful absence of parents and the children's adjustment to a different culture are well caught; and, towards the end of the novel, Sabrina and James hear that their much-loved home has been partly destroyed by a bomb (though their parents are unharmed). Published when victory in the war was far from certain, the book celebrates the strength of family ties and reassures its readers that mothers, fathers and other loving grown-ups will be there to see you through, and that happier days will come again. As if by way of further assurance, the book closes with Sabrina singing her brother to sleep with a comforting hymn. The bond between Britain and America in wartime is also confirmed – the title page and the endpapers picture a clasped handshake within a circlet of stars. Since the book was published in both countries in 1941, in her genteel way P. L. Travers may have been urging American entry into the war.

In peacetime, Nurse Bunty Brown is a bit of a card – fizzing with life, somewhat mischievous and a beacon of light on her hospital ward. But in *Bunty of the Flying Squad* (Barbara Wilcox, 1943) she finds herself kneeling by the bed of the dying Mrs Atkins, a young mother whose husband is away soldiering. With more rapid help, she might have been saved and Bunty determines there and then to raise money for an ambulance. Watching her, a bewildered older nursing sister marvels at her energy: 'Bunty was young, and it was her war, the war of young men and young women.'

Barbara Wilcox had already given her readers two books of Bunty's exploits (*Bunty Brown: Probationer* and *Bunty Brown's Bargain*), and although this novel is largely about nursing matters and fund-raising for the ambulance, the war provides the impetus for Bunty's endeavours. Unusually in wartime, the novel condemns unthinking hostility to all Germans. After an air raid has brought St Bernadine's onto an emergency footing, she encounters a German refugee, Paul von Eckermann, as a patient. 'To a good nurse, a patient has no nationality, no age, no sex' and although some of the nurses grumble 'at nursing a German and suspected him of being a spy', Bunty knows he has suffered terribly at the hands of the Nazis. One nurse's harshness reduces Paul to his old nightmares; Bunty explains to her patient, ' "She thinks in compartments and puts Englishmen in one and Germans in another" ', and buys Paul a Bavarian musical box to cheer him up. Eventually, the intrepid Bunty decides to persuade Gregory Button, a wealthy widower, to adopt Paul, despite the older man's initial dislike of all things German. Button owes something to Scrooge in his misanthropic characterization and he dismisses Bunty's suggestion:

> Bunty's quick temper flared up. Her cheeks blazed, her blue eyes stormed. She stamped her foot.
> 'How can you say such silly things?' she cried, 'You can't say you don't like *any* Germans; they aren't all the same. Some are horrid and some are nice, like us. And you can't detest refugees. Why, it's a misfortune anyone might have the way things go on now. You or me or anyone.'

In a crowded dénouement, Bunty not only makes a go of the ambulance, but the lonely millionaire agrees 'to have Paul on appro', and her brother comes safely home on leave from the RAF and falls for her best friend. Meanwhile, as if Bunty's cup were not already brimming over, Sir Ramsey Street, the gruff but warm-hearted middle-aged consultant, normally given to 'barking' at junior staff, proposes to her in a bluebell wood.

Like many novels of its period, the book is self-aware in its address to a child reader. Its characters may be two dimensional and adult readers may judge its relentless high-spiritedness to be irritatingly naive, yet its values are positive and unusually liberal, given the wartime context, and the episodic structure must have made inviting reading for the bed-time child reader.

The war was also reflected in other, better-known series of books; given the shortage of paper, publishers may well have decided to stick to trusted favourites. Mumfie, Katharine Tozer's engaging little elephant (a favourite on BBC Children's Hour) joined the Home Guard in *Mumfie Marches On* (1941). Gwynedd Rae's equally popular small bear, Mary Plain, helped the Local Defence Volunteers catch an enemy spy. Muriel Pardoe wrote twelve 'Bunkle' books, also popular in dramatized versions on Children's Hour. Half a dozen of the books involved the de Salis family in the capture of spies. Major de Salis is secretly employed in Army Intelligence and Bunkle – so named by his older brother and sister because he talked such nonsense – finds himself caught up in a series of exciting adventures, though the safe hands of his parents are never too far away. At one point in *Four Plus Bunkle* (1939), 'the whole difference between war and peace in Europe, and the safety of England' are in the children's hands.[21]

Elinor Brent-Dyer's Chalet School had to flee its Tyrolean home in *The Chalet School in Exile* (1940). Unusually, in children's fiction, Brent-Dyer included an incident in which an elderly Jew is persecuted by a mob and the situation is saved only by the intervention of the school's science mistress. A Jewish goldsmith, Herr Goldman, is pursued by a Nazi mob. Jo Bettany intervenes, trying to reason with the 'hooligans', one of whom she knows.

> 'He's a Jew! Jews have no right to live!' declared Hans Bocher sullenly. 'Give place, Fraulein Bettany, and hand over the old Jew to us! Better take care, or you'll be in trouble for this. Let him go! We'll see to him!'

Jo and her friends, and their teacher, escape through the efforts of the parish priest, Vater Johann, but subsequently the mob kill both Jew and priest.

Elinor Brent-Dyer's novels may well have been intended to alert her young readers to the evils which their fathers were fighting against. She was a Roman Catholic, and must have been well aware of Pope Pius XI's condemnation in 1937 of Hitler as 'a mad prophet possessed of a repulsive arrogance'.[22]

The School chose the Channel Islands as its new home which consequently meant yet another upheaval when the Germans occupied the islands, but not before a schoolgirl spy has been dealt with and Jo and her companions have survived a machine gun attack by a U-boat. The Chalet School found its third home on the Welsh borders, not too far from the Margaret Roper School in Herefordshire, where Brent-Dyer was Principal. The girls are encouraged to be international in their outlook – after all, the school had recruited its pupils from throughout the Empire and Europe. The Head reminds the girls that they had, before the war, committed themselves to a Peace League:

'You have not, I hope, forgotten our Peace League? As things are, we can do very little for those of its members who are still in enemy country. But remember, they are Chalet School girls, who have been trained in the same ideals as you have. God alone knows what these girls may be suffering now, and there is only one thing we can do to help them. Let us do it with all our might. We mean to gain the victory; for, make no mistake, this evil thing called Nazi-ism that has reared its head above the world like a venomous snake must perish as all evil must. There are many in Germany, more in Austria, who hate it as we do.'

(from *The Chalet School Goes to It*, 1941)[23]

The Head's firm line receives confirmation, literally from the heavens. One night, while she is fire-watching on the lawn, a German plane, with pinpoint accuracy, drops a cylinder containing a message at her feet:

'Chalet School, hail! The brother of two old girls greets you. They have bid him tell you they will never forget the Chalet School Peace League, and they will love you always. Their brother joins them, though he is forced into this abomination. Karl Linders.'

Brent-Dyer, like Barbara Wilcox, distinguished between the Nazis and the ordinary people of Germany and Austria who, like Karl Linders, 'hated Hitler and all his works'.

Another popular writer of girls' school stories, Dorita Fairlie Bruce, author of the *Dimsie* series in the 1920s, took a more straightforward view of all things German. In *Toby at Tibbs Cross* (1943), the eponymous heroine is sure that 'however much he may try, it is difficult for a German to look like anything else'. Yet again, there is a German spy to be caught – the local vet who is cunningly injecting 'cow plague' into the local cattle. The home fires need to be kept burning with menfolk away at the war, and Toby and her friend Charity run a farm together in the teeth of labour shortages and air-raids.[24]

Biggles inevitably tangled with the Nazis on numerous occasions. In *Biggles Defies the Swastika* (1941), he finds himself in occupied Norway. By temperament, he prefers to fight it out in the open, in uniform, and it goes against his grain to pose as a Norwegian (he'd picked the language up 'after seven weeks of concentrated effort'), behaving submissively even when struck by a German corporal. The story is well plotted, rapid in action, and addicted readers were no doubt pleased to find most of the regular cast in action – Biggles' cousin, the

Honourable Algy Lacey, Ginger Hebblethwaite, the sturdy young Yorkshireman and the sinister Erich von Stalhein. 'Tug' Carrington, a tough, embittered East Ender and the 'silly ass' figure of Lord Bertie Lissie, monocle wedged in eye, had not yet reported for duty ('Lissie's a devil with a Spitfire and a wizard with a gun, but I'm afraid he's as mad as a hatter'). Any of the uncertainties which troubled the youthful Biggles of the First World War have gone. He is cool under pressure, clear about his priorities, a brilliant flyer, incomparable in a scrap and a leader Algy, Ginger, Tug and Bertie, and thousands of readers, would follow anywhere.

Biggles was so popular that W. E. Johns was asked by the War Office to create two more characters to encourage recruiting – a field Johns understood since he served as a recruiting officer in the early years of the war. Johns proudly added a note to his Foreword in a post-war reprint of *Biggles of the Camel Squadron* (1934). 'In 1944, one of our leading fighter pilots, asked by a reporter from a Sunday newspaper to what he owed his success, answered, "Biggles". The reporter naively headed his article, "Who is Biggles?" I gather a lot of people answered his question.'

'Gimlet' King of the Commandos was, said Johns, 'not as gentlemanly as Biggles' but, he continued, 'kid gloves are about as useful to a commando in his job as roller skates would be to a steeple jack'. Somehow khaki lacked the glamour of Air Force blue, and Gimlet never approached Biggles' popularity.

A more interesting newcomer was Flight Officer Joan Worralson ('Worrals') who arrived in the *Girl's Own Paper* in 1940 and in book format in *Worrals of the W.A.A.F.* (1941). Eleven fast-moving novels appeared before 1950, six of them set in wartime. As we shall see later in this chapter, Worrals is not grounded yet, even in the new millennium. She was warmly welcomed by reviewers in the newspapers: 'The kind of grand stuff which the schoolgirl of today will jump at,' enthused *The Western Mail*. As early as 1934, Johns had written: '[Women] are going to fly ... make no mistake about it, the average girl flies as well as the average man.' Worrals shows few signs of conventional feminine weakness, and must have made a particularly welcome heroine for girls wishing for a more active role in wartime. '"Men! They can take care of themselves, but we're poor little lambs who can't be trusted to find our way home unless the sun is shining"', she complains in *Worrals of the Islands* (1945). In fact, before the end of the first page of the first novel, *Worrals of the W.A.A.F.*, she had been spoiling for a scrap: '"Men can go off and fight, but girls – oh no",' she grumbles to her friend 'Frecks' Lovell, who serves as an apprehensive foil to the nerveless Worrals. She gets the fight she is looking for, as she and Frecks tangle with spies; a taut finale involves Worrals at the controls of a plane with German markings, a spy's automatic aimed at her head, under attack by Spitfires. Worrals remains cool.

Of all the heroes and heroines of series novels, Richmal Crompton's William Brown saw things from a perspective closest to that of the readers themselves; though William's particular corner of the Home Counties had, even then, a period feel very different from the neighbourhoods familiar to most of those who loved the chunky red books and the comic illustrations by Thomas Henry which were an integral part of a reader's delight. William always had a keen eye for the latest faddish movement, from the League of Perfect Love to the New Era Society. In *William the Dictator* (1938), when he sees 'a man in a black shirt standing on a wooden box in the middle of the village, just outside the Blue Lion', William is quick to spot the opportunities open to a leader with absolute power over his uniformed followers. The cover of the book shows a smirking William giving a fascist salute, wearing an armband 'of a peculiarly virulent green' secured from his older sister Ethel in return for running an errand to the post office. As always, William's project comes to an unexpected conclusion. His attempt to found the Greenshirts results in a splendid picnic with someone else's hamper for William and the Outlaws and, as usual, they have the satisfaction of thwarting the Hubert Laneites and their rival Blueshirts.

William had a good war. Once hostilities began in 1939, the Outlaws hurled themselves into the war effort, collecting paper for salvage and throwing their usually unwelcome weight behind the local Home Guard, Air Raid Wardens and Fire Fighters. *William and the A.R.P.* (1939) actually appeared before war was declared; William organizes 'detramination' exercises and engineers the unauthorized evacuation of an unwilling pair of twins. As war went on, the Brown family became more involved. Even the dizzy Ethel joins the VAD and can enjoy only the occasional attentions of infatuated servicemen from the nearby aerodrome. The equally empty-headed Robert becomes a Second Lieutenant in the Army, allowing William to boast of his brother's single-handed exploits which promise to bring the war to a rapid conclusion. The Outlaws' greatest wish inevitably is to capture a spy, and in this they enjoy some accidental success (although they suspect many other innocent citizens of espionage). Often sporting an inverted colander on his head as a steel helmet, William became involved with the black market, unexploded bombs and, as the war comes to an end, a Victory Pageant which inevitably results in a free-for-all scrap. [25]

The contrast in social attitudes evident in children's literature produced during the two world wars is revealing. Between 1939 and 1945, young readers were not left in any doubt about the justice of the cause, but there was little of the jingoism, the harking back to days of Empire, the implicit pressure for older boys and girls to prepare themselves for active service. (It may well be true that the age of the implied reader of books and papers for young people was lower by 1939.) For the most part, novels featuring child characters and younger readers' picture books shielded them from the bloodshed of the war. In storypapers and books dealing with combat, the old certainties were less secure and this war is no game for Jessie Pope's British sportsmen 'on tour' which our side is sure to win. The fighting heroes are no longer culled from our major public schools – neither are they chirpy working-class lads who know their place (firmly in the 'other ranks') and do their best. Heroic qualities transcend social class. Obedience to orders is important, but anyone relying on rank or breeding alone is duly humbled. This is not to say that novels and storypapers abounded in working-class heroes – these were to appear after the war in stories written in Labour's brave new Welfare State. The threat of German invasion had been so close at Dunkirk, and the public was perhaps more accurately informed than in the First World War by wireless and broadsheet. Many people had witnessed with their own eyes the dogfights of the Battle of Britain over South-East England, or known the devastation of German bombing. Even if the information through radio and daily papers was censored to a degree, many teenage children as well as adults followed the ebb and flow of war closely, plotting troop movements on maps of Africa and mainland Europe provided by the newspapers.

1945–1970

Lost Children

The immediate post-war years were marked by continuing austerity – food rationing, shortages of coal and steel, and a rate of income tax as high as in wartime persisted in Britain even in the early 1950s. Nevertheless, this was a time for looking forward rather than returning to the horror of war, and those concerned with the writing or publishing of children's reading matter seemed determined to play an optimistic part in reshaping the world. Jella Lepman founded the International Board on Books for Young People (IBBY) almost literally in the rubble of occupied Germany;[26] the Board's Hans Christian Andersen Medal, open to writers around the world and awarded for a lifetime's outstanding contribution to literature for children, was established in 1956; since 1966, an illustrator's medal has also been awarded.

The winner of the award in 1962 was Meindert De Jong, American by residence but Dutch by birth. During the war, De Jong was an official war historian with the USAF in China, and *The House of Sixty Fathers* (1956), based on his wartime experiences, is one of the few distinguished books about the war to appear in English-speaking countries during the period 1945–1970. The story of a young boy's lonely search for his family in war-torn China, dodging Japanese patrols, was based on factual events. Tien Pao is an engaging, humorous character, resilient by temperament; eventually, he is adopted by his 'sixty fathers', the men of an American bomber squadron. In a moving, even lyrical concluding chapter, the little boy is reunited with his parents. As she greets her son, Tien's mother says,

> Ah, tomorrow, and tomorrow, and then will come a day when there will be no more shooting, and no more running from the shooting, and no war. There will come a day when the little family of Tien will go back to their village and live in peace. Ah, tomorrow and tomorrow.

The year 1956 was also the publication date of Ian Serraillier's *The Silver Sword*, another notable book which concerned children searching for parents separated from them by war. Serraillier's band of children make their way across Poland and Germany *en route* to Switzerland where, they hope, their father has found safe refuge from the Germans (see Chapter 4, pp 169–72). Like *The House of Sixty Fathers*, Serraillier's book has been a favourite class reader for almost half a century.

Anne Holm's *I Am David* (published in Denmark in 1963 and in Britain in 1965) tells a rather different story of a lost child. The setting is again post-war Europe, but the detail is left deliberately vague, which lends a sense of the universal to the wanderings of David, the central character of the story. He escapes from a prisoner-of-war camp, perhaps in the Balkans, perhaps in Greece, and spends much of his time as he travels northwards on foot across Europe wondering whether 'they' – the camp authorities – will catch up with him. In the camp, he has known only one kindly mentor, Johannes; and he has hated 'the man', the ambiguous camp commandant who – to David's confusion – has enabled him to escape. When in difficulties on his journey, David brings to mind Johannes' words – especially the notion that he must 'be himself':

'You are David. And if you never allow other people to influence what you're really like, then you've something no one can take from you – not even *they*. Never mind what others are like – you must still be David. Do you understand what I mean?'

David's journey is an allegorical 'progress', for it enables him to learn who David is. He can remember nothing but the prison camp, and although this has given him a useful knowledge of several languages, as well as Johannes' teaching, he is essentially a blank slate, waiting for a character to be inscribed upon it by experience of the outside world. In this way, David (a youth confronted by odds of Goliath proportions) stands for all refugee children – and to a degree all children as they find out who they are in a confusing world. Slowly, David learns to trust where trust is merited. He learns to receive, for many of the people he meets are kind to him; and he also learns that he has much to give. He develops an awareness of beauty, and begins to know how to have 'fun'. Very much the wiser, David comes to Denmark and, in the last paragraph of the book, finds his way to the address of a woman in Copenhagen whose name he has been given by another woman he has met on his journey – coincidence abounds in this book, which is one of the means by which a sense of allegory, rather than realism, is established.

Then David said in French, 'Madame, I'm David. I'm … ' He could say no more. The woman looked into his face and said clearly and distinctly, 'David … My son David.'

The book has been seen as 'sentimental to a fault'[27] and it is true that the philosophy of 'being yourself' which drives the narrative has a sixties simplicity. Nevertheless, allegory paints in bold strokes, and these broadly sketched ideas may make their impact upon young minds.

With these rare exceptions, 'quality' children's literature in the victorious Allied countries was not much concerned with the war or its aftermath. In the 1960s, writers such as Joan Aiken, Susan Cooper, Peter Dickinson, Leon Garfield, Alan Garner, Madeleine L'Engle, Penelope Lively, Andre Norton and Phillipa Pearce produced work much praised by specialist children's literature critics – themselves a new breed in the field. Their narratives offered escape from everyday life, if not escapism, through fantasy, historical and science fiction novels. However, towards the end of the decade, through the work of John Rowe Townsend and Aidan Chambers, a beginning was made in providing stories about the realities of readers' own environment; and Jill Paton Walsh produced *The Dolphin Crossing* (see pp166–9) and *Fireweed* (see p104) in which her characters landed on the beaches of Dunkirk and wandered through the bomb-damaged houses and streets of the London Blitz.

Popular Literature

Marcus Morris, an unconventional Anglican clergyman, launched his excellently produced comic *Eagle* in April 1950. Significantly, its cover story *Dan Dare, Pilot of the Future* was set in Space; many devotees believe that its artwork, by Frank Hampson, has never been surpassed. *Eagle* was not interested in looking back to the recent war, though it has been argued that Dan was virtually Biggles in a spacesuit.[28] The Thomson storypapers took a policy decision in 1945 to drop all stories about the war,[29] but in the early 1950s a new hero emerged whose values belonged to a post-war culture hostile to the privileges of class, even though his adventures all took place during the war itself. Sergeant Pilot Matt Braddock, VC and Bar, appeared in Thomson's *Rover*, where his chronicler was his navigator, Sergeant George Bourne:

> Many people disliked [Braddock], and some even hated him for the ruthless way in which he swept aside anything he regarded as red tape or useless discipline, but even his bitterest critics had to admit that, in the air, Braddock had no equal.

His popularity was such that Thomsons' produced a hardback collection of his stories, *I Flew with Braddock* (undated). Braddock's disregard of hierarchies and rules, balanced by his insistence on tight discipline in the aircraft, made him a different kind of hero. The storypapers were now running boarding school serials told by working-class scholarship boys (*Smith of the Lower Third* in the *Wizard*) and a very popular athletics serial in the *Rover* featuring *Alf Tupper, The Tough of the Track*, a welder who worked and slept under the railway arches during the week and outran the toffs from the local private club at the weekend. Such stories took every opportunity to ridicule pomposity and unearned status. Braddock is in constant opposition to many of his immediate superiors, but the men at the top recognize Braddock's qualities and respect him for the excellent pilot that he is. ' "Fifty men can win the war, Braddock, and you're one of them," ' says the Air Marshal in charge of Bomber Command, perhaps modelled on the famous real-life 'Bomber' Harris. It is the middle-ranking, self-important officers whom Braddock regularly exposed. A television documentary made in 2000 suggests that Braddock's anonymous writers may not have been far from the truth. In interviews, several Sergeant Pilots who fought in the Battle of Britain agreed that they were consistently treated as second-class citizens by some of the commissioned pilots of privileged backgrounds. The 'Few', they observed, were a less united band than the myth usually celebrates.

In 1961, the editor of the Amalgamated Press *Knockout* comic – no doubt impressed by the continuing success of Biggles, Braddock and Rockfist Rogan (still flying in the Press's own *Champion*) – published *Battler Britton*, the adventures of Wing-Commander Robert Hereward Britton, DSO, DFC and Bar, Croix de Guerre. Despite his pedigree (his father was a Lieutenant Colonel and his mother the daughter of a baronet in the diplomatic service) and his Cambridge education, Battler was essentially classless. No doubt his spell in the Peruvian Navy and a period with the French Foreign Legion had levelled his social horizons. Unlike Biggles and Rockfist Rogan, and even Braddock, Britton is a killer. He is no sadist, but he does delight in shooting up columns of 'mallet-faced' Nazis who go down like so many fairground targets, with barely time to utter a strangled *Schweinhund*. The Japanese are 'sawn-off, toothy little men', no match for Battler, who escapes with consummate ease from their prison camps in broad daylight, having broken in only a couple of hours earlier to check out the details of some information with the prisoners of war.

Battler Britton, like Braddock, proved so popular that his adventures were reproduced in hardback format, along with factual information about aircraft from the Great War ('Weirdies of World War I'), brief introductions to contemporary test pilots and accounts of specific actions from the 1939–1945 war. Half the stories were in print, the others in picture strips, and it was this latter format which led to a development in war literature for the young which has largely been ignored by critics of children's literature.

From 1951 Fleetway Publications produced pocket-sized comics some 68 pages long which originally included picture-strip versions of the classics. Issue 1 retold *The Three Musketeers*. It was to this series, *The Thriller Picture Library*, that Battler Britton was promoted from *Knockout*. Such comic books proliferated in the early 1960s, most of them wholly dedicated to war. Fleetway added *War Picture Library* (1958) and *Battle Picture Library* (1961) while Thomson produced *Commando* (1961) to an identical format. Other publishers joined in: Pearsons (*Picture Stories of World War II*, 1960), Famepress (*Attack*, 1962), and many more. They are action-filled, exulting in the pride and skill of the warrior – a well-muscled, square-jawed British, Commonwealth or American serviceman, usually something of an individualist, for whom the cowardly or devious enemy is no match. Such characters were echoed in comics for younger children such as *Film Fun* where Scoop Donovan, War Cameraman, outwits and outpunches the Jerries or the Japs, week by week.

In the early years of these comic books, a recurrent theme was that of the protagonist who has yet to find himself, or who is mistakenly thought a coward by his peers – a narrative line which must have been of particular appeal to uncertain adolescents. War offers such a character the opportunity to discover and demonstrate what it is to be a man. The main focus remained the Second World War in Europe or the Far East, although there were occasionally titles such as *Dogfight Dixon, RFC* (set in the First World War).

It might have been thought at the time that these stories were a passing phenomenon, perhaps a last farewell to days of action now distant enough to be celebrated as times of glory for a generation with no direct experience of the war. The truth proved to be very different. War comics developed dramatically in the 1970s and some of the series titles mentioned above are still on the newsagents' shelves in the new millennium. *Commando* No 3326 (70 pence), published in May 2000 and entitled *The Final Hunt*, shows a trio of German soldiers, teeth clenched, charging towards the reader, guns blazing. Plots have become less clear cut. The setting is Russia in 1943, and we follow events from the perspective of Sergeant Sepp Luther, a battle-hardened veteran of the *Fallschirmjäger* (paratroops). The enemy this time is the amoral SS – 'our' Germans dissociate themselves from Nazism and are clean-fighting soldiers. But the celebration of virile action and ruthless killing is much as it has always been in these comic books. They cannot be ignored by those studying the treatment of war in reading matter for children and adolescents. It may well be that such comic books have made a far wider impact in shaping the responses, and perhaps attitudes, of readers than the quality fiction under-standably preferred by parents, teachers and librarians.

The Jewish Experience

If young readers in Britain were being offered quality literature which avoided direct reference to the fighting, and pulp fiction which exulted in violence, some of their contemporaries on the European mainland were discovering another kind of post-war reading altogether.

Until the gates of the concentration camps were opened by the liberating armies, little had been known for certain of the realities of the treatment of the Jews – not by the general public or even by the servicemen themselves. A version of *Anne Frank's Diary* was first published in 1947, edited by her father Otto, the only member of the family to survive the Holocaust. The book is discussed in Chapter 4, pp 153–5, but it is worth noting here that the book was available in an English translation (as *The Diary of a Young Girl*) in 1952. Its widespread use in school classrooms did not begin until the 1960s. Teachers and parents may have felt unsure about the suitability of the subject matter for young readers; but in the mid-1960s English teachers began to see social issues – including racism and even genocide – as appropriate topics for their classrooms. In Germany, however, the examination of the national conscience was a more urgent matter, and Hans Peter Richter's *Friedrich*, published in 1961, was selected for the 'Distinguished List' of the German Children's Book Prize in the following year.

Friedrich Schneider is the best friend of the narrator, and the book begins in 1925 when the two boys are born. Year by year, incident by incident, the growth of the Nazi Party and its influence upon the everyday lives of the boys is recorded. For young readers, the impact of daily events upon characters of the same age as themselves is readily understandable. The narrator breaks a shop window with a ball – Friedrich gets the blame as 'a good-for-nothing Jewboy' despite the narrator's protests. Friedrich meets a girl he likes, but he dares not sit with her in the park on the green bench for, as a Jew, he is allowed to sit only on a yellow bench. The pressure on both boys increases month by month. Friedrich's parents and their rabbi are taken by the Nazis in the middle of the night, and the boy goes into hiding on the streets. In 1942, as the Allied bombers pound their city each night, Friedrich comes in desperation to the narrator's family. They dare not take him with them to the air-raid shelter, though he begs them to do so. Later, terrified, he comes to the shelter and implores the warden, the Jew-hating Herr Resch, to let him in. He is turned away; in the morning, he is found huddled in a doorway, his eyes closed, his face pale.

> Herr Resch lifted his foot and kicked.
> Friedrich rolled onto the stone path. A trail of blood went from his right temple to his collar.
> I clutched the thorny rosebush.
> 'His luck that he died *this* way,' said Herr Resch.

And there the book ends. Richter's *I Was There* followed in 1962, describing the experiences of three members of the Hitler Youth. It was another ten years before English translations of the two books were available and *Friedrich* especially became a book very widely used in secondary schools.

In the next 30 years, a considerable number of novels and picture books, many of them in translation, recorded the terrible shedding of Jewish blood in European streets, in cattle trucks, or in concentration camps (see Chapter 4).

1970–2000

Jill Paton Walsh's *The Dolphin Crossing* (1967) and *Fireweed* (1969) were precursors of numerous texts treating the subject of war written during the last 30 years of the century. Perhaps prompted by a *fin de siècle* need to set the record straight for younger generations, some writers returned to the desperate waste of men and the impact upon the lives of women during the First World War. In this chapter, we touch only briefly upon this area, since we consider the topic fully in Chapter 2. In their treatment of later wars, writers have been more concerned with the suffering of civilians in war than with combat itself, most notably in the Holocaust; with the experiences of children in wartime Britain and America as well as in the actual theatre of war on the European mainland; with later conflicts such as those in Vietnam, the Falklands, the Gulf, Bosnia and Sub-Saharan Africa; and, especially in the case of picture books, with the folly of war exposed through allegory and satire. Significantly, many of these texts arrived in North America and Britain in translation from continental Europe. By contrast, comic books and a limited number of paperback books have continued to celebrate the warrior hero in battle – the favoured arena for the modern gladiator remains the Second World War. Chapters 3 and 4 look in detail at the fictional treatment of this war in Britain, and on the European mainland.

The 1914–18 War

The final page of *In Flanders Field: The Story of the Poem by John McCrae* (1995) offers an image of a button-hole poppy and Kipling's familiar admonition, 'Lest We Forget'. The register and content of the book are such that the creators' intentions are clearly to inform and to warn ('Often, voices of peace ... may *scarce* be heard, but they *can* be heard ... if only we will listen'). The artist, Janet Wilson, and the author, Linda Granfield, are Canadian, and their text is dedicated to members of their families who fell or were wounded in Flanders. Granfield traces McCrae's life from boyhood in Ontario to his wartime service as a doctor and his death in France in 1918. The circumstances in which McCrae wrote his famous poem are described; he was much stirred by a close friend's death which, as a doctor, he could do nothing to prevent. The poem and the poet's life story are illuminated by factual information about the war, reinforced by Janet Wilson's strongly textured paintings of the trenches, operating tables in field hospitals, grieving relatives at home, and rows of tombstones in the war cemeteries. Posters, photographs and sketches by McCrae further complement the text.

This picture book reflects much recent literature about the Great War in its emphasis upon suffering and loss of life. There is none of the partiality or jingoism of the literature (described earlier in this chapter), actually written between 1914 and 1918 and in the years immediately following the war. There is a recognition of the courage of the soldiers and of the women who staffed the hospitals close to the front lines. The text, like many of those we discuss in Chapter 2, takes the reader into the front line; and, because we have the hindsight of history, and know that this was not in fact the war to end all wars, we feel more keenly the futility of the enormous loss of life, and the ironies of McCrae's last stanza:

Take up our quarrel with the foe:
To you from failing hands we throw
    The torch; be yours to hold it high.
    If ye break faith with us who die
We shall not sleep, though poppies grow
    In Flanders fields.

Other texts reflect the shifting roles of women, both in direct support of the fighting men and at home. The developments in women's education and their increasing sense of independence have interested contemporary writers such as Ruth Elwyn Harris, whose Quantocks Quartet of novels set during the first 40 years of the century depicts the struggles of a talented young artist to defy the conventions of feminine duty and attend the prestigious art school at the Slade (see pp 74–9); while Marjorie Darke's novel about the First World War, *A Rose from Blighty* (see pp 73–4), opens with one of its central characters imprisoned for her suffragette activities. The challenge to the rigid barriers between the classes is evident in such texts as Linda Newbery's trilogy *Some Other War* (see pp 67–73) and K. M. Peyton's *Flambards* (see pp 79–80) series. In these texts, a nostalgia for the lost pre-war world is coupled with the excitement of progress and shifting social values.

The Second World War
Many of the young characters of novels set in the Second World War are deprived of the security of parental love and familiar surroundings. On the Home Front, a number of novels dealt with the separation from

parents experienced by evacuees; perhaps the most outstanding are Nina Bawden's *Carrie's War* (1973) (see pp. 85–6) and Michele Magorian's *Goodnight Mister Tom* (1988) (see pp. 92–5). In contrast to newspaper articles which appeared early in the new millennium about the damaging psychological effects of evacuation, most children's authors have preferred to show the experience as being finally positive.

A sense of what life was like in wartime Britain is evoked brilliantly in several of Robert Westall's stories, such as the Carnegie Medal winner *The Machine-Gunners* (1975) (see pp. 99–104) and *Blitzcat* (1989) (see pp. 105–8). These stories deal with extraordinary events in a wartime setting, but everyday life is graphically shown in the course of Raymond Briggs' affectionate picture book account of the lives of his parents, *Ethel and Ernest* (1998) (see pp. 108–9). The diminutive Raymond is among those evacuated to the countryside while back at home his father builds the family's Anderson shelter ('"Mind my antirrhinums, Ernest"') and his mother goes to work in a warehouse. Together, they listen to the wireless announcing the dropping of the atomic bomb on Hiroshima: '"Well, at least it will put paid to wars,"' says Ethel. '"Eh, why?" "Everyone will be dead the first day."'

For children in mainland Europe, separation from parents was often of a grimmer order. Many of the finest novels open up the tragedy of the Holocaust – which is made accessible even to young readers through picture books such as *Let the Celebrations Begin* (by Margaret Wild and Julie Vivas, 1991) (see pp. 149–50) and the outstanding *Rose Blanche* (by Roberto Innocenti and Christophe Gallaz, English text by Ian McEwan, 1985) (see pp. 150–3). Some of the most harrowing accounts are by survivors of the death camps such as Livia Bitton-Jackson's *I Have Lived a Thousand Years* (1999) (see pp. 139–42), Uri Orlev's story of a Polish ghetto, *The Island on Bird Street* (1984) (see pp. 157–9) and Christa Laird's *Shadow of the Wall* (1989), a description, based upon historical fact, of the work of Doctor Korczak, who gave his life for the children of the Warsaw ghetto (see pp. 159–61).

The experiences of other victims of war are recorded in such texts as Tatiana Vassilieva's *Hostage to War* (1994, English translation 1996), an autobiographical account of a young Russian's enslavement as a labourer by the Nazis (see pp. 147–9) and Donna Jo Napoli's *Stones in Water* (1997) whose hero is also conscripted to work for the German war effort – this time literally taken from a cinema seat in Northern Italy (see pp. 145–7).

Nuclear warfare has been considered obliquely in children's novels in post-devastation dystopias such as Robert C. O'Brien's *Z for Zachariah* (1974) and Robert Swindells' *Brother in the Land* (1984).

However, the bombing of Hiroshima has been directly described in Toshi Maruki's challenging picture book *The Hiroshima Story* (1983). Judith Elkin's translation begins with a simplicity the informed reader cannot help but find poignant and ominous:

> It was almost 8.15.
> The people of Hiroshima woke up to a beautiful bright morning.
> The sky was clear and the shallow rays of early sunlight glittered through the morning air.

We follow the breakfast routines of 7-year-old Mii-chan and her parents to the moment when 'a violent flash of white-hot light cut open the sky'. From this point on the text is extended by illustrations which echo the most graphic medieval representations of Hell: piles of mud-green bodies, tortured figures caught up in swirling flames, double-page expanses of waste land. Mii-chan survives, though fixed for ever as a little girl seven years of age. Finally, in a sudden break from the preceding text, Mii-chan's mother speaks directly to the reader:

> Our suffering was no accident. Without your will to prevent it, it could happen again.

Only a small proportion of quality prose fiction for children has involved its readers in the combat zones of the war. Readers with a taste for the violence of action were still catered for by the comic papers. In fact, some of the pocket libraries of the 1960s expanded in the 1970s into quarto-sized magazines such as *Battle* and *Warlord*, published weekly and also produced as 'Holiday Specials' and Annuals. Brightly coloured strip cartoons are noisy with hugely muscled heroes beating the living daylights out of snarling 'Nips', and 'Krauts' shouting '*Verdammt Amerikaners*'. By the early 1970s, the cool glamour and dry humour of James Bond was very much in vogue and though these hulking fighters have none of his suavity, they do have the same aura of the gambler who dices with death and always wins – usually with a pithy one-liner to go with it. The dialogue of the comic books, often uttered under heavy fire, consists of the kind of well-polished wit which gives a sense of high-spirited gaming to the bloody exploits. These publications usually include 'real life' photographs from the 'war archives' and information about particular operations or the machinery of war – there might be illustrated pages headlined 'The Chindits – Special Unit of World War Two' for example, or 'Up the Gunners – British Artillery of World War One.'

Puffin Books, recognizing an undoubted readership for action-packed war stories, introduced their *Warpath* series in 1999. They are produced to a precise pattern by J. Eldridge: 144 pages, 'Following in the footsteps of fighting heroes' and, like the comic books, including photographs and factual information. Each hero, perhaps in a curious bid for ease of readerly identification, is called John Smith. These are clearly written, exciting stories which avoid caricaturing the enemy without for a moment allowing us to forget whose side we are on. Deaths occur regularly, but there is no exultant celebration (' "I know it's awful, but it's them or us, Chalky" '). In *Tank Attack*, when Monty comes to take command of the Eighth Army in North Africa, there is no ambivalence about his enormous personal ambition as there is in Aidan Chambers' *Postcards from No Man's Land* (1999) (see pp. 155–7). The series is an undemanding 'read', and although characters may tend to 'jabber' or 'bellow' their dialogue, and 'grin' rather frequently, the series may well draw less willing male readers into books. Many classroom teachers would be grateful for that.

Even Biggles flew on in new editions, including a series of graphic novels originating in Sweden in which he acquired a wide-eyed blonde sidekick named Bebe Sunday. At the end of the century, some 30 Biggles titles were in print in the United Kingdom, many of them accompanied by audio-cassettes; and early in 2000 it was announced that an entrepreneur had secured the film rights to the Biggles titles. In fact, Biggles is still turning up in surprising corners of the literary globe; a visit to a Prague bookshop in July 2000 revealed a shelf packed with some 35 Biggles titles in Czech translation in cheaply produced hardback editions. Even more surprising was the discovery of *Worrals z W.A.A.F* by 'Will Earl Johns' in which a pouting, tawny-maned Worrals gazes out at the reader from the front cover with the cool composure of a catwalk model, hips thrust forward, long fingers poised on a gleaming belt buckle adorned by a lion rampant. Her shirt is torn at tanned shoulder and breast. Behind her, on the tarmac, her Spitfire is ticking over. Presumably the publishers are aware of – or have created – a market; at the end of *Biggles A Tajemny Vetrelec*, they advertise four of George. E. Rochester's 1930s novels of war in the air during World War I.

Warnings, Allegories and Satires

The peace protests during the Vietnam War in America and Britain, the continuing possibility of nuclear war in the 1970s and 1980s, and the outbreak of the Falklands War prompted a number of distinguished authors and artists to create some remarkable allegorical and satirical picture books – not all of them for very young readers.

Michael Foreman's *War and Peas* (1974) exposes the folly of stock-piling arms, the unequal division of food resources and the need to help poorer countries to sustain themselves. Like Don Quixote with his Sancho Panza, a skinny lion king, seeking help for his drought-stricken people, sets off by bicycle with his Minister of Food, a hedgehog who worked in a grocery shop. They ask their neighbour, a revoltingly gross human king, for aid. The Fat King is surrounded by fat guards in riot gear, huge jars of cookies, mounds of jelly, milk shakes and cream cakes. Far from helping them, the Fat King sends the entire fat army into the animals' kingdom in pursuit of the lion and the hedgehog. The troops are so heavy their tanks sink into the sand, and when the animals pelt them with peas and the birds bomb them with seeds, the fat army is put to flight. The seeds grow in the tanks' tracks, helped by some timely rain and the Fat King is left burping by himself wondering what is this 'Peace' the lion keeps talking about ('"Never heard of it," said the Fat King. "What's the recipe?"'). Foreman had already published another allegory, *The Two Giants* (1967) which treated the ridiculous futility of a war between two giants who fight for completely trivial reasons. He was to return to the pity of war in *War Game* (1989), an illustrated account of the lives, and deaths, of young soldiers in the Great War (see pp. 57–61).

Raymond Briggs' two picture books about war are more ferocious in spirit, and are for older readers, some would say for adults. The end papers of *When the Wind Blows* (1982) are jet black; the book they enclose provides a frightening warning of nuclear war. Hilda and Jim (whom readers may have met in Briggs' *Gentleman Jim* (1980)) are a gentle, middle-aged couple who look back nostalgically to the Second World War:

> Evacuees ... London kids seeing cows for the first time ... Old Churchill on the wireless ... Vera Lynn singing away ... Workers' Playtime ... ITMA ... Spitfires and Hurricanes in the blue sky over the cornfields ... the White Cliffs of Dover ... Old Jerry coming over every night ... those were the days ... .

Responding to government advice, Jim faithfully carries out the procedures recommended in his copy of *The Householder's Guide to Survival*. When the bomb drops, the couple's defences are inevitably useless and they die a ghastly but touchingly resigned death as the radiation takes effect, still confident that the Emergency Services will know what to do when they arrive. Much of the story is told in the tiny strips readers will know from Briggs' *Father Christmas* books. Here, the crowded pages are interrupted by what seem, by contrast, vast double-page spreads devoted to a single image: a nuclear missile stands on a distant plain, shadowy bombers and submarines home in on their targets. As the bomb explodes, there is simply an empty page, largely white with a pink glow bleeding to the edges. The overall impact of the colour of the strip pages changes too into a grimly predominant white, as the couple sicken into pallid decline. Against all of this, Hilda and Jim's unawareness of what is happening to them and their faith in government and past ways of proceeding become increasingly moving – knowing their fate as we do.

It is, again, the structure of *The Tin-Pot Foreign General and the Old Iron Woman* (1984) which creates the book's numbing impact. Briggs launches a savage attack on the triumphalism of Mrs Thatcher's handling of the Falklands War. '"I WON! REJOICE,"' sings the Old Iron Woman, as a wickedly caricatured Mrs Thatcher, drawn with the ferocity of Gillray or Cruikshank, blood blazing from her metallic nipples as if from pop-guns, her crazed eyes and serried ranks of bared teeth set in a cadaver's grimace.

Reading this book aloud, while showing the illustrations to groups of older students or adults, is a powerful experience for both reader and audience. Laughter erupts as the equally grotesque General and the Old Iron Woman send their battle fleets into action over 'the sad little island down at the bottom of the world'. In a noisily colourful double spread, the huge gleeful heads of the antagonists confront each other. The page is captioned, 'BANG! BANG! BANG! went the guns of the Tin-Pot Foreign General. BANG! BANG! BANG! went the guns of the Old Iron Woman.' Then, the turning page suddenly reveals a blurred figure of a soldier sprawling face down away from us. The picture is lined in black and the monochrome drawing suggests a rapid charcoal sketch. On the opposite page, set starkly on the silent white space, the text reads 'Some men were shot'. Laughter in a listening group dies on the instant, and there is commonly an intensifying silence, broken only by indrawn breaths of empathy, through the rest of the reading – and for some time after the book has been closed. Page by page, the blurred images press relentlessly home: 'Some men were drowned', 'Some men were burned alive', 'Some men were blown to bits', 'Some men were only half blown to bits and came home with parts of their bodies missing'. The book closes with the Old Iron Woman's Victory Parade – 'everyone went to Church and Thanked God' – in which the wounded were not invited to take part ('Some watched from a grandstand and others stayed at home with their memories and their medals'). This book went into paperback but was fairly swiftly remaindered and, for whatever reason, did not reprint.

Several picture books about war from mainland Europe have been published in English translations. The author and critic Umberto Eco wrote *The Bomb and the General* (illustrations by Eugenio Carmi, translation by William Weaver, 1989), a rather contrived story in which atoms themselves foil the General's ambitions by refusing to be used for making bombs. The General is reduced to making use of his uniform as a hotel doorman. Martin Auer wrote the text of *The Blue Boy* (illustrations by Simone Klages, first published in Germany in 1991 and appearing in Michael Hirst's English translation in 1992). It is a tale of a people 'who look just like us, except that they are blue' living on another planet. A terrible war destroys the city and an embittered 'blue boy', having lost home and family, sets out with a gun in search of whatever he might find. His travels through a fantastic wilderness and a voyage to the planet's moon finally prompt him to throw away his gun in his effort to understand the self-destruction of his people.

Nikolai Popov's *Why?* (1996) is perhaps the most likely of these allegories to appeal to younger readers. It is a wordless picture book organized throughout in double-page spreads. At the outset, a frog sits on a stone on the right-hand page, smilingly sniffing a flower picked from one of several plants evenly spaced across a serene field of green. To the frog's surprise, in the next spread, one of the plants on the left-hand page erupts into the air, blasted upwards by what seems to be a nozzle. It isn't a nozzle, we realize in the next spread, but the end of an umbrella held by an emerging mouse. The frog smiles across at the newcomer tentatively, but the mouse suddenly hurls itself upon the frog, ejecting it from its rock and grabbing the flower. Bigger aerial frogs zoom in to chase the mouse away. And so things escalate as the mouse returns in an armoured boot-car. Pitched battle commences, as each side brings up reinforcements and devises new weapons. Cunning ambushes are laid and the landscape is devastated. The green meadow is churned up until a battlefield reminiscent of the Somme is littered with the detritus of war – the wreckage of the armoured boots smoking in piles across the blackened pages. Finally, the two antagonists sit – bewildered – in their original positions, but now surrounded by a waste land.

The author's note reveals that he was a small boy in wartime Russia, his town bombarded by the Nazis. With his friends he played 'Cossacks and Robbers' on the streets and collected gleaming shrapnel after air raids. 'We didn't really comprehend their terrible origin – the deadly power that produced these shiny treasures – until a boy on one of these hunts found a special treasure that flashed and exploded in his hands, leaving him crippled for the rest of his life.' This experience, and the sight of German prisoners of war and limbless Russian peasants, along with his reading of Tolstoy and Dostoyevsky, Remarque and Hemingway, led Popov to a rejection of war and violence. He ends with a sentiment many who have written for children about war in the last three decades of the twentieth century would share:

> I have created this book because it seems to me that if children can understand the senselessness of war, if they can see how easily one can be sucked into a cycle of violence, they may become a force for peace in the future. I also hope that adults who share the book with children will re-examine their own thoughts on the futility of war.

Other Battlefields

Within Western cultures, through film, television and the printed media, a body of information is already held by most readers about the two World Wars. It is more difficult to write about wars in Vietnam, the Middle East or African states, or about civil conflicts in countries such as Chile or East Timor covered only fleetingly by the British and American news media. Nevertheless, Peter Dickinson's *AK* (set in a fictional African country) and James Watson's *Talking in Whispers* (Chile) and *Justice of the Dagger* (East Timor) have all been published in trade and educational editions. *Talking in Whispers*, in fact, is a set examination text and has been an immensely popular class reader for more than a decade. *AK* is remarkable, as Carol Fox has pointed out, in being one of the very few recent books about war in which a child is an active fighter – engaged in a struggle for democratic freedom – rather than a victim of war.[30]

Three writers – Rachel Anderson (*The War Orphan*), Robert Westall (*Gulf*) and Bernard Ashley (*Little Soldier*) – have brought distant conflicts into close focus by employing a broadly similar device; they alternate the familiarity of life in Britain with fighting in remote theatres of war.

Rachel Anderson's Simon is in the early years of secondary school – studious, thoughtful, highly self-aware, an only child of liberal parents. The book's opening sentences tell us much about him and the kind of narration we can expect from him:

> There was a small incident on the way home from school. I was stoned by four boys and I handled the situation badly.

The day holds more surprises for Simon. He is looking forward to an evening of homework ('It's the best part. Total control over yourself and your work. It's when you really learn something') when his parents tell him that he is about to have a new brother. That brother is, in fact, a Vietnamese orphan, and as the desperately damaged Ha moves into the family, Simon's own life is radically changed. Even his mind and his dreams are invaded by Ha and his experiences – which Ha himself will always be too restricted now to communicate directly. In this way, Rachel Anderson can interplay Simon's changing self in middle-class England with Ha's perilous existence in a Viet-Cong-held village. There is passion as well as skill in the writing, a book with the power to stop adolescent readers in their tracks and reveal new ways of thinking.

Robert Westall's *Gulf* also invites its readers to move between a secure British home and the hell of a battlefield through a kind of possession. The narrator, Tom, is a chip off his Dad's block – his father is larger than life, a builder, a rugby player, a good-humoured, loving and very physical man. Tom's younger brother Andrew, known as 'Figgis' (after Tom's imaginary friend who disappeared at Andrew's birth), is much more variable in his moods: his restless nights are disturbed by dreams. Figgis is a boy of painfully intense compassion – his empathy for others, especially those who are suffering, stretches into new dimensions with the outbreak of the Gulf War.

Figgis begins to talk in his sleep in Arabic, and Tom realizes that he is speaking as Latif, a boy soldier in Saddam Hussein's army. When Tom's Dad vehemently supports the Allied air attacks on Iraq, his wife loathes his 'gloating' attitude. Night by night, Figgis is drawn into the personality of Latif, trapped in his battlefield fox-hole with his comrades. Figgis can 'return' from Latif for increasingly brief interludes. Drained of energy, he is placed in hospital under the care of Dr Rashid, a psychiatrist who has more insight into Figgis's kinship with Latif than an Anglo-Saxon Briton might have. When Rashid is verbally abused by some school students, he tells Tom, 'I'm a member of the Royal College of Psychiatrists. I give them lectures. I have a big car and make much money. But I am still a Wog poofter. There is no exam I can pass that exempts me from being a Wog poofter.' Figgis is reduced to a small shrivelled figure in a psychiatric ward, as close to death as Latif on the battlefield. During one of his brief moments in his own skin, as it were, he tells Tom:

> 'I'm meant to be here, to see it all. To make up for all those who're watching on the TV as if it was a soap.'

And there, it seems, is the sustained anger which drives Westall's book – a rage against the presentational machismo of Stormin' Norman Schwarzkopf, the Allies' commander, the gung-ho belligerence of an otherwise decent man such as the boys' father, the fact that the suffering of the Iraqis goes unreported by the media. Eventually, with Latif's pathetic death in the desert, Figgis is freed. But he is changed. It is as if Figgis has died and a much more conventional, less feeling Andrew has taken his place. ' "[Figgis] felt too much for his fellow men. It is the rest of the world that is mad," ' says Dr Rashid. Ironically, the experience has profoundly affected Tom, the narrator. Figgis has taught him the nature of compassion, and as the two brothers face their futures, it is as though they have exchanged elements of their personalities.

Westall's criticism of the media's handling of the Gulf War, and his implied hostility to the war itself, stand in sharp contrast to his several novels set in the Second World War, of which *The Machine-Gunners* is the best known. Here, the justice of the cause is never in doubt, and there is even celebration, sometimes nostalgic in spirit, of the civilians' response to the impact of war. Westall's contrasting novels could well stand as representatives of the fictional treatment of the war of 1939–45 compared with later writing about Vietnam, the Falklands and the Gulf.

Like both Rachel Anderson and Robert Westall, Bernard Ashley enables his reader to move between the familiar context of Britain and a war zone, this time between the London streets and the potholed roads of an East African country almost destroyed by tribal warfare. Like Ha, Kaninda is badly damaged:

> There was nothing left for Kaninda at 14 Bulunda Road: no mother, no father, no sister, no place to live, no life. He either went on standing still, shaking; or he walked round in circles; or he stood and shouted his head off, screamed for the soldiers to come back and put bullets and machetes into him too.

He is not traumatized in the same way as Ha, for he becomes a hardened, Kibu guerrilla, possessed by a single intention – to kill his tribal enemies, the Yusulu. Kaninda is captured by the UN, however, and finds himself transplanted to a housing estate south of the Thames (an area which Ashley knows well from many years teaching there). The youths on these streets think themselves hard, dramatizing their neighbourhood wars into colourful importance. The realities of the wars obsessing Kaninda's memories provide a sharp contrast – all the sharper since the family which has taken him in is headed by Mrs Captain Betty Rose, so busy with her evangelizing work for God's Force – a kind of Salvation Army without the good works – that she ignores the anxious needs of her own daughter Laura and takes no time to reach out to Kaninda's earlier experiences. Kaninda's tribal war flares up in London, for in his school is a Yusulu boy. Towards the end of the novel, Kaninda holds Faustin N'gensi at knife point, but his enemy does not flinch:

> My family was killed the worst way. Atrocity. No mistake, boy. I hate, too – but I don't hate you ... Tribal war did it. War takes us all in its hand and smashes us on the rocks.

Slowly, Kaninda turns his knife away. The perspective he has found in his new environment has allowed him to re-order the past.

The basic rhythms of the novel – shifting between the clashing cultures – make for a compelling story. Stories in which characters learn from each other, or grow up through their experiences can easily become trite or pious. Ashley is far too tough and honest a writer for that. *Little Soldier* brings home the brutalizing effects of war and, to a different degree, the brutalizing effects of gang warfare in the inner city. Bernard Ashley researched this novel in Africa and – as there has been for 30 years in his work – there is an intensity about this story which urges tolerance based on knowledge.

The war in former Yugoslavia has already produced powerful texts, some of them by children suffering the war themselves. Zlata Filipovic's *Zlata's Diary* (1994) written in Serbo-Croat, was translated into French in 1993 and into English the following year. It is an account of her daily life by a child in Sarajevo, hiding in cellars and shelters as the city is pounded by bombs and shellfire. Els de Groen's *No Roof in Bosnia* (1997) follows the struggle for survival of a group of teenage children who have escaped from Sarajevo to the mountains.

Children's literature often provides particularly clear insights into the values of a period. The French critic Paul Hazard noted in 1932, 'England could be reconstructed entirely from its children's books.'[31] As he looked back on the likes of Henty, Kingston, Brereton and an ever-increasing number of public school stories, Hazard believed that British children were urged by their books to 'Love your country, strive to maintain the strength and grandeur of England' and, thus assured, to believe that Britain's 'absolute superiority over all the other nations of the world is indisputable'. Nevertheless, Hazard concluded his section on British children's books by suggesting that 'children's books repudiate instinctively antagonisms and hatred, mixing indissolubly with a sense of patriotism a sense of humanity'.

If he were able to survey the texts produced for children about war in the last three decades of a century of bloodshed, he would surely note how 'a sense of humanity' had largely displaced the certainties and jingoism he saw in the books of the nineteenth and early twentieth centuries. He would also see a nation far less at ease with itself, and far less sure of its cultural identity than the one he described in 1932; and the complex, ambivalent reactions to the Falklands and the Gulf wars could well be said to confirm Hazard's notion of a nation reflected in its children's books. In the treatment of the two world wars in recent novels and picture books, however, young readers are invariably urged to examine the nature of violence and suffering, persecution and endurance, hatred and loyalty, selfishness and sacrifice. They are asked to share the writers' condemnation of war and the repugnant beliefs which lead to conflict, and to feel compassion for the anguish imposed upon the innocent many by the powerful few.

Notes

1. M. Cadogan and P. Craig (1978), *Women and Children First: The Fiction of Two World Wars* (p29), in which the authors combine scholarship with humour.
2. In C. Cullingford (1998), *Children's Literature and Its Effects*, p. 71.
3. For a full exploration of this area, see M. Green (1980), *Deeds of Adventure, Deeds of Empire*; and P. Parker (1987), *The Old Lie*.
4. In P. Parker, p. 211.
5. In 'Football and War', *The Boy's Own Annual 1914–15*, p. 95.
6. In Parker, p. 248.
7. See W. O. G. Lofts and D. J. Adley (1970), *The Men Behind Boys' Fiction*, p. 151.
8. In P. Warner (1978), *The Best of Chums*, p. 51.
9. In C. Cullingford, pp. 81–7.
10. In Cadogan and Craig, p. 60.
11. In Cadogan and Craig, p. 61.
12. See S. Sims and H. Clare (2000), *The Encyclopaedia of Girls' School Stories*, p. 214.
13. In Cadogan and Craig, p. 62.
14. See D. Butts (1989), 'Imperialists of the air: flying stories 1900–1950' in J. Richards (ed.) (1989), *Imperialism and Juvenile Literature*, pp. 126–43.
15. See J. Richards, 'The lost boys', pp. 216–29, in *Happiest Days* (1988), and G. Fox (1991), 'Tell England and the perfection of death', in *Children's Literature in Education*, Vol. 22, No. 4, pp. 257–74.
16. See M. Fisher (1986), *The Bright Face of Danger*, p. 362.
17. For facsimiles of several of the comics mentioned in this section, see D. Gifford (1988), *Comics At War*.
18. For a detailed account of the publishing of 'little books' in the Second World War, see M. Eve (2000), 'From better little books to Baby Puffins', in *Children's Literature in Education*, Vol 31, No. 2, pp. 125–43.
19. See George Orwell, 'Boys' Weeklies', in *Critical Essays* (1940). For an account of Frank Richards' fine reply to Orwell, see Mary Cadogan (1988), *Frank Richards: The Chap behind the Chums*.
20. See Cadogan and Craig, p. 215.
21. See Fisher, p. 141.
22. See O. D. Edwards (2000); 'The Battle of Britain and Children's Literature', in J. Dronfield (ed.), *Burning Blue*, pp. 163–90.
23. Ibid., p.173.
24. See Cadogan and Craig, p. 226.
25. See M. Cadogan (1990), *The William Companion*, pp. 198–200.

26. See J. Lepman (1969), *A Bridge of Children's Books*.
27. In P. Hunt (ed.) (1995), *Children's Literature: An Illustrated History*, p. 263.
28. We are indebted to Tony Watkins of Reading University for this comment.
29. We are grateful to the late Mr Colin Morgan for his generously given advice and information concerning the Thomson papers.
30. The comment on *AK* is one of many insights in an invaluable reference source for books dealing with war, *War and Peace in Children's Books*, prepared by an international team from Belgium, Portugal and the United Kingdom, funded by the European Economic Community. The team made a selection of 200 titles, with annotated details provided for each book. The co-ordinator of the British team is Carol Fox of the School of Education, Brighton University, Falmer, Brighton, East Sussex, BN1 9PH. We are grateful for her help in our own work.
31. See P. Hazard (1932) (English trans. 1944), *Books, Children and Men*.

CHAPTER 2

The First World War

The closing decades of the twentieth century saw a proliferation of novels for young readers which examined the Second World War and its aftermath, but over the same period relatively few novels have been published for this readership which dealt with the First World War. The success of Sebastian Faulks' *Birdsong* (1993) and Pat Barker's *Regeneration* (1991) – and its sequels – signifies the depth of adult interest in literary fiction about the First World War. The opening of *Regeneration* which portrays the continuation of war as 'evil and unjust' reflects the attitude towards the war prevalent in contemporary children's novels. Those novels for a younger audience published in recent years rarely seek to paint an overtly patriotic picture of the nation at war or to promote the values espoused by First World War novels written earlier in the century. Contemporary novels are frequently critical of the planning behind the war, painting a grim picture of the huge loss of life suffered by both sides in the trenches and on the battlefields. For many authors the First World War is depicted with a curious blend of sorrow, excitement and bewilderment. The tension between the sense of emancipation – particularly for young women or for those who had worked as servants before the war – and despair at the seemingly endless loss of life, is at the core of many recent British children's novels about the First World War. The patriotic mood of the time in which the public desired its young men to act heroically and its young women selflessly is contrasted poignantly with the blood, sweat and tears of the battlefield scenes. Late twentieth-century children's novels present their protagonists not as heroic or saintly figures, but as ordinary people caught up in terrible events. Often uncertain of the ethics of the war they fight, frequently afraid and exhausted, the young heroes and heroines exhibit moral as much as physical courage. Above all they demonstrate the inner strength, resourcefulness and determination of ordinary people, rather than the glamorized heroics of earlier novels. Late twentieth-century children's novels rarely deal with the crude equation that bravery on the battlefield is what makes a man a hero, and even fewer portray an empathy with the idea that young women should remain patiently at home while the men go off to fight the war. Instead many of the novels are concerned with the protagonists' attempts to find a *modus vivendi* which allows them to retain their own personal integrity in impossible situations and against the backdrop of a war which is notable for its lack of organization, compassion and morality. The struggle of ordinary young men and women to reconcile national duty with personal ethics, inner self with outer world, is at the core of many children's novels about the period. For young heroines the attempt to find a way of living that is compassionate, brave and useful often reflects a pre-war interest in women's social and political rights, whether the right to vote as in Marjorie Darke's *A Rose from Blighty* (1990) and Linda Newbery's *Some Other War* (1988), or the right to an education as in Ruth Elwin Harris' *Quantocks Quartet* (1986–94)

A. J. P. Taylor's influential book *The First World War* (1963) gave an account of the conflict presenting the generals as ignorant, the politicians as incompetent, and the massacres of thousands as senseless. He describes 'a pattern not foreseen by anyone in a responsible position before the war started: not a short war of quick decisions, but a war of deadlock and prolonged battering which seemed as if it might go on indefinitely. No one had prepared for this; no one knew how to handle it' (p. 47). At Verdun, 'both sides … fought literally for the sake of fighting. There was no prize to be gained or lost, only men to be killed and glory to be won' (p. 126). Taylor's picture of 'brave helpless soldiers; blundering obstinate generals; nothing achieved' is one which has permeated recent British children's fiction of the First World War. In her book *The Bright Face of Danger: An Exploration of the Adventure Story* (1986) Margery Fisher has examined the change in portrayal of the First World War, the move away from patriotism and a heroism concerned only with physical bravery (as exemplified in the Biggles books for example) towards a more contemplative consideration of war. Recent novels about the war are concerned not with heroics or bravery under fire, but with the difficulties for the heroes and heroines of reconciling an inner self which demands integrity, kindness and morality, with the harsh and brutal demands made by the external world. At the close of the twentieth century authors and publishers are concerned not to inculcate an active sense of patriotism in their young readers, but rather to educate them about the misery of war. Their subject matter is no longer the vainglorious heroics of earlier novels, but war and the pity of war. With the late twentieth-century move away from belief in patriotism and towards humanism, away from state and church and towards individualism, and away from external heroics and towards inner consciousness, it is unsurprising that children's fiction should reflect these trends and move towards a critical examination of the war itself coupled with a psychological examination of those who lived through it. The novels discussed in this chapter are those contemporary classics of children's literature which most comprehensively reflect the prevailing attitudes towards the First World War to be found in contemporary children's fiction.

On the Battlefields

With the move away from the adventure story format and towards the inner lives of characters, the depiction of young men at war has become more complex. Young women may be portrayed as brave, compassionate and sympathetic in their lives away from the trenches, but the portrayal of men whose task is to kill or be killed, and who can no longer cling to the easy morality of the action adventure story has become increasingly unpopular. Few late twentieth-century children's novels concentrate primarily on the lives of young men in the trenches, preferring to juxtapose scenes of the battlefield with those set in hospital wards or on the home front.

War Game

Michael Foreman's *War Game* (1989) is one of the few recent children's books to depict life in the trenches. A poignant and powerful picture book, it raises through illustration issues that are arguably more difficult to convey in words to young readers. The book has also been published on the Puffin list with black-and-white illustrations, in an edition that – as well as being cheaper to produce – is presumably intended to appeal to children who may consider themselves too old for a full-colour picture book. Although this version is in widespread use throughout British schools, it is inevitable that the loss of colour and reduction in size of the illustrations lessens both the power and poignancy of the original full-colour version.

War Game opens with a group of young men playing a game of football in an English village; Will dreams of scoring for England and the illustrations show the young men in brightly coloured football kit playing under a blue summer sky. When the game ends the young men begin to talk of enlisting. The watercolour illustrations are now in muted pastel colours and are accompanied by black-and-white wartime pictures of the posters which encouraged men to enlist. A second chapter ironically entitled 'The Adventure' sees the boys enlist at the town hall urged on by cheering crowds. While the British flags retain the bright colours of the opening illustrations, the people are shown in shades of grey and brown, foreshadowing, perhaps, the impersonal nature of the boys' new life.

At first, joining the army does indeed seem an adventure, though the astute reader may foresee the impending disorganization of the war, anticipated in the detail of the short supply of uniforms. Even when the boys first get to France there is still a sense of normality and the illustrations show women and children working the fields just as they do at home in Suffolk. It is only as the boys get closer to the front that the illustrations suddenly and shockingly reveal the horrors that await: the viewpoint changes to ground level and the colours become predominantly brown and grey. One illustration is a full-page spread showing lines of refugees and wounded and exhausted soldiers, all fleeing the battlefields. The visual image is striking and immediately powerful, inviting readers to consider the state of mind of the young men who find themselves in this harrowing situation. The narrative, however, becomes less concerned with the lives of individuals, distancing itself from the four young men and conveying a general picture which moves away from Will and Freddy, posted as sentries in the trench, to the routine of trench life for all the ordinary soldiers, and outwards to the position of the army as a whole, bogged down in their fixed positions in the mud as the weather grows worse. The move from personal to general allows the reader to speculate about the role of the individual soldier, likely to end up dead in No Man's Land without, seemingly, contributing to any advance by the army as a whole. The narrative is interspersed with brief factual accounts of life for the soldiers while further factual details sit outside the main body of the text, focussing attention on the emotional aspects of both narrative and illustrations, which again use predominantly browns and greys, except in depictions of the sky. Both words and pictures concentrate on the proximity of one front line to the other, 'so close that whenever the fighting died down, each army could hear the other's voices and could sometimes even smell their breakfasts. They all knew that they were sharing the same terrible conditions.' The word 'all', with the sudden intervention of the omniscient narrator aware of life in the German camp as well as the British, marks the beginning of a change in narrative focus leading the reader to view the Germans not as wartime enemies but as fellow sufferers. Words and pictures portray a change in relations, with singing across the lines and shouted Christmas wishes.

The book then depicts the famous football game said to have been played in No Man's Land on Christmas Day 1914 between the British and German troops. The game acts both as a reminder of the happy home life enjoyed by the soldiers only months before and as a bitter-sweet indicator of the poignancy of war. It is 'wonderfully disorganized, part football, part ice-skating, with unknown numbers on each team. No referees, no account of the score.' The parallels with the war are implicit, a disorganized conflict involving every type of warfare from cavalry to airplanes; it is a fight in which there can be no referee and which everyone will lose. The stupidity is tacitly emphasized by the pre-game reminder that the British and German men have lived and worked alongside one another before the outbreak of war. As in many recent children's novels about the war, there is a sense – here implicit rather than stated overtly as in Michael Morpurgo's *War Horse* (1982) – that, left to themselves, the ordinary men in the trenches could end the war without the bloodshed or brutality. Officers are held to blame when events take a turn for the worse:

> Some of the British officers took a dim view of such sport ... Boxing Day passed without a game. The officers were alarmed at what had happened on Christmas Day. If such friendly relations continued, how could they get the men to fight again? How could the war continue?

The implication is clear: officers must make sure the war continues, while the troops are anxious for it to end. The shift to the officers' viewpoint is made manifest in the use of the clichéd upper-class phrase. With the next page turn comes the return to warfare, muted colours, and wartime advertisements. This time the British ad for cigarettes to be sent to the troops as Christmas presents is paired with a German one, also showing Christmas presents for the troops. The Germans can no longer be thought of as an alien enemy, only as fellow participants in a futile game. The pairing implicit in the advertisements is re-enacted vividly in the final pages of the book, which return to the footballing imagery of the opening. As the British front line moves forward to attack, Will watches Freddy dive full length, then curl up 'as if clutching a ball in the best goal-keeping tradition' – though both Will and the reader know that it is not a football that Freddy clutches. Amidst scenes of utter chaos and misery, Will finds himself in a shell hole, close to death. The final pages of this picture book are a triumph of understatement, a vivid reminder that text and illustration combined allow young readers to comprehend and to internalize even the most terrible of events:

> The whole line went down. Earth and sky turned over, and Will found himself in a shell-hole, staring at the sky. Then everything went black.
>
> Slowly the blackness cleared and Will could see the hazy sky once more. Bits of him felt hot and other bits felt very cold. He couldn't move his legs. He heard a slight movement. There was someone else in the shell-hole.
>
> Will dimly recognized the gleam of a fixed bayonet and the outline of a German.
>
> 'Wasser. Wasser,' the German said.
>
> It was about the only German word Will knew. He fumbled for his water bottle and managed to push it towards the German with the butt of his rifle.
>
> The German drank deeply. He didn't have the strength to return the bottle.
>
> 'Kinder?' he said. Will shook his head. The German held up three fingers. Will tried to shake his head again to show that he did not understand, but the blackness returned.
>
> Later he saw a pale ball of gold in the misty sky. 'There's a ball in Heaven,' he thought. 'Thank God. We'll all have a game when this nightmare's over.'
>
> At home when he had a bad dream he knew that if he opened his eyes, the bad dream would end. But here, his eyes were already open.
>
> Perhaps if he closed them, the nightmare would end.
>
> He closed his eyes.

The contrast between the understated, predominantly monosyllabic language of the first part of this extract and the sudden vivid image of the golden ball in the sky suggests something akin to an out of body experience. Will seems to be distanced from the pain and suffering that we know he must be enduring, and the change from the physical description of his wounded legs to the spirituality of the great ball in the sky implies a progression from earth towards heaven, a suggestion which is reinforced by the illustrations which pass from a horrifying close-up of the German, almost threatening with his bayonet and bald head, through an image of Will haloed by the golden ball, and outwards to a wider perspective of the battlefield. The many shell-holes become smaller and smaller until the final pages show the holes covered in snow and the poppies growing in No Man's Land.

Throughout recent British children's literary fiction of the First World War the racial stereotypes embraced by some aspects of popular culture are refuted. Where Germans do appear in contemporary British novels about the war they are portrayed as no different from their British counterparts. For the most part all the soldiers are shown to be ordinary men caught up in the horrors of war. Between British and German soldiers there is almost invariably a degree of mutual respect. Each buries the other's dead and when they meet they find much in common.

War Horse

Michael Morpurgo's *War Horse* takes as its protagonist a horse sold to the army for use in the cavalry. When the horse is captured by the Germans the narrative shows life on both sides of the front line, drawing attention to the similarities between the two sides. As in *War Game*, the parallels between the British and the Germans are made explicit. Here Joey, the horse, has survived a terrifying attack across No Man's Land, only to be taken captive by the Germans. For him there is little difference between the two sides:

> I had seen the same grey faces looking out from under their helmets somewhere before. All that was different were the uniforms – they were grey now with red piping, and the helmets were no longer round with a broad brim.

Later, when Joey becomes trapped in No Man's Land he serves to bring the British and the Germans closer together. After watching the horse desperately trying to find his way through the wire to one side or the other – it matters little to him which – a British and a German soldier move into No Man's Land, enmity suspended in their desire to help the horse. While other troops watch and cheer, the two men converse together, discuss the horse's injured leg, and resolve its fate with an amicable toss of a coin. The atmosphere is closer to that of a game than a war and parallels are drawn between their conversation and the war as a whole. As in other writing about the war, there is a pervading sense that the continuation of the war is the fault of the generals and politicians, and that, if left to ordinary people, it could be swiftly ended. Here the Welsh soldier who has rescued Joey says to his German counterpart:

'Jerry, boyo, I think if they would let you and me have an hour or two out here together, we could sort out this whole wretched mess. There would be no more weeping widows and crying children in my valley and no more in yours.'

Throughout *War Horse* our attention is drawn to the madness of war and to the way in which it turns normal values upside down. The German soldier Friedrich is viewed as mad by his fellows because he talks to himself, but he points out to the horses the insanity by which he is surrounded, insanity made manifest in his companions' inability to think for themselves and willingness to follow orders without thought:

'I am the only sane man in the regiment. It's the others that are mad, but they don't know it. They fight a war and they don't know what for. Isn't that crazy? How can one man kill another and not really know the reason why he does it, except that the other man wears a different colour uniform and speaks a different language?'

The armies' attitude towards the horses acts as an image for the madness of the war as a whole. Strong healthy horses are worked into the ground when a little foresight would keep them well for future use. At the end of the war we see how little sense has been learned by the officials when the order comes through that all the remaining horses will be left in France because there is no way of taking them back to England. Although Joey's own future is optimistic, the mood of the book as a whole, in which the slaughter of men at war is replaced by the slaughter of horses in peacetime, is a sombre one in which it is made apparent that nothing has been achieved and little learnt. The only consolations remain individual acts of kindness. Even without a central human figure the book still dwells on the need for personal integrity during wartime, contrasting the individual human kindness shown to the horse with the harsh brutality of the world at large.

Voices of Danger

Alick Rowe's novel *Voices of Danger* (1990) is rare among contemporary fiction in that it concentrates almost exclusively on depicting the demands made on young men in wartime. It examines the lives of boys at war, and, as with both *War Game* and *War Horse*, it too portrays a shift in mood from optimistic patriotism to elegiac questioning. The book opens in a choir school in the spring of 1916 where it depicts the conventional world of the boys' public school, a world in which boys are accustomed to obeying orders, and where authority is rarely questioned, even when it is vested in older boys rather than masters. This is a world where the hierarchy is determined by age and social background rather than by merit, and where ideals of patriotism and glory abound. The whole community is 'eager to raise money to provide comfort and memories of home to the local men fighting far away for King and Country in France'. In many respects the school represents a microcosm of army life with its attention to rank and seniority and its reliance on tradition and authority.

However this is not to be a book that follows the standard patterns of school or adventure stories with their clear demarcations of good and evil, bravery, cowardice and heroism. Instead the novel opens with a description of the would-be hero – a chorister – stealing from the collection box. Neither Alex, the chorister, nor Seb, his best friend, fit the traditional mould of middle-class, monied young men who will go straight from school to become officers in the army. They run away from school, Alex in disgrace, and enlist in order to avoid having to return. Once in the army, war appears initially to be merely a continuation of the school pattern of obedience to orders and respect for one's superiors. Their first task in France is to be 'general dogsbodies', an echo of the fagging familiar from school. The two boys are removed from the front line when their age is discovered, and are taken instead to help with the running of Pavé, a unique depot behind the lines. Once the boys are established in the depot they – and the reader – have a space in which to adjust to the differences between life at war and the familiar pattern of home and school. At Pavé life is neither ordered nor regimented; the very success of the depot lies in its ability to do whatever is needed whenever it is required. Its flexible structure comes both to represent and to mirror the boys' changing attitudes to the war, their growing ability to live outside the world of rules and regulations, and their increasing need to question the ethics of the war.

During their time at Pavé, Alex and Seb are exposed to a wider view of the world and a different view of the war. Two of the boys in particular provide strong contrasts to Seb and Alex: Ted is a nervous young man, embarrassed about changing his clothes in public and happiest when looking after the pigeons in the loft. Reuben, on the other hand, is shown to be a troublemaker. His belief in a dubious set of supposedly patriotic values eventually leads to the downfall of Pavé and the brutal deaths of almost all its inhabitants. Alex and Seb – and the reader – are also given a new and critical view of the war by Cocky, the RSM in charge of Pavé. Cocky's view of war is central to the shift in perception undergone by the boys. An older man who has been in the army since he was a boy, he replaces the earlier authority figures of master and prefect, and demonstrates to the boys the possibility of combining loyalty and bravery with bitter cynicism. Cocky is known for questioning orders which he feels 'would put his men in unnecessary danger' and characterizes the war as 'Old Men killing Young Men'. He has, however, a strong army record, is a 'good leader of men' and has been 'an example in courage and in attitude towards authority'. His anti-war attitude, endorsed as it is by his own experience, carries considerable weight. Cocky's anger over the way in which the war is being managed is given further authorial endorsement in the chapter in which tanks are first used. His curious blend of cynicism and kindness is here shown at its strongest. In the camp everyone is excited at the prospect of the new weapons, but Cocky is unconvinced. The account of the ensuing action, told partly from the boys' perspective, partly from Cocky's, and at times with the dispassionate voice of an official report, is central to the view of war presented in the book. While everyone else is convinced that 'after such weapons as the tank there could never be another war', Cocky remains sceptical: ' "If we're daft enough to fight this one to the bitter end, we're too daft to change." ' He nevertheless allows the boys to go and see the tanks which so excite them. When the tanks are put to use, however, Cocky's own views are directly juxtaposed with the failure of the official plan, clearly signalling to the reader that his are the views to which we should give credence:

> The tanks … were to have ripped away every obstacle that had created the deadly stalemate of trench warfare. Supported by infantry, they were to have punched great gaps in the German defences through which the Cavalry stood poised to pour, eager to gallop spectacularly into that untrenched and undefended countryside beyond the front lines and capture headquarters, railheads, ammunition depots. By the end of the day, British GHQ expected to draw a new front line across Picardy. That was the plan.
>
> 'Plan,' said RSM Allcock scornfully. 'They sit on their aged arses and think they're playing chess.'

The contrast between the emotive description of the official plan with its dramatic verbs and clichéd images, and Cocky's monosyllabic coarseness emphasizes the gulf between theory and practice. The chapter, which had opened with the excitement at the arrival of the tanks, ends with a picture of their failure, an image made all the more dramatic since it is couched in sparse factual terms which contrast sharply with the tone of the official plan:

> Forty-two tanks had been able to muster at their starting-point, ready to spearhead the big push. Just over half of them had been able to move when required and of the twenty-five that began the attack, only eight saw the action through. Dotted around the battlefield, seventeen tanks lay ditched, destroyed or broken-down.

From this point on the impetus of the novel changes from the portrayal of war itself to the portrayal of the boys' reaction to war, their attempts to maintain integrity and to retain a degree of sanity in the face of the appalling conditions and senseless massacres. Having seen at first hand the brutality of war, and having learnt from a trusted mentor that war is neither planned nor managed, Alex and Seb have to return to the thick of the fighting in the trenches. When they meet up with Lionel Tarrington, once the school bully and now their commanding officer, the change in both Seb and Alex is marked. While Tarrington, new to the front and over eager to prove himself, expects the old school-boy values and hierarchy to be preserved, neither Alex nor Seb can return to the old world, speaking out in defiance of Tarrington and declaring, ' "We're not at school any more. This isn't sport; not a game." ' As the two boys struggle to reconcile themselves to life after Pavé, Seb remains quiet, internalizing his misery and 'keeping the door of self-control locked and barred'. Alex, however, increasingly takes refuge in a form of madness, unable to find a way of living to which he can reconcile himself and becoming intent instead on death and destruction. Seb tries to save Tarrington's life on a night-raid, destroying his own choir-school voice by giving the dying Tarrington the only gas mask, but Alex is still intent on murdering the former bully. Excited by danger and driven to push himself further and further, there is no morality underlying his actions, just a basic animal instinct:

> Alex ... knew he was mad and that people believed he was half in another world. Fine. Let the unearthly part work for him. He no longer needed sleep and was fed more by danger than by food and drink. He was mad. Good. He opened his mind to whatever it was he could find in the ravaged landscape ... It happened, the familiar rush of anger rose through him as he moved. Every sense began to tighten. His nerves stretched taut as wire. His skin felt

wafer-thin and as tense as a drum. The adrenalin began to pump
... I am a spirit, he thought. I am an angel. I could fly.

Alex is shown to have little need for the bodily comforts of sleep, food
and drink, all things which we have seen Seb seeking for himself and
Tarrington. After the rescue Seb returns to England, where he lies in a
bright room with clean white sheets, a contrast with the bloody red
used in the image of Alex in battle:

> He yelled he was a spirit, was an angel and could fly as he jumped
> towards the dug-out where the Germans screamed and scattered.
> His bayonet glinted red in the flames.

Seb is able to achieve inner peace, his growing sense of self evidenced
in his increasing ability to write music. The need for inner courage
rather than obvious heroics is made explicit after the return of Roy, a
boy who was taken prisoner by the Germans at Pavé. Staring sadly into
the fire Roy recounts to Seb how he told everything to the Germans
who interrogated him, '"They knew enough anyway. There didn't
seem any point in being a hero."'

When Seb meets Alex again the latter is both physically and
emotionally unrecognizable. His face has been symbolically blown to
pieces, leaving him living physically behind an electroplate mask, just
as emotionally he has taken refuge behind madness. In a novel which
uses repeated images of watching, and which examines the difference
between appearances and reality, the metal mask behind which he
hides becomes a symbol of his isolation from the world around him. His
madness becomes an emblem of the madness of the whole war, his
physical injury an image of the inability of the world to see the cruelty
of war.

Throughout the novel music is used as an indicator of characters'
emotional states. The choirboys' cracking voices at the beginning of
the novel foreshadow the physical and idealistic division that takes
place between boys and school. Cocky's defiant mixture of bravery and
cynicism is epitomized by his love of Elgar; although many view Elgar
as an archetypal and patriotic English composer, Cocky rejects 'Pomp
and Circumstance', preferring instead the 'Serenade' to soothe and the
'Introduction and Allegro' to steel him. The book culminates in the
first performance of Seb's new piece of music, a piece written in
memory of Alex but which becomes an elegy for the whole war. The
music is symbolic in more ways than one. Performed in the village
church, it is initially viewed by the local people as critical of the war
and therefore unpatriotic, but it eventually gives the entire community

an implicit understanding of the futility of war. It also re-enacts the movement of the book, away from conviction and patriotism towards uncertainty and doubt:

> The march followed. At first it was jaunty, swaggering – full of hope and glory – but after a while, without any of the hearers knowing exactly how, it became a funeral march, slow and sombre. Then it was not even that, and the instruments fell silent one by one, until only the drummer was left. Now his rhythm faltered and his beats became confused, quieter and quieter like a blind man wandering into the distance.

The piece ends with the singing of 'Dear Lord and Father of Mankind / Forgive our foolish ways ... ' a sentiment that echoes the theme of this book, and of many other contemporary novels about the First World War.

Women at War

Some Other War Trilogy

In the *Some Other War* trilogy (*Some Other War*, 1988), *The Kind Ghosts*, 1991), *The Wearing of the Green*, 1992)) Linda Newbery pairs a young man in the trenches with his twin sister working as a member of the Voluntary Aid Detachment, thus counterpointing the inhumanity of life in the trenches – and the difficulties for the hero of developing his own integrity in such brutal situations – with the slightly more humane hospital setting. The trilogy takes as its theme the dichotomy between the public perception of the war and its true nature, its theme expressed openly by Alice's fiancé who is subsequently killed:

> 'As far as the public and the newspapers are concerned, it's all heroism and derring-do, running the straight race and putting the foe to flight. It's as if the reality we know about – the bungled decisions, and the maiming and disfigurements, and the hopeless slaughter – all that belongs to some other war.'

We see images of men being encouraged to go to war by those who remain at home, and of crowds cheering the wounded as they return from battle. While the older generation clings tenaciously to its view of a heroic war, the younger men and women who are directly involved learn that the reality of war is something quite different. Repeatedly, in this as in other First World War novels, we are shown how newspaper headlines report victories while hospitals are crowded with casualties, many of whom will never recover. Young readers are encouraged to question both the 'truth' of newspaper reports and the assumptions of those who remain ignorantly at home.

The pairing of the two central characters, the twins Alice and Jack, inevitably invites us to contrast their lives before and after the war as well as the role they play in the war itself. Before the war both were servants, Alice working in the house and Jack in the stables of the local landowner. During wartime Alice trains as a nurse while Jack enlists voluntarily – partly, like the protagonists of *Voices of Danger*, in order to get himself out of potential trouble at home. For much of the first two novels, alternating chapters give Alice's view of life in the hospitals and Jack's of life in the trenches. Of the two Alice is the better educated and more widely read. When she writes letters they are eloquent and well composed, whereas Jack's betray a struggle with language. Meanwhile the third person narratives are paired so that, in the main, Alice's is the internalized, contemplative view of war while Jack's is the active, externalized one. While this pairing might suggest that Jack's narrative would be the action adventure story and Alice's the tale of romanticized heroics, the distinction between the two is gradually broken down, giving a critical view of war and of the stereotypes that accompany war fiction.

From the opening of *Some Other War*, Jack, who initially appears to be a typical adventure story hero, clearly demonstrates his physical bravery, jumping his horse over a hedge that his master, Philip Morland, cannot manage. Initially Jack is depicted as lacking in sensitivity but having great physical courage. When he is caught mocking Philip he demonstrates no sense of shame at what he has been doing, merely grinning as he remembers the episode, despite the knowledge that he came close to losing his job and his livelihood. The two early incidents between Jack and Philip are echoed later in the novel revealing the changes wrought by the war on each character, and specifically Jack's development from thoughtlessness towards concern for others. Jack, now a soldier, is again discovered mimicking Philip, by now his commanding officer. On this second occasion Philip has come to summon the men whom he is taking on a trench raid when he catches Jack mocking him in front of his men, just as before the war he had found Jack mocking him before his servant. Although Philip now appears to have an even greater degree of mastery over Jack, the night ends with Jack saving Philip's life in an act of bravery which, particularly when juxtaposed with Philip's comparative cowardice, recalls the incident at the beginning of the book. The complex interweaving of the two events in the men's lives affords the reader an insight into the development of Jack's character in the course of the war and his departure from the mould of traditional adventure story hero. As he struggles to persuade Philip to move, Jack himself recollects the incident when Philip shied away from jumping the hedge at home:

> He started to pull Philip by the arm, and Philip gave him a look of such blind panic that Jack was suddenly reminded of the time when he'd lost his nerve facing the hedge on Galliard. Well, they'd got a big hedge to face here all right, both of them … History was repeating itself with a vengeance.

The incident is significant not only for its presentation of Jack's character and its subsequent effect on events, but also because it suggests the changing nature of the social order. Before the war Philip held power over Jack as his master; in wartime his power has apparently increased – just as did Tarrington's over Seb and Alex – and he behaves, like Tarrington, as if attention to petty rules and regulations is all that matters. However this incident marks a turning point. Philip and Jack here have to function as individuals, regardless of their rank in the army or place in society. Each man is dependent on himself and his fellow to survive and Jack is proved the stronger of the two. The incident demonstrates the theme, recurrent in novels about the First World War, of the irrelevance of pre-set rules and of petty social divisions, and the need to think and act independently and regardless of social status.

During the course of the war we see Jack developing in sensitivity towards others and becoming increasingly inclined to question the ethics of the war itself. Initially he is shown as a person little able to internalize what goes on around him. He is – or thinks he is – in love with an empty-headed and faithless young woman, yet he remains oblivious of her true character. It is only when he meets Stephen, an army friend with whom he enjoys a friendship that encompasses mutual understanding, empathy and shared values, that Jack begins to perceive the failings in his relationship with Harriet. His relationship with Stephen also leads Jack to think more deeply about the world around him, allowing him to distance himself a little from the rough joviality of army life, and to question in a more complex fashion the wisdom of the war they are fighting.

Initially Jack watches his companions questioning the war not on grounds of morality but of tactics. The questions asked by the men are those of the ordinary soldier frustrated with the generals, ' "What happened at Gallipoli? What happened at Neuve Chapelle? Same as'll happen here in a day or two. More slaughter and they'll report it in the

papers as a victory.'' This early questioning is given narrative support
by Alice's experiences in the hospitals where an empty ward is a sign of
an impending 'Big Push'. At first Jack is shocked by this cynicism,
never having encountered anything like it. Then his meeting with
survivors of the fighting around Loos, who were caught in their own
poison gas released into the trenches when there was no wind to blow
it away, reminds him of his companion's criticism of their own leaders:

> Jack was shaken by these reports having believed that poison gas
> was an evil weapon, used exclusively by the Germans, and finding
> it difficult to reconcile this picture of chaos with the orderly
> advances he had practised at home and at Base Camp.

At this stage Jack still clearly associates the Germans with evil and is
shocked to discover that his own side is capable of being equally
immoral. However his concerns still lie primarily not with the war as a
whole, but with his own role in it:

> he wanted to go over the top. Only then would he know how he
> would acquit himself in battle, whether he'd be able to keep his
> nerve and follow his instructions, or whether he'd funk it and
> make a fool of himself and get shot for cowardice.

As Jack learns more about the war, his concerns extend to those
around him. Early on in the second book of the trilogy he looks at
another man new to the army who is experiencing the same longing to
go 'over the top' that he himself felt in the first book:

> Jack remembered how he himself had felt – almost wanting to get
> on with it, to test himself, to find out whether he would be steady
> under fire. *Steady under fire* – there was a bloody stupid phrase.
> The army didn't allow for ordinary human feelings. To be a
> perfect soldier you'd have to have no imagination at all – then
> you'd have no trouble staying *steady under fire* like a target on a
> shooting range.

Jack comes to question both the way in which the war is being fought
and the ethics of the war itself. His colonel quotes the words of Sir
Douglas Haig:

> There is no course open to us but to fight it out. Every position
> must be held to the last man: there must be no retirement. With
> our backs to the wall and believing in the justice of our cause,
> each one of us must fight to the end.

The newly arrived colonel's view of this as 'brave words, bravely spoken' is in marked contrast with Jack's own response:

> Many of the men the Colonel faced were seasoned troops who had been beaten back from Meteren and Bailleul and Estaires. Jack wondered what fighting spirit they could possibly have left, backs to the wall again as if it had ever been any different.

While the generals and the politicians are shown to be fighting an increasingly futile war, with ever growing lists of casualties, Jack develops an internal morality that inevitably leads him to question the war: 'He felt sickened, weary. *Thou shalt not kill*, he thought, until it was wartime, and then *Thou shalt kill*.' Jack's internal monologue is juxtaposed with a description of a dead German soldier looking up at Jack as if to emphasize the futility of it all. However, Jack does not allow himself to dwell upon what has happened, reverting once more to his role as the man of action rather than contemplation, 'There was no time for thinking; there was Sanders' wounded arm to be seen to, and hours of work after that; digging in, consolidating the new line.' As Jack's thoughts turn from the huge moral dilemma to the immediate task of planning the next few hours we see that, whatever his views on the rights or wrongs of the war, he will continue to follow instructions and to do as he is told, regardless of his inner views. Although Jack is not made brutal by the war he fights, we watch him actively deciding to ignore the horror of what he does. For him there is no option but to go on fighting and he has therefore to evolve strategies for dealing with the day-to-day events of his life. He consciously decides to stop thinking about the individual Germans that he fights, though his underlying morality is shown when he insists on burying the dead Germans as he would their British counterparts.

Jack's attempt to remain humane on the battlefield is shown to be part of a larger pattern in *The Kind Ghosts* when Alice, her friend Lorna and Philip Morland visit the battlefields of France after the war. Alice is comforted by the sight of the graves dug by German soldiers for the British dead. To an attentive reader there is a clear point to be made in the mirroring actions which reflect the similarity rather than the differences between the two sides. The humanity Jack himself develops in wartime is shown to be not merely a short-term response to the horrors of war, but a characteristic which remains with him after the war. The contrast between Jack, who is changed by the war, increasingly able to rely upon himself and to react to individual situations with honesty and integrity, and Philip, who even after the war still seeks to live according to a set of superimposed social values, is apparent when Jack cannot understand Philip's desire to go on shooting for sport. Jack is shown to have grown in sensitivity through his wartime experience and to have developed a way of living which applies to peacetime as well as to war. Philip Morland, on the other hand, now seems less concerned with issues of class and with petty rules and bureaucracy, but Alice knows that what he still wants is the 'carrying on [of] the traditions set by his father and grandfather'. In its examination of the effect of war on the British class system the trilogy is reminiscent of the *Flambards* series; the unconventional Jack exhibits many of the same characteristics as Dick, while the upper-class Stephen, unable to forget the old values appears, like Mark, to have changed little as a result of his experiences.

Alice is an independent young woman. Determined to take an active part in the war, she combines looking after her family with a caring and nurturing role as a nurse. Just as Jack is contrasted with Philip, Alice is set in opposition to Harriet, Jack's wife. The two girls were servants together before the war. Harriet's concerns both during and after the war reflect her own narrow and limited world. Her ignorance of and lack of interest in the horrors experienced by Jack and his fellow soldiers are shown in her response to his nightmares. Rather than showing any sympathy at his distress she complains of being woken by his shouting. Her lack of concern for the misery that haunts her husband is contrasted with the sympathetic ear Alice provides for her fiancé Edward when he returns home depressed by what he has witnessed.

With inside knowledge of the war provided by her hospital experience, and with the first-hand accounts from both Jack and Edward, Alice is fully aware of the futility of the war. A likeable character whose views we have come to respect, she questions the wisdom of the war, sees for herself the atrocities experienced by the troops, and reminds the reader that war is not about heroism or bravery in combat but about ordinary people. Facing impossible conditions, Alice struggles to maintain her integrity and succeeds in doing so, earning our respect for her views as well as her actions. With the growth of Alice's character the novel becomes a far more complex one than it first seems. From her hospital perspective Alice is able both to have an overview of the war and to consider its effects on individual men as they arrive wounded. The account of Alice's own exhausting and harrowing work is juxtaposed with the men's account of the horrors of life at the front:

> There was no time for gentleness. The men simply had to be
> processed like items on a factory production line. Normally, at

least some of the men arriving at the base – the less seriously injured – were pleased to find themselves in hospital, away from the fighting. Now, they were unanimous in speaking as if the war was lost.

'The Germans'll be here in a few days time,' they told her ... 'They'll be in Buckingham Palace this time next week.'

The men told of Peronne and Bapaume being retaken; the Germans had swept through the Somme battlefields with derisive ease, striding through Martinpuich, Guillemot, Contalmaison, Beaumont Hamel. The names were familiar from the dreadful summer of 1916, representing ground gained at such enormous cost, yard by desperate yard ... Alice could have wept, but there was no time to do anything other than work.

A Rose from Blighty

Life as a VAD is repeatedly seen in children's fiction to offer a particularly poignant mix of excitement and misery. For Alice Smallwood it offers the chance to leave behind the life of a servant and the narrow world of the village where she has grown up. It also opens her eyes politically to the true nature of the war. As VADs, the heroines of children's fiction have to come to terms with the realities of war, the contrast between the men's accounts of the war fought on the battlefields and its portrayal in the newspapers at home. For Julia Purcell in Ruth Elwin Harris' *The Dividing Sea* (1989), for Emily Palmer in Marjorie Darke's *A Rose from Blighty* (1990) and for Alice Smallwood in *Some Other War*, being posted close to the front lines brings them face to face with the reality of trench warfare. The heroines' work as VADs allows the authors to present the horror of war to young readers from the viewpoint of young women who, although they are appalled by the injuries they witness and critical of the planning behind the war, display both mental and physical courage.

Both Alice and Emily come from a working-class background and the war is clearly seen to bring about a change in their future social expectations as well as in the daily patterns of their lives. The horrors they encounter are unbearable, yet at the same time their work offers a form of freedom never experienced before the war. Despite the many restrictions which govern their out-of-hours activities both are able to experience a social freedom rarely afforded in their previous working week. Both Alice and Emily form friendships with young women of a higher social class, and both become engaged to marry the brothers of their new friends. In each case the fiancé dies in the war and the girls have to plan for a future which encompasses neither the certainty of marriage and children nor the old role as a servant or seamstress. The novels are also alike in their portrayal of the link between the suffragette cause and the role of women in wartime. Alice herself is not directly involved with the suffragettes, but espouses their views and helps her friend Laura with her work for Sylvia Pankhurst. Laura was a suffragette before the war, and the implication in *Some other War* as well as in *A Rose from Blighty* is that the same qualities of conviction, bravery and determination shown by the suffragettes are the qualities which give the heroines their strength as VADs and women their changing role in the political world.

The Quantocks Quartet

Ruth Elwin Harris' *Quantocks Quartet* tells the interlinked stories of two different families, their different characters, backgrounds and social situations allowing a complex consideration both of war itself and of the characters' evolving views of the war. Each of the four novels in the series is told from the viewpoint of one of the Purcell sisters (Frances, Julia, Gwen and Sarah), describing not only their lives, but also those of the neighbouring Mackenzie family with whom they form close friendships. Gabriel, Geoffrey and Anthony, the three Mackenzie sons, all enlist while their sister Lucy remains at home looking after their parents. The first three novels in the series, *The Silent Shore* (1986), *The Beckoning Hills* (1987) and *The Dividing Sea* (1989) overlap in their account of the First World War though each considers different aspects of the conflict.

Although each novel concentrates on different times in the girls' childhood, all contain an account of a momentous outing made by the eight children to the Quantock hills. The outing becomes in memory part of a halcyon time before the tragedy of war intervenes. It comes to symbolize life before the war, the companionship between the two families and the carefree nature of their lives. An important part of the memory is the pleasure of the very English countryside, which remains a powerful image throughout the novels. In each individual's memories of the day we see re-enacted the distortion of facts and the selectivity that later characterizes the adults' view of the war. None of the characters talks afterwards about the tensions that pervaded the early part of the day, and which the reader is shown in the first account of the outing: Lucy's struggle to persuade her mother to let her abandon her domestic duties; the tension between Sarah and Frances; the knowledge that they will return home to the wrath of the adult world.

In all the accounts the day is marked by Anthony's marching recitation of Coleridge. Sarah likens Anthony to a Greek god, or Achilles 'marching against the wicked men of Troy', the imagery an early foreshadowing of the war that is to come. As the incident is narrated for the first time in *The Silent Shore*, the first book in the quartet, we hear Anthony recite only the triumphal aspects of Coleridge's 'Kubla Khan':

> So twice five miles of fertile ground
> With walls and towers were girdled round ...
> But O, that deep romantic chasm which slanted
> Down the green hill athwart a cedarn cover.

The poem seems both to echo and to buttress the image of triumphant rural England, protected and romantic, which pervades the early images of war when would-be heroes enlist full of idealistic notions of fighting to defend England. Here the link between Xanadu and the landscape around is made explicit, ' "He was thinking of Aisholt when he wrote that," Gabriel said. "He wanted to live in Aisholt but Mrs. C. wouldn't agree." ' However, when the incident is described again in *The Dividing Sea*, the book most closely concerned with the portrayal of war, we are told that Anthony has been quoting chunks of 'The Ancient Mariner' all day, the chilling images it evokes very different from the triumphal 'Kubla Khan' recalled in the earlier book.

Throughout the series, the literature read by the protagonists provides an indication of their frames of mind and an insight into their characters. Anthony is a classicist, inspired by Greek poetry and historical accounts. After he enlists he still sees the war in epic terms, sending home letters,

> full of Homeric allusions in an attempt to beat the censor; unable, as the rector wryly remarked, to decide whether he was taking part in a modern day crusade to free Byzantium from the Turks or a reenactment of the Greek expedition to Troy.

Even after his death the Homeric allusions persist, his family imagining for him the heroic life he would have enjoyed. It is only when his brother Geoffrey dies that Sarah realizes how far from reality her vision has been:

> Geoffrey's death was worse than Anthony's for it brought her face to face with the reality of Anthony's loss ... Anthony had been sailing forever in her imagination on mythical seas: Jason among the Argonauts, Agamemnon with his Greek princes, Odysseus

exploring the far islands. Never once had she thought about the scene on the beaches. Now she thought of little else.

Had she really believed that some time in the future he would return to her, older, weather-beaten, and experienced? Had her work, her absorption in books, been like Penelope's tapestry – a refusal to face the truth?

The books that Sarah reads are shown to be integral to her personal development. She and Anthony study the classics and Gabriel provides her with Henty, Harrison Ainsworth and Conan Doyle as an antidote to the Victorian tragedies she has been reading: he is determined that she won't grow morbid. Sarah herself becomes a writer, as does Gabriel who writes very successful thrillers with a classical setting – a genre that seems to combine his love of the classics with a conventional view of the division between good and evil that permeates both the books he gives to Sarah and his own view of the war. Geoffrey's concept of the world is less easily reflected in classical literature. When he quotes Coleridge he remembers the 'slimy things', thinking 'The Ancient Mariner' 'horrible' and preferring instead Coleridge's poem 'Love', a romantic antidote to the horrors of war that surround him. While Gabriel and Anthony share a love of the classics and an uncomplicated view of war, Geoffrey, who comes to loathe the war and to question its ethics, shows little interest in the Greek classics, but asks for a copy of Coleridge's poetry which he reads in the trenches. For all the characters, development of the imagination as well as of moral sensitivity is directly linked to the books they read. When Sarah complains of her nightmares the servant Annie – who herself reads romances – blames her early reading:

> 'That was your mother's fault,' Annie said, 'letting you read whatever you wanted, fairy tales and suchlike. I told her 'twas a mistake. "Grimm by name, grim by nature, that's what I always said."'

Images of painters, paintings and music too are also used to represent the protagonists' mental states. Frances' independence and desire to rebel are shown in her appreciation of contemporary artists, while the more conventional Julia likes to listen to Mozart and Beethoven on the hospital gramophone.

In the third book, *The Dividing Sea*, Julia Purcell enrolls as a VAD, determined to go to France. Julia comes from an unorthodox middle-class background and her decision shocks her sisters and their guardian. Like Alice Smallwood and Emily Palmer she is given greater understanding both of the physical reality of war and of the mental implications for the men caught up in it through her work in the hospital. Again the book demonstrates the repeated pattern of eager excitement followed by critical questioning and sometimes cynical disbelief. Julia's fiancé Geoffrey is, like his brothers, initially eager to go to war, filled with schoolboy enthusiasm. Even after some time at the front he retains this enthusiasm:

> 'You must see,' [Geoffrey] said patiently. 'It's the biggest thing that's ever happened. It'll go down in the history books. We'll slaughter Fritz; everyone says so. It'll mean the end of the war. *Of course* I don't want to miss it. And even if we do get into it before it's all over it's not the same thing. Besides, it's my birthday soon. Wouldn't it be tremendous to go over the top in the greatest battle of all time on one's birthday?'

Julia, who has been working in a field hospital, does not share Geoffrey's eager anticipation, feeling 'sick with apprehension' at the prospect of the big push. The summer sunshine 'full of promise' mocks the futility of the war as Julia and her companions prepare the hospital for a new consignment of wounded and dying men. As the novel progresses Geoffrey comes to share Julia's doubts, becoming extremely depressed after the death of his friend in the mud of the battlefields, his misery apparent in his silence towards Julia and his withdrawal when he goes home on leave. Like Alice, Julia herself returns after the war to a sense of unbearable emptiness and displacement which makes the memory of war all the more poignant: 'Hillcrest seemed remote. She felt as if she were looking at it through the wrong end of a telescope.' Like *Some Other War* and *A Rose from Blighty*, *The Dividing Sea* is concerned not with accounts of glory on the battlefield, but with the horror and misery of war and with the development of inner strength needed to survive with morality intact.

Julia's unorthodox sister Frances, a painter who wraps herself in her own world and appears sometimes to have little knowledge of what goes on around her, is clear from the outset about her view of the war, arguing forcibly against the patriotic and clichéd views held by the wife of her guardian:

> 'Stupid little boys playing games, that's what it's about. Fooling around with guns, showing off, getting carried away. Well, they've gone too far now – it's too late to pull back now isn't it? What do you think matters, Mrs Mackenzie? Trade? Battleships? Power? You don't care if Rheims cathedral's been destroyed, or

> Kreisler's lost an arm or all the manuscripts of Louvain have gone
> up in smoke. None of that matters so long as we can beat the
> beastly Germans. We stand up in church and roll off the Ten
> Commandments and then what? Half the men in England are
> given guns and told to go off and murder the Hun. The world's
> gone mad.'

Frances' tirade outrages the conventional Mrs Mackenzie who
counters with trite phrases about 'England's hour of need' and 'duty'.
At this stage even Frances' sisters are shocked by her outburst, but as
the series progresses the deception of 'the old Lie' becomes increasingly
clear and Frances' views become more widely understood. When
Geoffrey returns home shell-shocked after the death of his friend, his
account of the war shows Sarah – the youngest Purcell sister – all its
horror and inhumanity. He demands, 'What are we fighting for
anyway?' and in the ensuing conversation the questionable link
between church and war is considered:

> 'I don't know. God, I think.'
> 'There can't be a God – He wouldn't let such things happen.
> Or perhaps there is and He's helping them.'
> 'England then. We're fighting for England.'
> 'But England's not – it's not what I thought it was.'
> She could think of nothing to say or do that would help. In the
> hollow emptiness of the church she prayed wordlessly for some
> means of comfort. None came.'

In many novels of the First World War the church stands in the
background, its representatives often urging young men from the pulpit
to go and fight as they do in *War Game* or *Voices of Danger*. The return
of characters from the battlefields and hospitals to the church at home
frequently marks the failure of those who remain behind to understand
the reality of the war. In *Some Other War* Edward makes explicit the
gulf between the supposedly patriotic sermons and the true nature of
war:

> 'I don't think I can stand another church service,' he exclaimed.
> 'The sententious moralizing – the attempts to justify the senseless
> slaughter of war as if it springs from some divine inspiration.'

With the church no longer able to provide a set of moral codes by
which characters may live their lives, it becomes increasingly important
that individuals develop their own set of values, a personal code which
takes into consideration the impossibilities of absolute morality in

wartime, the ignorance of authority figures, and the meaningless nature of all previous sets of rules and values.

Social Changes

Throughout children's literature, the First World War is seen as a time of change both internal and external. Characters' inner emotional and intellectual growth is matched by the enormous external social change; masters and servants fight alongside one another in the trenches, women take on jobs only previously open to men and can no longer expect to fill their lives with marriage and children, and the British class system is altered irrevocably. For almost all the young people caught up in the war, serving abroad enables them to see their country from a distance, to form a detached approach to the view of Britishness, of fighting for King and Country that prevailed before the war. During the course of their wartime experiences they not only begin to question the wisdom of their leaders, but also to distance themselves from the social hierarchy so dominant at home. The enormous social changes are often made manifest through their effect upon one particular house, most commonly a large house where the household encompasses people from more than one social class.

Many British children's novels therefore begin well before the war, exploring the contrast between life for those in the house before and after the war. In all these novels the house performs many functions. In part it affords the opportunity to link together the fortunes of people of different social backgrounds, class and age. It also draws together parents and children, those who have been accustomed to living as servants or masters all their lives and a younger generation who will begin to question the wisdom of this divide. The house also represents at once both stability and change, a physical symbol of the childhood the young men and women have left behind and a constant reminder that the world outside is changing fast. After the war the house may be either a potent symbol of the changes in society, or a reminder to those who have been away that little seems to have changed in rural England.

Flambards Series

The house as motif for the social changes brought by the war is perhaps most obvious in the original three books in K. M. Peyton's Flambards series. *Flambards* (1967), *The Edge of the Cloud* (1969) (winner of the Carnegie Medal) and *Flambards in Summer* (1969) span the period from 1908 to 1917, the first and last set predominantly at Flambards itself, the country house which becomes Christina's home. After the enormous success of the television series in the late 1970s a fourth novel, *Flambards Divided* (1981) was published. The first three books chart a pattern in which the heroine Christina moves from childhood to adulthood and from dependence to independence. The undercurrent of social change brought about by the war runs through the novel. The house itself comes to embody both stability and change, a symbol of the childhood Christina and her cousins have left behind and a constant reminder that the world outside is changing fast. After the war the regeneration of the house acts as a metaphor for Christina's mental state, the restoration of the old house mirroring her struggle to construct a new life after Will's death.

When Christina first arrives at Flambards she knows that she is expected to marry her cousin Mark and use her money to prop up the decaying family home. An intelligent child, Christina has no say in her own future and is not told directly what is expected of her; she finds out when she furtively reads a letter her aunt is writing, ' "The next thing we shall hear ... is that she will be married to Mark, and Flambards will be back on its feet again for another few years. How else, save through an advantageous marriage, will the poor place be propped up much longer?" ' The house itself reflects Christina's own emotions. When she first arrives she sees an unkempt garden and a bedroom which is shabby and old-fashioned, but whose general effect is 'pretty and homely'. To Christina it is a welcome refuge; although the house may not be well looked after she finds comfort within it, lamps lit, vegetables prepared for supper and cold apple pie – a dish which often symbolizes homeliness in British children's fiction – waiting in the pantry. However, as Christina comes to question the ethics of life at Flambards, where servants are taken for granted and physical cruelty is an accepted part of everyday life, we are made more conscious of the shabbiness of the house; the curtains fall apart as Christina pulls them leaving the shreds hanging forlornly on the rings. By the end of the novel when it has become apparent that Will and Christina have a future together only if they leave Flambards, the house no longer appears comforting. Christina sits waiting for Will to arrive in a room which is 'silent and gloomy, only the branch of candles which Mary had left at the top of the stairs guttering dismally in the draught'.

The second novel, *The Edge of the Cloud*, in which war draws closer, is set almost entirely away from the house. Christina returns to Flambards only once for Uncle Russell's funeral, and there is almost no description of the 'decayed old house' other than that of the 'wild garden flaunting its tumbled roses in the sunshine'. As Christina shares in the excitement so many novels depict at the beginning of the war, the house, and everything connected with everyday life, fades into insignificance:

> It was as if all the sorrows and excitements of their own lives were now very small and of no great importance, for what was happening was out of their hands. And – more strange still – it was not sad and terrible that the country was on the brink of going to war, but terrifically thrilling.

Without active descriptions of the horrors of trench warfare this view of the war remains largely unchallenged. However, when Christina herself returns to Flambards as a widow – Will is killed in the gap between the second and third novels and her cousin Mark has been reported missing – the effect of the war is evident in the dilapidated state of the house, a symbol for the misery of Christina's own war-torn life. Christina, now 21, rich and in charge of Flambards, repairs the house, its physical refurbishment reflecting her own regeneration. To some extent Christina herself exhibits not the typical fictional values of those who have stayed at home, but an open-mindedness and compassion comparable with the attitudes demonstrated by Julia Purcell and Alice Smallwood. She is the first in the village to take on a German prisoner-of-war and flouts convention by bringing her illegitimate nephew to live at Flambards. Eventually she plans to marry the former servant Dick, a move that before the war would have been deemed socially unacceptable and which Christina's cousin Mark still cannot understand. While the events of the third novel take place during wartime, its immediate effects are gradually distanced from Christina's own life and the preoccupation of the novel remains with social change rather than war itself.

A Little Love Song and The Rinaldi Ring

Many novels set during the First World War examine not just the changing social world, but the more open-minded morality adopted in wartime. In particular this is demonstrated as an increased sexual freedom. Julia Purcell and Alice Smallwood experience, while working as VADs, a degree of social and romantic licence never previously afforded them. For both girls, despite the strict rules of the ward sisters, the war brings the opportunity to spend the night with their fiancés, behaviour that would have been unthinkable without the freedom from accepted social mores and distance from the prying eyes of their villages afforded by the war. In each case the night spent with their partners – a short time before the death of the fiancé in both novels – stands as a symbol for the mental 'growing-up' that they have had to do in wartime, and for the need to act according to their own beliefs rather than according to social conventions. For Alice and Julia, able to ignore stifling pre-war morality, the nights spent with their lovers bring peace and happiness, their physical pleasure mirroring their emotional state. For other heroines, however, the First World War is shown to bring only short-term sexual freedom which leads to long-term suffering. Both Michelle Magorian's A Little Love Song (1991) and Jenny Nimmo's The Rinaldi Ring (1999) (short-listed for the Carnegie Medal) look back within the narrative to the First World War, describing the life of an unmarried young woman whose family consign her to a mental asylum because she is pregnant. In A Little Love Song Miss Hilda's restricted life during the First World War is contrasted with the comparative freedom experienced by Dot, pregnant with an illegitimate child in the Second World War. Diary extracts reveal Miss Hilda's state of mind, showing the narrow-mindedness of those who remain at home in wartime and contrasting their petty restrictions with the emotional and intellectual – if not physical – freedom experienced by Miss Hilda herself. The Rinaldi Ring is a much darker novel in many respects. Locked away by her parents because of her disgrace, Mary Ellen at times really does seem to be going mad, her grieving insanity mirroring the misery of the contemporary hero who has lost his mother. While Miss Hilda develops – though at an enormous cost – the emotional stability that allows her to survive the horrors inflicted on her by her narrow-minded and cruel brother, Mary Ellen is never fully able to reconcile herself to her situation and dies on Midsummer Day, falling into the river as she dreams of her dead fiancé.

Tree by Leaf

Cynthia Voigt's novel Tree by Leaf (1988) examines the lasting effects of the war on the men who fought in it. Clothilde's father returns from war disfigured and isolated from his family. Although the astute reader may be aware that the father's reluctance to return could be connected with the life he has inflicted upon his family during his absence, the well-read reader may also expect this moral American family to bear their changed circumstances nobly since the tale contains many echoes of Little Women. Eventually, we see that it is the redemptive power of family love which helps Clothilde's father to recover from the traumas of war, the symbolic kiss that his daughter gives him upon his ruined face the turning point in his difficult and complex journey. The horrors of war are portrayed visually throughout the novel, culminating in the image of the father as a man with a 'monster face'. Earlier her father's drawing had given Clothilde a graphic sense of the nightmare that he was experiencing when he sent her a picture of himself having to shoot their beloved horse. Although Clothilde remains distant from and largely unaware of the war itself, its effects are central to the complex portrayal of family relationships, the strong family bond eventually overcoming the suffering dealt by war.

Throughout the twentieth century children's authors and book publishers have sought to educate their readers, instructing them (with varying degrees of subtlety) in the importance of family love, of loyalty to friends and comrades, and of doing what is 'right'. The beliefs of each generation, and hence its fiction, are imbued with that generation's ideals. It is inevitable, perhaps, that novels written shortly after the war should depict the conflict through the eyes of heroic soldier figures, while novels of our own time should question more closely the ethics of the war, presenting those who lived through it as ordinary human figures with whom the readers should empathize, rather than seek to emulate. At the end of the twentieth century young readers and adults alike are encouraged to question the ethics of war, the demands made on young men sent to war, the role played by young women in wartime, and above all, perhaps, the place of the individual within society.

During the 1990s British publishers struggled to keep children's books about the First World War in print, partly perhaps because the National Curriculum for primary schools focused on events still within living memory, concentrating specifically on the Second World War in preference to the First, and partly because adults are still uncomfortable with presenting to young readers the image of a nation state determined to prolong a territorial war regardless of the human cost involved. Linda Newbery's excellent *Some Other War* trilogy was remaindered by Collins, as was Marjorie Darke's *A Rose from Blighty* and Voigt's *Tree by Leaf*. However, the late 1990s revival of interest in 'modern classics' has brought about the reissuing of, among others, K. M. Peyton's *Flambards* series and Alick Rowe's *Voices of Danger*, and the rejacketing of Ruth Elwin Harris' *Quantocks Quartet*. The demand from young readers for the publication of the final novel in the *Quantocks Quartet* testifies to the interest shown by children themselves in the period. With the republication of several contemporary classics, the 'trickle down' effect of adult literary interest in the period, and the approach of the centenary of the declaration of war, it seems likely that over the next decade children's literary fiction about the First World War will again come to prominence.

CHAPTER 3

The Second World War: The United Kingdom and North America

In recent years the 'Home Front' during the Second World War has become an increasingly popular subject, for authors and readers alike. Several novels have been published which deal with the mass evacuation of children out of British cities and a number of novels have sought to re-examine the plight of children who, while remaining at home – both in North America and in the UK – nevertheless found themselves facing moral and ethical dilemmas which reflected those encountered by the adult world at war. While novels of the First World War examine the position of young adults performing adult tasks in wartime, many novels set during the Second World War seek to understand what happens to children and to childhood itself in wartime.

A recurrent theme is the apparent powerlessness of children in wartime, their seeming inability, initially at least, to influence adult decisions, sometimes even to make their own views heard or understood. This is particularly apparent in the many novels about evacuation, where children are transported around the country like parcels, uprooted from home and family and sent to live with strangers without any say over their destination. The image of the evacuee arriving powerless at a strange place is one that is repeated time and again in children's fiction, the impersonal nature of the billeting process often forming a marked contrast with the subsequent emotional and moral development of the children involved.

Evacuees

Carrie's War
Nina Bawden's classic novel, *Carrie's War* (1973), demonstrates a
pattern which has since been adopted by many children's novels about
evacuation, whereby the heroine's progress from initial powerlessness
towards emotional maturity is paralleled by her developing response to
her new environment and those who inhabit it. Carrie and her brother
Nick are sent from an informal middle-class home in London to stay
with Welsh shopkeeper Mr Evans and his sister, 'Auntie' Lou. Here,
amidst the ordered life of Mr Evans' pristine home, the children
discover a complex web of family relationships, which their arrival –
together with that of Carrie's new found friend Albert who is billeted
with Mr Evans' other sister – is to change forever. Here the children's
initial sense of impotence is coupled, in Carrie's case, with a terrible
feeling of responsibility for those around her. The novel examines
themes of guilt and responsibility, and of absolute versus relative
morality. The perspective is that of the older sister for whom personal
feelings of insecurity are paired with a need to take responsibility for
the younger brother. Several novels – *Carrie's War*, Kit Pearson's *The
Sky Is Falling* (1989), Marita Conlon McKenna's *Safe Harbour* (1995) –
depict the evacuation of a younger brother with an older sister from
whose viewpoint the narrative is told, the older sister's sense of
responsibility (often closely allied to a sense of retrospective guilt)
suggesting wider questions about the war as a whole. For Carrie the
duty of care for her younger brother extends to concern for the adults
in the world around her, her compassion even including the formidable
Mr Evans who is disliked by almost everybody else.

Much of the novel deals with the twin issues of power or
powerlessness and responsibility, themes that echo the wider wartime
setting in which individuals bear responsibilities but hold little power.
Carrie gets off the train with her brother in the small Welsh mining
town, laden down with suitcases and struggling to manage everything,
her metaphorical burdens mirrored by her physical ones. As she sits
waiting to be chosen for a billet her sense of powerlessness develops
into one of shame and fear that no one will want them. Later the
oppressive, rule-conscious atmosphere of Mr Evans' immaculately
clean household adds to her burdens as she tries to abide by Mr Evans'
rules and to behave fairly to everyone. Her brother Nick, meanwhile, is
not unduly troubled by concern for the well-being of others, adhering
to his own absolute morality and seeing every issue in black and white.
While Carrie alternates between sympathy for the lonely Mr Evans and

anger at his apparent greed and coldness, Nick is brutally honest, both to Mr Evans' face and behind his back. Albert too, less given to romanticizing than Carrie, believes her to be naive in her sympathy for Mr Evans. Carrie's sense of responsibility carries with it the burden of isolation: Nick doesn't trust her not to sympathize with Mr Evans and so the secret of Auntie Lou's engagement is hidden from her. In her attempts to behave fairly to everyone, Carrie ends up feeling isolated and lonely. Years later her oldest son realizes that her constant worrying may well be a legacy of this period. She is:

> more afraid than most mothers. Not stopping them doing things, she wasn't silly like that, but you would look at her sometimes and see the fear holding her still. Especially when they were happy. As if she were afraid of a happy time stopping. He thought, perhaps because *this* happy time had come to an end all those years ago, and she blamed herself for it.

There hangs over the novel a brooding sense of the powerlessness of being a child, especially a child in wartime. When Mr Evans' older sister dies and the livelihood of those who have cared for her is threatened by Mr Evans' actions, Carrie tries to act as a grown-up but Albert is clear about the limitations of childhood. Thwarted in his desire to talk to a solicitor because of the impossibility of being a child, he can nevertheless understand the adult's view:

> 'I mean, what would you do if you were a lawyer and a boy came in and started yapping on about missing Wills like in some kid's story. I could just hear Mr Rhys saying *Run away little man, back to your comics*.'

Later Carrie, upset and frustrated by the impossibility of resolving the problem, takes action impetuously and thoughtlessly, hurling the ancient skull that acts as a symbol for the well-being of the house into a bottomless pond, her action explicitly linked to the war around her:

> Carrie's thoughts were like bits of jigsaw whirling around in her head. Several pieces but all fitting in, one to another. Albert throwing a stone and it falling. Bombs falling on cities, houses crumbling like sandcastles. Horrible, but somehow exciting to think of.

Like the other fictional children considered in this chapter, Carrie is physically removed from the war but its effect on her is nevertheless both profound and lasting, shaping her adult life, as her oldest son notes, for years to come.

War Guests Trilogy

Like *Carrie's War*, Kit Pearson's *War Guests* trilogy (1989–1993) describes the evacuation of a brother and sister, this time to Canada, remote from the war and from the Kent countryside where the children have grown up. The period of evacuation, covered in the three novels, *The Sky is Falling* (1989), *Looking at the Moon* (1991) and *The Lights Go on Again* (1993), sees Norah growing from determinedly patriotic childhood into contemplative adulthood. Here Norah's changing attitude to the war becomes a marker of her increasing maturity. The first book, *The Sky is Falling*, opens with 10-year-old Norah thinking of the war as a game, 'The war was the most exciting thing that had ever happened in Norah's ten years, and this summer was the best part of it.' At this stage the adults collude in seeing the war as a game and it is unclear whether it is because of Norah's age alone that she views the war in this light. Even when the adults are visibly anxious about developments in the war, the news announcer continues the analogy with a game, giving the 'scores' of the battle in the sky 'as if it were a football match'. The weather too, a cypher for Norah's mood throughout the series, echoes the children's sense of excitement and anticipation:

> There was a bright edge to everything; even the weather was exaggerated. The coldest winter in a hundred years was followed by a short spring and an early summer. As the war news grew worse and the grown-ups huddled anxiously round the wireless, day after day dawned hot and clear.

The book opens in a summer of unusually clear blue skies, skies whose absence of cloud cover brings a degree of safety to the residents of Kent. The grown-ups predict that 'Hitler and the rain will come together' but even before the bombing starts in earnest the unexpected debris that falls from the sky heralds the beginning of Norah's own impending upheaval:

> For the last month things had been falling out of the sky: stray bombs meant for the coast or the airfields, German propaganda leaflets that ended up being sold at raffles; and distant floating parachutes like tiny puffballs.

As Norah's departure approaches – she has guessed but does not know for certain that she is to be sent away – the things from the sky fall closer, no longer remote objects viewed in the distance, but tangible items landing close to home:

> Yesterday a pilot's boot had plummeted into the grass behind the
> Lookout ... Every day this week they had seen dogfights, as the
> clean sky became covered with a cobweb of the tangled white
> contrails of fighting planes.

Finally a German plane lands close by and the time comes for Norah
and her brother to leave England.

In England Norah and her friends have played at taking on adult
roles in the war. Forming a group they call the 'Skywatchers' they
watch the Kentish sky for German planes, determined to do as good a
job as any adult. War becomes an extension of their earlier childhood
games, their own objectives clear and the morality of warfare
unquestioned:

> At first the fort had been a good place in which to play Cops and
> Robbers. But this spring it had been named the Lookout when
> the Secret Society of Firewatchers was formed. Now they were on
> the alert for real enemies: the Good Guys were the English and
> the Bad Guys were the Germans.

A sense of patriotism and a strong feeling of national identity pervades
the fort as the children emulate the adult world; newspaper pictures of
'enemy' planes line the walls, their reading matter – no longer
necessary since they have become such experts – is a copy of *Friend or
Foe? A Young Spotter's Guide to Allied and German Aircraft*, and a
government propaganda leaflet is attached to the trunk of their tree.
The subject matter of the leaflet, however, acts both as a reminder of
the proximity of war and as an indicator of Norah's likely emotional
state when her parents tell her that she and her brother are to be
evacuated to Canada. Entitled 'If the Invader Comes', the government
propaganda – aimed, of course, at adults in time of invasion –
nevertheless now seems relevant to Norah with its proclamation, 'If
you run away ... you will be machine-gunned from the air'. The leaflet
dwells on the physical danger of running away, but to Norah the moral
weakness is as much to be feared as the physical cowardice, 'it's braver
to stay here, not to run away!' Norah is desperate to play a helpful role
in the war: 'children are *useful*. I watch for paratroopers every day, just
like the Observer Corps. I helped pull up the signposts. And I'll do
some of the housework so Mum can spend more time at the Hall.'
Norah who, despite the proximity of the shot-down German plane, still
views war as part of a game and fears not just the cowardice of running
away, but the dreariness of a country without war: 'a country without a
war seemed a very dull prospect'.

Part of Norah's anger at being sent away stems from the feeling that, instead of being the valiant skywatcher she feels inside, she is now being treated like the dependent child she appears, subject to adult decisions and packaged off like an object, but nevertheless expected to be grown-up enough to look after her younger brother. One of the themes of the trilogy concerns the relationships between adults and children, the question of when children become adults old enough to make their own decisions. It is a question of particular relevance to all novels about evacuation where children are removed from both the adult carers whose authority is familiar and whose limits are known, and from the set of social and moral codes individual to every family and with which they have grown up.

The second novel in the *War Guests* trilogy, *Looking at the Moon* (1991) deals primarily with the concerns of a young teenager. It considers the issues commonly found in young adult novels, the onset of puberty, the awkwardness of feeling in-between adulthood and childhood, and the difficulty of adjusting to the new teenage culture, but the issues presented here are more complex than in the typical young adult novel. For Norah growing up means not just adjusting to a new life-style as a 'teen-ager', it also means becoming accustomed to life in a new country and learning to understand a different set of values from those with which she has grown up. The novel is set in summertime; Norah, her brother Gavin and the two 'aunts' with whom they are living, have decamped to their summer home by a lake. The idyllic holiday setting takes the characters further away from the actions of war and closer to the kind of world portrayed in the *Swallows and Amazons* books which Norah read avidly in the early weeks of being an evacuee. On an island in the middle of a lake the children are to an extent isolated from everyday rules and concerns and are even left to spend a night there without adult supervision. However, real life is more complex than the Swallows and Amazons style exploits of which Norah has dreamt: reminders of war still abound and the prisoner-of-war camp on the other side of the lake acts as a constant reminder of war's proximity. War comes to the foreground with the arrival part way through the novel of Andrew, their older Canadian cousin. While 'the elders' are united in urging Andrew to join up, it emerges that Andrew himself has grave doubts as to whether war is morally right and, as the corollary of that, as to whether he should fight. While some of his doubts revolve around his personal sense that he would be unable to kill his fellow men, another part is to do with the ethics of war itself. As a child he has been unhappy with warlike games, pretending that his gun is not a gun but a camera, and hating the endless drilling he was subjected to as a cadet. His attitude contrasts with that demonstrated by Norah and her friends in the first book of the series where there seemed to be a natural progression from game-playing to the real war. Unlike the aunts and uncles intent on glory and victory, Andrew considers the human implications of the war:

> 'Nine hundred men slaughtered like cattle – for what? Doesn't it seem intolerable and absurd to you that whenever human beings disagree they go out and *kill* each other?'

Andrew's questions, coming at a time of growing maturity for Norah, encourage her to reconsider her own attitude to war. The ideas he expresses are new to Norah and her head is 'whirling' as she listens to Andrew's impassioned words but, initially at least, she counters with questions that echo the assumptions and expectations of those around her, '"But what about *Hitler*? Don't we have to beat him?"' She tries to explain to Andrew why she feels as she does:

> Beating Hitler had been ingrained in Norah's consciousness since she was nine. She remembered her own efforts to help. 'I used to watch for his planes in England,' she said softly. 'All my friends did. We thought war was fun then. I don't any more, but I still think we have to fight him. What would happen if he won?' Her voice rose in panic. 'What would happen to *England*? And to my family?'

Andrew cannot provide any answers to her questions, and in fact seems, as the novel progresses, to move further and further away from his own ideals, a pattern which reflects a more general character change from golden boy, beloved of all the relatives, to thoughtless young man. Although Norah supports his beliefs, she herself does not initially agree with them:

> She took a deep breath. All right, then. No matter how much she disagreed with him, she would accept his beliefs, if that was what loving him demanded.

As Andrew withdraws further from Norah, becoming increasingly preoccupied with an older girl and insensitive to Norah herself, he also appears to leave his pacifist beliefs behind, coming home without warning on the last night of the holidays dressed in uniform and ready for training camp. While the older relatives applaud his decision Norah feels betrayed by it, conscious not only of her own feeling of being let down, but of his betrayal of his own ideals:

How *could* he? He had broken his promise! He had betrayed her, but worse than that, he had betrayed himself – for she couldn't believe he had changed his beliefs so suddenly.

Thinking about Andrew's possible death brings home to Norah the reality of war, convincing her that,

War was wrong! She didn't care what the cause was. Aunt Catherine was right. It was wrong and wicked that the lives of boys like Andrew and Hugh could be extinguished as easily as snuffing out a candle.

Again Norah tries to argue with Andrew and again he cannot answer her arguments, made now in favour of pacifism. Although the change in Norah comes as a result of thinking about the effect the war will have on her and on those she knows, the views she develops here remain with her as she thinks about the wider issues involved. In school she writes an essay about pacifism, sticking to her beliefs even when she is suspended as a direct result of expressing them. At the end of the trilogy her pacifist views remain unchanged. Gavin tells Aunt Florence, ' "Norah and John [her boyfriend] say they are pacifists and that the Allies shouldn't have dropped the atomic bomb on Japan." '

The third novel in the trilogy, *The Lights Go on Again* (1993), takes Norah's brother Gavin as its central character. For Gavin, who can remember little of either England or pre-war life, the war represents a strange kind of stability. With its end come upheaval and uncertainty:

Lately, though, even his security in Toronto had begun to crumble. The war, which had been going on as long as Gavin could remember, was ending ... Of course Gavin wanted the Allies to beat Germany and Italy and Japan. But once the war was over there would be no reason for him and Norah to stay in Canada. They'd have to go back to England, to that place where he had felt so *unsafe*.

For Gavin the question of whether to return to England – where his parents have been killed – or to stay in Canada and be adopted, is linked in with wider questions of both family and national identity. Norah has retained her British accent during her time in Canada, and never ceases to think of herself as British, but Gavin looks and sounds like a Canadian, and, more importantly, he thinks of himself as a Canadian and not as an outsider. At first his decision is to stay in Canada after the war, living with Aunt Florence as if he were her own son. While he thinks he cannot remember England he is content with his decision, but almost as soon as it has been made memories of England begin to resurface until finally he realizes that he can recall his parents telling him to stick with his sister. Gavin knows that he cannot stay in Canada while Norah returns to England and, at the last minute, decides he must return with her.

As Gavin confronts the question of whether to leave Canada, his concept of self is challenged. He tries to reinvent a new family with his two best friends, who make a ritual pact to become blood brothers, drawing their inspiration from *Secret Water* (one of the *Swallows and Amazons* books which had brought Norah comfort in the first novel of the trilogy). Next Gavin tries to shed his role as good boy and befriends the school bully, helping him to steal from a local store, and being severely punished for his exploits both at school and at home. Gavin's grandfather doesn't condone the beating Gavin receives, but he exhibits an uncomplicated view of the morality involved; Gavin acted wrongly, knew that he was doing so, and received the standard punishment for his behaviour. Aunt Florence, meanwhile, is appalled at the punishment Gavin has received and determines to go to school and complain. The grandfather expects Gavin to think for himself, to live with the consequences of his actions, and, we may infer, to feel better in himself for having done so. Aunt Florence treats Gavin like a child, certain that he must have been forced into behaving badly and determined to protect him from the consequences of his own misdeeds. Her response to this incident is indicative of the life she plans for Gavin should he opt to stay in Canada: by adopting him she will ensure his financial security and domestic stability but he will be treated like a young child. England meanwhile offers physical discomfort but moral independence. To choose to stay in Canada, where he lives a life of physical comfort amongst people he knows and loves, is presented as a path of temptation for Gavin, one devoid of moral responsibility as well as physical hardship. To choose to go to England, where his parents have died, and where he will live in relative poverty with relations he does not remember, is to choose a course of action that is morally right, cementing as it does the value of family love on which the trilogy as a whole has placed such a high premium.

Goodnight Mister Tom

William Beech, hero of Michelle Magorian's enormously successful novel, *Goodnight Mister Tom* (1981), winner of the *Guardian* Award for children's fiction, typifies the initial sense of powerlessness and vulnerability shown by many children in novels about evacuation. When he first arrives in Little Weirwold as an evacuee he is unloved, uncared for and abused by his religiously fanatical mother. William Beech is handed over to Tom Oakley solely on the basis that Mister Tom, as Will comes to call him, lives beside a church. While, as an adult, Tom is 'entitled' to choose his child, the child himself has no choice over his future home, an emotionally forceful point that is made in *Carrie's War*, in Michael Morpurgo's *Friend or Foe* (1997), as well as in many other novels. William's vulnerable state is epitomized by the pathetic brown paper bag that he carries, containing all his possessions – no change of clothes or nightclothes, only a Bible, a few basic toiletries, a letter from his mother full of certainty that he will be naughty and, worst of all, the belt that he is to be beaten with. When Will first arrives he is certain that Mister Tom will beat him, convinced of his own naughtiness and the inevitability of punishment at the hands of the adult world. He gradually grows in confidence, his greater self-assurance mirrored in his learning to read, while the emotional freedom he enjoys in Little Weirwold is made manifest in his painting. Tom discovers that Will is a talented artist and encourages him to paint, giving Will the set of paints that had belonged to his dead wife. However, when William is forced back to London by a summons from his mother – a summons which he must perforce obey despite his reluctance and Mister Tom's concern for his well-being at the hands of his cruel parent – his mother is horrified at his paintings and refuses to have them in the house.

The book opens just before Will's ninth birthday and the main events of the story end just after his tenth. Time in the novel passes almost cyclically, the central action taking a little more than a year, perhaps echoing the year-and-a-day pattern found in fairy tales. The first birthday that he spends in Little Weirwold acts as a clear marker of the change in his life – from a miserable existence where birthdays are never marked to a life where friends and new family care for him, celebrating the anniversary of his birth. Will's mother regards the birth of his baby sister as something to be ashamed of, a visible manifestation of sin. When Will returns to London he discovers that the baby – about whose birth he had been left in ignorance – is kept hidden from view with her mouth taped over so that she cannot be heard. Will's desperate, and unsuccessful attempts to preserve the life of the baby neglected by his mother are compared with the love and affection shown by everyone to the new baby born in Little Weirwold. However, by the second birthday that Will spends in Little Weirwold we see that happiness does not come easily, that the pleasures of friendship bring pain too and that love may be accompanied by loss. Over the weekend of Will's tenth birthday Zach, his best friend, returns to London to see his injured father and is himself killed in the bombing. The final section of the novel sees Will learning to cope with his loss, and realizing that the strength he has gained through friendship can help him to deal with the pain as well as the pleasures of his new life. With the new spring comes renewed hope, and a fresh beginning. Fortune's wheel has turned for Will, and although we see that its continued turning may bring further sorrows (hinted at in Will's sudden awareness of Mister Tom's age), Will is now better equipped to deal with the misery that accompanies its turning. When visitors from outside the village come to discuss Will's future after his mother's suicide, Will is able to stand up to them and assert his own wishes. Destiny is no longer entirely controlled from outside but is seen to be affected – to some extent at least – by one's own actions.

Much of *Goodnight Mister Tom* is distanced from the daily horrors of life in wartime. The book opens with Will's arrival in the country, rather than his departure from the city as is more conventional for evacuation stories. In the first part of the novel the misery of war seems remote; we do not see the bombing in London and only those children who are happy in their billets are depicted in any detail. There is little sense here of the loneliness and discomfort of evacuation, but rather a strong image of the possibilities offered by both evacuation itself and life in wartime. Although Tom and Will build an Anderson shelter in their garden we never see the shelter in use. Its main function in the book is as a means of bringing together Will and his future best friend Zach. War is seen in this novel, and in Magorian's *A Little Love Song* (1991) as a social facilitator. Here it is directly responsible for Mister Tom's return to village life; in *A Little Love Song* it provides the rationale for a series of social activities enjoyed by Rose and her sister.

However, when Will does return to London the misery of his home life is linked with that engendered by war. Back in London Mister Tom's love is replaced by his mother's cruelty, and the physical safety of Little Weirwold is exchanged for the danger of the Blitz. The misery inflicted on the community by the bombing is juxtaposed with Will's personal misery suffered at the hands of his mother. The book depicts cruelty and misery arising in the main not as a result of the war, but rather as a result of Will's dysfunctional family. Will's mother treats him cruelly but the war offers escape for both him and Mister Tom; Mister Tom has chosen a lonely existence since the death of his wife but with war comes the opportunity for reintegration into local society. Only at the end of the book do we really see the human misery of war: Zach's death tests Will's newly learnt self-confidence and the happiness he has finally found with Mister Tom. Will's ability to draw and paint (a sign throughout the book of his emotional freedom) seems to vanish as Will grieves for the death of his friend. Only when he has to draw from a photograph of two young men whose situation parallels his relationship with Zach does he finally begin to accept Zach's death. In so doing Will learns again to take responsibility for his own life, making decisions about how he wants to remember Zach and what he wants to do in the future, his sense of liberation symbolically marked by his mastery of Zach's bicycle. 'He turned the bicycle and cycled back down the hill. It was even more pleasurable to ride after his sojourn on the hill. He was more relaxed, more at peace with himself.' The final chapter provides a reminder of the use of colour made throughout the book to reflect Will's new-found freedom. When Will undertakes his symbolic planting of seeds he wears Zach's multicoloured jumper, a reminder of Zach's individuality and Will's rediscovered zest for life.

The concept of pleasure heightened by adversity – an opposition found in books and films about the war for both children and adults – is perhaps at its strongest in the work of Michelle Magorian. Her novels portray extremes both of wartime suffering and of the delights occasionally afforded to those living through the war. The pleasure and the misery of war are often juxtaposed to heighten our awareness of the power of each. In *Goodnight Mister Tom* the chapter where Will, his friend Zach and Mister Tom himself spend a happy fortnight by the sea, a fortnight in which the concerns of war seem distant, precedes a chapter in which Zach and Will make friends with a man who has been severely handicapped by the war and who has lost both family and friends in the bombing. In the chapter after that the war comes yet closer to Little Weirwold with the death of Zach in the Blitz. Will frequently quotes one of Mister Tom's favourite sayings, 'everythin' has its own time' and there is a strong sense that the good and the bad are both parts of the same whole.

Growing Up in Wartime

A Little Love Song
Michelle Magorian's *A Little Love Song* (1991) presents the Second World War as a time of pleasure as well as sorrow, a time of greater open-mindedness and freedom than had been seen either in the pre-war years or in the previous war. The novel is set in and around the village where Tom, Will and Zach had holidayed, their landlady now a friend of the heroine and, with its holiday setting, it is perhaps unsurprising that the overall mood should be predominantly one of joviality in adversity. Its protagonists are older than many found in

Second World War children's novels; no longer children, Rose and her sister Diana inhabit a grey area between childhood and adulthood in which war brings new and unexpected freedom.

The book presents a picture of a patriotic nation, doing its bit to help the war effort and determined to have fun despite the war. It portrays war as a time of extremes of both misery and jollity, its depiction of frivolity in the midst of pain echoing the mixed views expressed by Aunt Louie in Michael Foreman's autobiographical picture book, *War Boy* (1989): 'Even today Aunt Louie cries when she talks about "all those lovely boys". And then, drying her eyes, she says, "Oh, but we had the time of our lives." Like *War Boy*, *A Little Love Song* celebrates the strength of the British people as they struggle with shortages and rationing, but in *A Little Love Song* the stereotyped British character is also mocked. The sometimes overt sense of patriotism is here counteracted in the character of Alex who is experiencing severe shell shock. His character is implicitly paired with that of his cousin Derry – a younger, over-zealous boy whose head is filled with patriotic ideals and who has little understanding of how Alex has suffered. To the readers Alex is portrayed as the more sensitive of the two: he takes an interest in Rose's writing, a topic which irritates Derry while Derry himself only considers Rose attractive once he realizes that other people find her so. Derry's interest is expressed largely in terms of sexual desire rather than concern for how Rose thinks or feels. Alex is clearly the more thoughtful, better educated and kinder of the two and our sympathy for his gentler views about war is perhaps inevitable, while Derry's hotheaded patriotism looks increasingly thoughtless and unsympathetic in comparison.

A Little Love Song particularly examines the effect of the war on young women. At the start of the novel Rose and her sister hover on the verge of adulthood, uncertain whether they are really old enough to fend for themselves for a whole summer. The two argue about whether they can stay on their own, the naturally cautious Diana finally persuaded by her more exuberant younger sister. As in Westall's *The Machine-Gunners* (1975) the question of when one becomes an adult, or can be judged ready to live independently, is central to the novel. At the start of the novel Diana, used to being looked after, is unsure whether they will be able to fend for themselves, and equally worried about what people will think of their arrangement:

> 'Who's going to cook our meals and wash our clothes? ... And who's going to chaperone us?' asked Diana.
> 'We can chaperone each other.'

'But what would people think? Two girls on their own?'
'We're not girls.'
'You are.'
'But you're not. A lot of people are married by your age.'

Set against a backdrop of war, food shortages, bombing in the cities and the arrival of the American GIs, this is primarily a coming-of-age story. In the course of the summer Rose evolves from awkward schoolgirl to independent womanhood. The story is romantic and at times very funny, though not free from tragedy. The lives of the young women in the Second World War are contrasted with the tale of Miss Hilda in the First World War, who had an illegitimate child and was as a result consigned by her family to a mental asylum. Now, during the Second World War, Rose's friend Dot is also pregnant with an illegitimate child, but although she faces prejudice from the villagers, Dot knows she will be able to survive, supporting herself and her child – albeit only if she conforms to the views of society and gets herself a pretend wedding ring.

The book presents wartime as an opportunity for greater independence – especially for young women – and as a time to enjoy oneself away from the restrictions of adult supervision. The two young girls, housekeeping for the first time, find plenty of humour in their attempts to be domesticated. One of the funniest moments in the book comes when Rose determines to do her bit to help with the household war effort while at an American dance. The week before the dance has been spent in Dot teaching Rose to jitterbug – the outrageous American dance a symbol of the girls' determination to enjoy themselves despite the war. When the day of the dance comes Rose prepares herself with care, the difficulties of getting ready for a first date amidst the austerity of war dwelt upon in detail. She dyes her old dress, uses her new and luxurious scented soap and dons her blackout bloomers, 'they were a bit cumbersome but at least they weren't patched or darned'. When Rose reaches the dance Derry, her tight-lipped British partner, regards the noisy chatter and (presumably American) music as 'rather vulgar'. Derry's terse reservations about both the dance itself and the presence of the American soldiers accentuates how far removed from the usual wartime austerity this joyful scene is with its waving flags and loud music. Even at the dance, however, Rose cannot forget the privations of daily life. The Americans have brought in oranges for the dance and as soon as she sees the peel, Rose has only one thought, ' "Marmalade," she thought. "If I can collect enough peel, Diana could make marmalade." ' Rose stuffs the peel into her bloomers, covering the lumps with her dress. However, when British austerity – in the form of the blackout bloomers – meets the new American freedom – signified by the dancing of the jitterbug – disaster strikes and Rose ends up revealing first her peel-filled bloomers and then the carefully collected peel itself, which spills out in all directions, catching the attention of the entire room in a dramatic and entertaining display. However, what might have been disaster ends happily since the incident breaks the ice between the British and the Americans. Even the disapproving Derry is won over when he sees the positive reactions of all around.

The question of whether Rose is child or adult – an issue central to the book – forms an important part of the evening. Older sister Diana is initially reluctant to let her go, ' "I don't know. I think seventeen is a bit young to start meeting men" ', and once there Derry persists in treating her like a child, refusing to let her taste his cider or dance with a young man who isn't an officer. Derry appears to embody the old stereotyped British middle-class value system, values that Rose is beginning to divorce herself from. The contrast between Rose and Derry – she determined to live according to her own values, he wanting to stick to the long-established rules, unwilling to dance with Rose himself, but not prepared to let others partner her – is sharpened when she accepts an offer to dance without reference to him. The American GI responds to Rose as an individual, even devising an eccentric way of dancing specially to suit her, and bringing her the cider that Derry had refused. He and Derry stand as icons for their two cultures, Derry representing the emotionless stiff upper-lip of the British middle class, which is already seen to be outdated, and Tony the open easy-going freedom of America.

War Boy

Michael Foreman's autobiographical picture book *War Boy* (1989) gives a nostalgic view of the war as seen through the eyes of a small boy living in rural Suffolk. Like *A Little Love Song* it depicts the war as a time of fun, particularly exciting for the small child who revels in the excitement without being fully conscious of the danger. The young boy enjoys the attention from the troops who drink tea at his mother's shop and the thrill of the approaching 'doodlebugs':

> Local people flocked to the cliff tops each evening to see the spectacular show as the doodlebugs came over the horizon to be met by the barrage of coastal guns (now largely 'manned' by ATS girls). A direct hit would result in a tremendous orange flash.

Although set in Lowestoft, a vulnerable British town on the east coast, the book concentrates not on the bombing or the deaths in the town, but on the small child's sense of novelty, the little boy's enthusiasm for wartime memorabilia, the cigarette cards that show you how to deal with a bomb (if you have collected enough of them) and the details of spotting enemy planes. The illustrations show a world in which, for much of the time, the adults too appear smiling and friendly, taking the young Michael on fishing trips, providing him with miniature versions of their own uniform, and jitterbugging at the local dance. As in *War Game* the illustrations show posters of the period, government reminders to wear gas masks, cigarette cards and evacuation notices, but here the mood, unlike that of *War Game*, is a jovial one. War only becomes 'personal' when a lone raider drops bombs on houses and a restaurant in the town, 'one enemy plane, looking for someone to kill'. Here the illustrations become much darker and the text reflects the fear felt by boy and adults alike, the exhaustion of the firemen worn out by the unpredictable hit-and-run raids and the lack of warning before they arrive. Later bombings are presented in a more exciting light, with an illustration showing the boys running to escape the Fokker Wulfes juxtaposed with *Spotter's Guide* depictions of the different German planes, suggesting a return to the childhood view of war as a time of excitement and novelty.

The Machine-Gunners

Robert Westall's acclaimed novel *The Machine-Gunners* (1979), winner of the Carnegie Medal, is, like *A Little Love Song*, closely concerned with the transition between childhood and adulthood, charting the parallel demise of adult authority and the children's own reworking of the adult world. Chas McGill, brought up to respect his parents, creates his own world, a world which at once defies and simultaneously embodies the rules of the adult world. After Chas steals a machine-gun from the wreck of a German plane, he and his friends disobey the laws of the adult world to create their own camp. The camp is beautifully made, a model of how such things should be built. It is, however, also dangerously close to the real thing, and once the adult world intervenes the camp is brought to an end for the children. The irony of the novel is that Chas and his friends mimic the adult world at war, creating a camp that would be admired were it to have been built and used by adults, but which in children's hands is deemed unsafe.

The Machine-Gunners depicts Chas and his friends moving from childhood and dependence towards adulthood and independence. At the beginning of the novel we see Chas as a schoolboy collecting war memorabilia. His life is bound by rules and regulations or, rather, by the need to evade such rules. The novel opens with his discovery of the wreckage of a German plane, but his ability to explore his new find is limited by the need to get back to school in time for lessons. On his way back he encounters his mother who issues further reminders of the need to obey school rules while worrying about his health. Parents and schoolteachers still wield a degree of authority, homework has to be done before the raid begins and, although Chas has no objection to breaking the rules, he cannot bring himself to lie to his father about what he does: 'What was even luckier was that Mr McGill never questioned Chas about the gun himself; he was the only one Chas could never have deceived.' Gradually, however, the sets of rules which govern the children's lives are removed, piece by piece. School is closed by a bomb and with the closure of school Chas and his friends find themselves removed from one of their governing sets of regulations with time suddenly on their hands. With Mr and Mrs McGill increasingly preoccupied with the war Chas finds it easier to get round them, exploiting their absorption in the daily difficulties of wartime life and using his increasing self-awareness to test the limits of their own values. When he arrives home announcing that he has been to Benny Nichol's house Chas encounters disapproval from his parents – disapproval stemming from their adult knowledge of the relationship between the widowed Mrs Nichol and the sailors billeted on her house. Chas, however, is determined not to let the unique venue afforded by the Nichol house slip out of his grasp:

'Where *you* bin?' asked his mother.

'Nichol's house.'

'You *what?*'

'I've been to Benny Nichol's house. He's got a goldfish six inches long, in a pool.'

Mr McGill put down the newspaper with its glaring headline *Invasion Imminent* and took off his reading spectacles.

'What you been up to now? ... You are *not* to go there again. And you aren't to play with that Nichol boy again.'

'Why not?'

'Never mind why not. Because I damned well say not.'

'Look, tell me why. You always tell me why I can't do things.'

His father looked at his mother, and his mother at his father. They both seemed acutely embarrassed.

'We can't tell you. You're too young to understand.

'But it's a marvellous place to play ... ' sensing their

embarrassment, Chas pressed on unmercifully.

'You can play anywhere else if you like. But not at the Nichol's house, and that's final.' Mr McGill vanished again behind the *Daily Express*. Mrs McGill went on with her ironing. Chas knew a brick wall when he saw one. But he also had a taste for getting round brick walls.

The juxtaposition of the terrifying newspaper headline with his parents' struggle to maintain 'decent' standards of behaviour illustrates both the relative ease with which Chas can get round rules in wartime, and the close proximity of the war to everyday life.

In place of the rules and timetables set by the adult world, the children begin to develop their own sets of regulations and codes of conduct, rules which are in many cases stricter than those of their adult counterparts. The rules – which combine domesticity with attention to security and display an internal sense of logic and morality – are read out every day in the camp and everyone has to swear to keep them, an attitude markedly different from that shown towards adult authority. Shortly after we first see the children swearing to observe the rules, Nicky's mother is killed and it becomes increasingly obvious that the children will have to adopt adult roles if they wish the camp to continue. With Nicky – already established as the most vulnerable of the group – now orphaned, the rest of the children recognize that they will have to take on the adult tasks of caring and providing for him if he is not to be handed over to the authorities:

'I don't want to leave this place. I mean ... all this is mine now. And I'd rather be with you than strangers.' [Nicky] held out his hand. Chas felt very strange. He had prickles up and down his spine. He felt bigger and stronger than ever before, and yet more frightened at the same time. He clasped the proffered hand in both of his.

'We'll have a meeting. We'll see you through.' ...

So they brought the gun out of its wrapping, and laid Granda's Union Jack on it, and everyone put their hands on it and swore to look after Nicky. In the swearing, Fortress Caporetto became more than a game; it became a nation. And the Germans ceased to be the only enemies. All the adults were a kind of enemy now, except John.

The use of the Union Jack here is a powerful reminder that the children, although defying adult rules, still subscribe to the same set of national values endorsed by their parents. The fortress continues, run to a formal set of rules and dependent on the strict observance of those rules by all who inhabit it. The children are successfully creating a microcosm of the adult wartime world.

The activities of Chas and his gang are paired with those of teacher Stan Liddell and his Home Guard. In the opening pages of the novel Stan and Chas come into humorous conflict with one another in the classroom and we see Chas triumph. Later Stan's Home Guard operation is set against the building of the camp. Both groups seek to defend their territory against invaders, both share the same patriotic ideals, and both are dependent on the strict observance of rules by all involved. However, while Stan's Home Guard inhabits ramshackle buildings and has to make do with donated firearms or those left over from the First World War, the children's fortress is beautifully built, strongly fortified, and contains a real German machine-gun, if only the children can work out how to put it back together. As the children's world becomes increasingly well ordered, even able to cope with the arrival of a real life German airman whom they treat as a prisoner-of-war, the adult world becomes increasingly fragmented, its disorganization culminating in the chaotic response to the imaginary German invasion. Usually law-abiding adults become hysterical, trying to flee the area or go into hiding, and the Home Guard struggles with a comical password system and the unplanned movements of the Polish Free Army. Meanwhile the children repair to a well-prepared and well-ordered fortress where they have food to last and defences that will withstand almost anything, and where the machine-gun has finally been repaired and left in full working order. In the face of the invasion believed to be in progress, their efficient and well-run camp contrasts starkly with the shambolic and even cowardly response of the adult world.

However, when the invasion fails to materialize and the adult world restores itself to normality, the children at the fortress find their world beginning to crumble, falling apart from within as well as threatened from without. As the adult world wakes to a 'working Monday morning', Chas – who should have been on duty against the supposedly imminent invasion – wakes to find the fortress unguarded. He looks back on the previous night:

> What had they talked about? What it was like to be hurt; what it was like to be dead. There had been a stupid argument about God, which had ended in Nicky attacking Cem, and the usually calm Cem fighting back viciously. Audrey had declaimed the

Agincourt speech from *Henry V* which she had learned by heart, and then *she* had burst into tears. What an awful stupid night.

Like their adult counterparts, the children mistake the soldiers of the Polish Corps, who are out looking for the missing children, for Germans, and in using the machine-gun which forms the heart of the fortress they inevitably bring about its destruction.

Although the discovery of the fortress leaves the children in disgrace with their parents, it is clear throughout the book that they have done nothing more evil than to mimic the adult world, recreating it more successfully than it has created itself. Their crime lies not in what they have done but in doing it as children rather than as adults. The end of the book sees an even wider gulf between adults and children than that which existed at the beginning when the children were bound by the adult rules:

> [Stan] looked at Chas.
> 'Will you tell me how it all started?'
> 'No, sir. You wouldn't understand. Grown-ups never do.'

The moment recalls one in the first chapter where Stan Liddell made a decision to laugh at Chas' joke rather than risk his enmity. Now the well-meaning Stan can offer Chas sympathy but little else. He cannot even promise that Cem and Chas won't be sent to a reform school or Nicky and Cem to a home. All the sympathetic representatives of the adult world can offer is the comfort of treating the children as if they were adults:

> The children ... led [Stan] and Sandy inside. They answered every question with monosyllables, and shut faces. Only when Sandy boomed, 'This is a good 'ole. A very good 'ole indeed! Well made to last, I could 'ave done with this 'ole in the Somme in 1917,' did their faces break into peaked grins that vanished as soon as they appeared.

Chas' final words to each of his gang, spoken adult to adult, stand in contrast with the comments made to each of the children by their parents, comments that assume the children's inability to take responsibility for their own lives:

> 'You're not to play with that McGill again,' said Mrs Jones in a savage whisper.
> 'That Cemetery Jones always got you into trouble,' said Mrs McGill.

The complete failure of the adult world to understand the complexity of the fortress or its morality – more sound than that exhibited by the adults who buy black market petrol and ignore their responsibilities to their families – underlines the prevailing theme of the book, that of the inconsistency, immorality and lack of understanding to be found in the adult wartime world.

Fireweed

Jill Paton Walsh's classic novel of the Second World War, Fireweed (1969), also takes as a central theme the position of children growing into adulthood in wartime. Bill and Julie meet in war-torn London, each having escaped from evacuation and determined now to survive without adult help. Each can fill the other's needs; Julie has money but cannot manage on her own, while Bill has no money but a stronger instinct for survival. Until the adult world interferes they manage well, but when they encounter a schoolteacher one night the teacher, certain that they are still to be treated as children, orders them back to school.

> 'I'm over fourteen,' [Bill] said, 'you can't make me go back to school.'
>
> 'If you were at grammar school, your father signed you up for longer, I'm sure,' he said, getting curt and angry now. 'And your sister is under leaving age. Come on now, your name and address.'

Ironically, in his attempts to bring them back into the safe adult world the teacher leaves them more vulnerable, forcing them to quit the shelters with his threat, 'We've got someone in every shelter for miles, do you hear?' His dictatorial style and assumption that they should be treated like children forms a sharp contrast with the new-found and hard won independence and freedom enjoyed by Bill and Julie. Although the school teacher may treat them as children, Bill and Julie themselves are fully aware of the duties involved in adulthood, building themselves a home in the cellar of a bombed house and taking in a young, probably homeless, child. As they act out a parental role the teenagers are both acutely conscious of their responsibilities and aware that their position as children themselves leaves them unable to fill those responsibilities.

The Adult World

Blitzcat
While Chas and his gang achieve independence through an adult
preoccupation with war, the heroes of Robert Westall's *Kingdom by the
Sea* (1990) and *Time of Fire* (1994) have independence thrust upon
them with the bombing of their homes in the Blitz. In *Blitzcat* (1989)
the narrative as a whole takes on a more adult tone with the use of the
cat as central figure and the almost complete absence of child
characters. *Blitzcat* won the Smarties prize for books for 9- to 11-year-
olds when it was first published in 1989. Its position as a children's book
has sometimes been questioned by adult critics who consider both its
subject matter and narrative stance too old for a children's book. John
Rowe Townsend, in his influential book *Written for Children* (1990),
raises the question, 'Is this really a children's book?' and answers:

> If the episodes were to be regarded as the substance of the novel,
> with the cat as a mere linking device, there would be a strong
> case for classing it as adult. But if, as a young reader must, you
> identify with the cat, it becomes a children's book, for you are
> moving, vulnerable and uncomprehending, through a dangerous
> adult world.

This story of a cat who travels across Britain in search of its master
during the Second World War is a powerful vehicle for the exploration
of the themes of war found in many of Westall's books. The cat's
travels around the country allow the author to examine several aspects
of the war and its effects on different kinds of people. In the opening
chapters the narratorial perspective is closest to that of the cat, but as
the novel moves on the cat is distanced from the narrative viewpoint
which approximates those of the cat's various carers. The book uses
major events in the war as part of its plotting, covering the return of
soldiers from Dunkirk and the bombing of Coventry and examining the
effect of the war on those whose lives are involved in these incidents.
Westall is critical of the planning behind the war, as is clear in the
presentation of the troops returning from Dunkirk, exhausted and
demoralized. The women discuss the men's sorry state:

> 'It's the ones who won't stop crying that I can't stand. I mean,
> they're safe home, now … You'd think they'd cheer up.'
>   'Shell shock it is … '
>   'I don't reckon half of them will ever fight again.'

We are sharply reminded of the unorthodox nature of this

conversation by the comments made by another character, couched in the propaganda of the time: ' "Mrs Barstow," said the bossy woman sharply, "that's treason. The Germans are doing well enough without your help. Careless talk costs lives." '

There seems little to suggest here that the evacuation of Dunkirk might be regarded as a success. Equipment supplied to the forces is also criticized. From a police sergeant – a man who ought to be a visible face of government – we learn that Blenheims are considered 'flying death-traps; too slow, not enough guns'.

In *Blitzcat* Westall depicts the bombing of Coventry and its aftermath, describing vividly the horrific sounds and smells of the city going up in flames – roasting beef from the cold storage warehouse, cigars from the burning tobacconists, all compared ironically with the smell of Christmas. We learn of the mass graves where 50 people are buried at once because they can't be recognized. The mingling of mutilated bodies is an image that recurs in the book, one which is in stark contrast to the scene of bodies mingling in sex shown earlier in the novel. Most vivid of all, however, is the contrast between the lack of preparation for an attack on the scale of the Coventry bombing, the chaos it causes, and the disorganization of the officials, all set against the efficiency and speed with which racketeers begin to take advantage of the refugee families. The bombing of Coventry is likened to the events taking place on the front line. Viewed through the eyes of Ollie, the livery stable owner who has looked after the cat and now finds himself taking charge of a group of people fleeing the devastation, the scene looks like an image from the war zone:

> They began to overtake people. Mothers dragging crying children along. Men with bundles of bedding on their shoulders, or in prams. At first, the groups parted when they heard the rumble of the carts and Ollie's warning shouts; parted without looking back, without looking up. They seemed oddly familiar. Ollie thought he had seen them before somewhere. But where? In a dream? Then it came to him. In the newsreels at the cinema. In Holland, France and Belgium. Refugees, fleeing. Good God, he thought. It's happening here, in England. Hitler's doing it in England now.

Ollie's calm leadership is contrasted with the refusal of an avaricious farmer to let the refugees stay on his land. Although the narrative endorses Ollie's success as a leader and as a tradesman who ends up making money during the war, the role of profiteers in the war is questioned. The book portrays the curious mixture of affection and aggression brought out by wartime and epitomized in the character of

Sergeant Smith, a man brutal yet kind, rough but thoughtful. Sergeant Smith is in charge of the group of men billeted on Mrs Smiley, whose husband is an officer. She is both attracted and repelled by the lower-ranked, lower-class Sergeant who feeds the cat at the table but is considerate enough to order his men to help Mrs Smiley with the housework. Sergeant Smith – his name perhaps intended to denote the ubiquitous nature of his character – is both revered and feared by his men, the legends about him springing up quickly and all indicating his potential brutality:

> They [the soldiers] were nervous of the Germans, but they were far more nervous of their new Geordie sergeant. He was a tall, thin man, with a big black moustache and tattooed arms. He'd survived Dunkirk. They thought him slightly mad. He'd taken a Luger pistol off a dead Jerry, and they said he lay in bed and trimmed his toenails by shooting bits off them with it. They said he was bomb-happy after seven days on the beaches. They said he didn't give two buggers for anybody, British or German.

However Sergeant Smith does care for others; he befriends the cat, Lord Gort, and his relationship with the animal has distinctly Lawrencian overtones, emphasizing his masculinity and her vulnerable femaleness, the physical relationship mingling pleasure with pain, and watched by Mrs Smiley:

> Mrs Smiley watched the sergeant's hands stroking the cat. He had big hands, but well-shaped, with long, slim, clever fingers that now twisted the cat's ears, now gripped her by the nape of the neck, now dug along her twitching back like a living comb. Mrs Smiley could almost have sworn he was hurting the cat except the cat was purring loudly and rubbing her cheek against his clever hand in ecstasy. How strange, thought Mrs Smiley, that ecstasy should be so close to agony.

Later Sergeant Smith takes Mrs Smiley under his protection, first encouraging his men to protect her, then providing for her care and comfort and finally making love to her on an ancient hilltop fortress, a place where past and present are brought together, the union 'blessed' by the cat, who has never before shown an interest in Mrs Smiley but now behaves affectionately towards her. Earlier Mrs Smiley, having watched a German plane crash to the ground, considers the war, seeing it as 'a black tunnel, in which they were all together, British and German. In which there was no way out but dying.' Now the timelessness of the place acts as a reminder of the transience of war – and of human life – in contrast to the permanence of the landscape around:

> Her body pressed against the dry warmth of the hill; she felt all that ancient mass beneath her; all those enduring years, William the Conqueror must have passed; Napoleon across the channel. People must have been terrified then, but up here only the wind, and the grazing of sheep, and the peewits calling.

The timelessness of the setting gives their coupling less significance in everyday terms, but also a greater universal resonance, suggesting a picture of an archetypal man and woman, thrown together by war but able to conquer their fears with love, a reminder perhaps of the sentiment expressed in Thomas Hardy's 'In Time of the Breaking of Nations', written in 1915:

> Yonder a maid and her wight
> Come whispering by:
> War's annals will cloud into night
> Ere their story die.

The closeness of agony and ecstasy, of love and violence, is a theme that runs through the novel: Ollie's care for his refugees comes precariously close to the profiteering of other men; the new kittens are born in Coventry just before the bombing, and then later the liveliness of one of the kittens encourages a young woman novelist who has lost her husband to live and to love again. Many of the episodes used in this novel are ones that Westall returned to in his collection of short stories about the War, *Blitz* (1994) where he again examines the fine line between earning a living and profiteering, the apparently absurd pomposity of those who impose rules and regulations (particularly when invasion may be imminent) and the close relationship between love – especially physical love – and death in wartime.

Ethel and Ernest

Raymond Briggs' award-winning *Ethel and Ernest: A True Story* (1998), although published as an adult book, has proved popular with older children and teenagers. Using the comic-strip style familiar to his readers, Briggs portrays the lives of his parents from their meeting in 1928 through to their deaths in 1971, the section on their lives during the Second World War showing the adults' bewilderment at the world around. Conversations about events in Germany or the impending war are juxtaposed with scenes of domestic life; Ethel's personal response to the situation in Germany is contrasted with Ernest's growing concern for what is going on around them. He asks her, 'Here Et, did you know if you're a Jew in Germany, you're forbidden to marry a German?' and she responds, 'I'd hate to marry a German,' turning her attention in the next strip to the luxury of the gas 'copper'. Later, as the two sit picnicking on the beach, apparently far removed from the possibility of war, with little Raymond building sandcastles at their feet, he tells her snippets from the newspaper, background to the war sitting alongside plans for 'tele-vision'. Ethel's unquestioning response ('They say Hitler's assured Holland and Belgium of his friendship.' 'Oh, that's nice'), though always tinged with the concern for domestic comfort, becomes more complex as the war continues, her confusion at the complexities of war giving her an understanding of its madness:

> Germany's always invading someone. I expect they'll invade Russia one day ... or Russia will invade Germany ... If they ALL keep invading one another, WE'LL end up invading someone.

Although her husband counters that Russia and Germany are 'in league', that she is being 'daft' and finally, 'you just don't understand politics', a few pages later the insanity of war is apparent as we see them in the Morrison shelter – which Ethel wants painted 'a nice pastel brown' to tone in with the furniture – Ernest again reading his newspaper, 'Blimey! Germany's invaded RUSSIA!' and Ethel's response, 'I wish I'd betted you sixpence.'

Ethel's struggles to understand the war, her desire to maintain everyday routines in her household, her vulnerability, all suggest the response of a child to war and echo themes to be found throughout children's literature about the Second World War.

Encounters with 'The Enemy'

Friend or Foe
In a number of novels about the war children not only look after themselves and their friends and family, but their responsibilities extend to making the complex moral decisions generated by chance encounters with the so-called enemy. The meeting with an individual German is a familiar device in British and American children's fiction, enabling the exploration of complex questions of individual morality and national identity. Michael Morpurgo's novel *Friend or Foe* (1997) is an evacuation story which examines themes of displacement and of national identity through the heroes' encounter with two German men. Tucky and David are London boys, evacuated to a Devon village.

Although both dread the evacuation they are billeted on Mr Reynolds, a farmer who, from his initial meeting with the boys, shows kindness and concern. He arrives late for the billeting process, is impatient with the bureaucracy and reminds the officials that life on a farm cannot work to a prescribed timetable. His early rejection of rules and authority, set against the regimented mass movement of children around the country, is indicative of the broad-mindedness and relative freedom that his home will offer to the two boys. The official planning for the evacuation is fallible – there is an extra child unplanned for – and the early episode in which Mr Reynolds opts to take both boys, rather than leaving one without a home and unwanted, stresses the value placed on human kindness in preference to official rules and planning. Furthermore, Mr Reynolds, unlike any of the other adults involved in the billeting, takes account of the boys' own feelings:

> 'I'll tell you one thing for certain, it'll be both of them or neither. There'll be no choosing. What about asking them? They might not like the look of me – have you thought of that?' No one said anything, so he asked them direct. 'Well, what do you think?'

Mr Reynolds goes on to describe himself and his lifestyle, offering the boys not only the theoretical choice, but also practical grounds on which to make their decision. Many novels about evacuation describe the children's misery at waiting to be chosen by their hosts, the awful feeling of waiting to be picked, but few portray the adults as either aware of or sympathetic to the children's plight. Adults normally are concerned with the smooth and efficient running of complex operations, not the small human acts of kindness, which make a child's life more bearable. In his attention to the child rather than the bureaucracy Mr Reynolds, like Mister Tom (see pp. 92.–5), becomes an instantly empathetic character; one who, in the chaos of war, will be a sympathetic presence for the child involved.

David and Tucky fit into the pattern of their new life smoothly and easily, experiencing few of the horrors depicted elsewhere in novels of evacuation. At school they are treated as novelties, subjects of interest rather than derision, and at home they enjoy an exciting rural life that combines pastoral idyll with domestic comfort. On their first morning they wake to the smell of eggs frying and porridge cooking. Mr Reynolds' wife Ann understands their possible sense of displacement: a French woman who has married an Englishman, her presence calls into question concepts of national identity and ideas about what constitutes 'home'. ' "I'm French," Ann said. "I was French until I married Jerry. Now I am English like you. But I still think of France as my country." '

For the boys the farm yields a whole host of new experiences, sufficient to make them forget all about their London homes. In contrast to the usual narrative pattern of evacuation novels, where several chapters may be spent in describing the first few days and weeks in the new home, the pattern here is reversed, the boys adapting to what seems a rural idyll so quickly that it takes only one chapter to describe the time from lambing to June.

The central action of the novel features the boys' sighting of a German plane over Dartmoor, a plane which they believe must have landed on the moor. Although Mr Reynolds believes their story and persuades the army to search for the missing plane, their failure to find it confirms everyone's disbelief in the boys. Tucky and David experience not just the frustrations of being children in an adult world – those same frustrations experienced by Albert Sandwich in *Carrie's War* – but also the misery of being marked out as different. Where the two boys had been integrated into the village community they are now almost ostracized, taunted by their school mates as 'townies'. Just before their discovery of the two German pilots the boys again experience for themselves the sense of isolation, distance from home and alienation from one's surroundings that the German men in enemy territory must also experience. Searching for the plane on the moor one last time David nearly drowns, surviving only because one of the Germans appears almost miraculously to pull him from the river. The man's decision to rescue David – taken at considerable risk to himself – leaves the boys in an ethical dilemma and the narrative explores issues of moral conflict, setting national loyalty against personal obligations. With their sense of unity frayed, David and Tucky are more understanding of the individual needs of the two Germans. Since one of the Germans has saved David's life Tucky is adamant that he deserves their personal loyalty:

> 'We got to help him, haven't we? He saved your life, Davey, pushed all the water out of you and he was risking a lot to light that fire for you. You owe him a lot, Davey. We both do.'

For David, questions of national loyalty ('These were the men who had bombed London and Plymouth and killed thousands') also revolve around personal issues, matters of fact becoming confused with the emotional picture David paints for himself of his own father's death ('perhaps these were the men who had shot down his father over the French coast and cheered as they watched him crashing into the French beaches'). Tucky recognizes that David's reactions stem from personal emotions, ' "They're Germans and the Germans killed your

Dad, so you hate them all, don't you, every one of them?"' David himself cannot reconcile these individual German men to the image he has in his own mind, 'Yet one of them had saved his life.' The two pairs, German men and British boys, are implicitly compared to one another; one of each pair has been hurt, one of each pair is wet and only partially clothed. Like David and Tucky, the two men are far from home. And with the recent failed search for the plane, the army and the locals have become hostile to David as well as to the two Germans.

However, David still cannot see beyond his own personal feelings, hoping to find glory and refute the locals in the discovery of the two men:

> Every instinct except one told him to give the Germans up, to call in the soldiers, to tell Mr Reynolds. After all, wouldn't Ann and Mr Reynolds be pleased? Wouldn't the laughing faces in the village be silenced? Wouldn't their stock be high at school? And wouldn't everyone have to eat their words about the 'townies'? And, apart from that, they were Germans, enemies. It was a duty to make sure they were captured.

The sentence about 'duty' stands as an afterthought, a way of justifying to himself a course of action that Tucky views as morally wrong, rather than as an end in itself.

David and Tucky's anxieties are partially relieved when the German who is ill decides to give himself up rather than impede his friend in his bid to escape. Tucky and David are then able to return to school with honour restored by the discovery of the man from the missing German plane, but their victory is marred by the knowledge that they are lying to those who have protected them. David 'felt no triumph, only relief ... The happier the evening became the more he thought of the lies and trickery that had made it all possible.' When the second German is discovered and David and Tucky confess all they find that Mr Reynolds supports their decision, '"'Tis never wrong to do what you feel is right, Tucky."' His simple sentiment provides the implicit moral behind the whole book, a story in which individual conscience must take precedence over national pride and official duty.

The Prisoner

Like *Friend or Foe* and *The Machine-Gunners*, James Riordan's novel *The Prisoner* (1999) describes the discovery of an individual German soldier by patriotic British schoolchildren. It is unique among British children's fiction in its detailed portrayal of the effects of the British bombing on German civilians, providing a complex examination of the morality of war which is usually found in Britain only in novels published in translation. Although the central events of the book happen within a 24-hour period the narrative structure is a complex one in which flashbacks and a story-within-a-story suggest the passage of a much longer period of time.

At the beginning of the novel Iris and Tom have a straightforward view of the war – the British are the good guys and the Germans the bad. Like Norah in *The Sky Is Falling*, Iris views war as a game, 'war was serious fun. It was the greatest game ever invented'. Iris is fiercely patriotic and wishes that she was 'old enough to kill Germans'. When she and her brother 'capture' a German pilot she feels no pity for him, agreeing to her brother's suggestion that they should help him only reluctantly. ' "Whose side are you on?" she said crossly. "Why should we help a German? We didn't ask him to bomb us." ' Like David in *Friend or Foe* her views are influenced not only by supposedly patriotic beliefs, but by her sense of personal outrage at what has happened to her own father, reported missing after his boat was torpedoed. 'She didn't understand her brother, not after what had happened to Dad. If Mum were here she'd surely claw the man's eyes out.'

However, as the German shelters with the children overnight in an old shed, he tells them of the bombing of Hamburg, describing vividly the horror of life for the German civilians living there. His tale shows the children the difference between 'Nazis' and 'Germans' which they have not previously considered. The story he tells begins in his childhood and shows the divisions that existed in Germany before the war, the bullying he experienced over his reluctance to join the Hitler youth movement and the change in his perceptions about the war as he witnessed the atrocity of the destruction of the city. For the children his story is given personal as well as national relevance when they realize that it is intertwined with that of a British prisoner-of-war who could be their own father. He describes the prisoner and the young German soldiers working together to save the lives of the civilians and the children begin to see the full horror of what happens in wartime. Their clear divisions between good and evil are destroyed by his story. For the reader his account is supported in the closing pages of the book by the discovery of his body sheltering the British children from the German bomb which killed him. For a British reader accustomed to novels which describe only the horrific effects of the German bombing of Britain and avoid descriptions of life in Germany, this is a particularly powerful novel. It provides a rare account of the war in which the utilitarian view of the bombing of German civilians, predominant in British children's literary fiction, can provide no justification for such horrific attacks. The book contrasts with David Rees' Carnegie Medal winner, *The Exeter Blitz* (1978), which gives a detailed account of the bombing of Exeter in one of the Baedecker raids ordered by Hitler after the British bombing of Lübeck. Here the British attacks on civilian Germany are consigned to the novel's introduction, while the brutality of the Germans – shown targeting the civilians as they run for the shelters – is depicted in detail.

Summer of My German Soldier

Bette Greene's classic novel *Summer of My German Soldier* (1973) also uses the device of the single German soldier to prompt questions about right and wrong, and about the relationship between civic duty and individual conscience. Concerned primarily with the friendship between an American Jewish girl and a German prisoner-of-war, it also considers the racism within American society, both between whites and blacks, and between Jews and non-Jews. To a contemporary reader the opening pages of the novel are more remarkable for their presentation of the solitary black man in a group of whites than for the portrayal of the 'Nazi' soldiers who, as prisoners-of-war, have been brought to the small town in Arkansas. The book looks at themes of community, loyalty and race. Patty Bergen – daughter of a small-town Jewish shopkeeper – begins to fall in love with Anton, the German prisoner-of-war who buys a pencil sharpener from her father's store, and whom she subsequently befriends when, having escaped from the prison camp, he is in need of food and shelter. She is eventually sent to a reform school for her 'crime'.

Against a backdrop of the Second World War the book sets up complex antitheses, implicitly comparing the prevailing anti-German feelings with the intolerance shown to the blacks, and also examining behaviour towards the Jews in this small town. In parallel with this discourse in hatred runs an implicit discussion on the nature of love, both romantic and familial. Patty is a lonely child, socially isolated partly because she is Jewish (her contemporaries are spending the summer at a Baptist camp) and partly through her father's strictness – he beats her brutally for disobeying him and spending time with a boy of a lower social class. Her father's brutality and her mother's vacuous nature leave her isolated from her family. When the novel opens her only friend is the family's black housekeeper, Ruth, a woman presented as both strong-minded and fair who adopts the maternal role left vacant by Patty's own mother. Patty's alienation mirrors that of the German soldier and allows her to empathize with his position. Anton himself, meanwhile, is presented as both sympathetic and likeable.

Although the locals think of all the German prisoners as 'Nazis', Anton's father has ridiculed Hitler to his university students and deplores the Nazi burning of books at the university. His son is presented not as any form of hero, but as an ordinary man, a medical student before the war, a man who has spent the war being 'mostly bored to death and occasionally scared to death'. To Patty, however, he offers the love and respect she has never received from her own family, coupled with the opportunity to escape the petty restrictions of day-to-day life. His respect for her views and his appreciation of the way she looks are set against her father's continual and frequently brutal criticism of her behaviour, and her mother's continual nagging about her appearance. Anton gives Patty an account of his life in Nazi Germany which shows that as a character he is eminently likeable, with an intellect and capacity for empathy which match Patty's own. Her parents, meanwhile, are portrayed as dogmatic, thoughtless, brutal and disloyal to both their daughter and their servant. They cannot see Patty's own worth, their prime concern is for appearances, and they do not stand up for their black maid when she is unfairly criticized by a white woman. Patty's parents are flanked by the inhabitants of the small town they serve, a group of people as small-minded as Patty's parents themselves. The white townspeople are shown *en masse*, their main preoccupations shopping and gossip. We see them either standing around to gather the latest gossip of local events, or as petty individuals who complain unjustly and who succumb to the empty flattery bestowed upon them by Patty's parents.

However, Patty's defence of the German soldier is not portrayed in unambiguous terms; she supports him initially not because she feels he is right morally, but because she is in love with him, and has been ever since he first walked into her father's store. Hers is not a logical but an emotional decision. However, decisions made emotionally can be as 'morally correct' as those made logically, and our sympathies, both logical and emotional, rest with Patty. As narrative time moves on, her father's dislike of her is set against Anton's care for her. Patty herself sees her decision not as a choice between right and wrong, but as a choice between the two men. Anton's delighted reception of the shirt she had lovingly bought for her father is in stark contrast to that father's own curt dismissal of the gift. The most marked contrast, however, comes as Anton recklessly abandons all fears for his own safety when he sees Patty being hurt by her father. The servant Ruth retrospectively places his action in a religious context:

'That man came a-running from the safety of his own hiding

'cause he couldn't stand your pain and anguish no better'n me. That man listens to the love in his heart. Like the Bible tells us, when a man will lay down his life for a friend, well, there ain't no greater love in this here world than that.'

In the wartime setting local prejudice and unchecked bullying have wider connotations. Anton explicitly compares Patty's father to Hitler:

'Cruelty is after all cruelty, and the difference between the two men may have more to do with their degrees of power than their degrees of cruelty. One man is able to affect millions and the other only a few. Would your father's cruelty cause him to crush weak neighbouring states? Or would the *Führer's* cruelty cause him to beat his own daughter? Doesn't it seem to you that they both need to inflict pain?'

Hitler in turn is placed in a wider context. While in other novels he may be seen as the face of the enemy, the autocratic dictator single-handedly responsible for the war, here Anton offers a different view: 'Leaders don't usually spring forth to impose their will on a helpless people. They, like department stores, are in business to give people what they think they want.' Even Patty's father unconsciously echoes this view, and Patty knows that, with an appropriately materialistic stance, it is a view shared by all the provincial shopkeepers: 'Remember what they say? My father, mother, the clerks in the store, and the salesmen with heavy sample cases from Memphis, St Louis and Little Rock: "You only get what you pay for."' Patty's personal decision to act according to her conscience and not according to a narrow-minded set of conduct codes is seen therefore as part of a wider struggle between good and evil. All people are shown to be capable of racism and prejudice; the white Americans who berate the German prisoners themselves perpetrate daily acts born out of prejudice and racism towards their Negro employees. The Jewish lawyer, who takes on Patty's case only because her father begs him to, is reluctant to defend her for fear her act will stir up further anti-Jewish feeling. He refuses to listen to her version of events – although we understand that this would have helped him to defend her – and lectures her instead, '"Young lady, you have embarrassed Jews everywhere. Because your loyalty is questionable, then every Jew's loyalty is in question."'

Patty's own actions are not born out of a sense of moral right but from the human emotions arising from the need to be loved and valued. She befriends Anton because she has fallen in love with him and because she wants his good opinion of her. Like those around her she is not morally perfect; the difference is that she knows and seeks to rectify her faults where her father ignores his own. In the novel we see the need for love breeding violence – Anton hears Patty's father pacing up and down repeating over and over again, ' "Nobody loves me. In my whole life nobody has ever loved me." ' With such a clear importance attributed to the value of love, Patty's decision to choose a course of action which stresses the values of love and friendship is one which readers are encouraged to support.

The novel offers no easy solutions to the complex problems of racial hatred and prejudice of all kinds, and ends with Patty still in the reform school, still uncertain of what the future may bring, though looking forward in hope of a better future. The value of human love has been emphasized throughout the novel, yet we know that Patty will have to return to a home where she is unloved and uncared for; her family have not visited her once in the reform school, though Ruth, with none of their privileges, has made the difficult journey. There are hints, however, that she will find her own way in the world, supported by the friendship of people like Ruth and Anton and the young woman journalist who offers her both friendship and the chance of publishing her first newspaper report. Patty's voice, silenced first by her father and then by the Jewish lawyer who will not listen to her story, will at last have a means of making itself heard.

Racism in Britain

The Lion and the Unicorn

A small group of texts deals with a subject often ignored in children's fiction, the treatment received by Jews and by foreign nationals at the hands of ordinary British people. Shirley Hughes' *The Lion and the Unicorn* (1998) is a complex picture book intended, perhaps, for readers of six to eight. It tells the story of a young Jewish boy evacuated to a stately home in the country. Lenny Levi's father is in the army and has left Lenny a badge bearing the emblem of the lion and the unicorn. His father reminds Lenny to be brave like the lion and Lenny tries to remember his father's words. The image of the lion suggests the need for physical rather than mental bravery but the book considers different kinds of courage: the mental courage of the unicorn becomes as powerful a force as the physical courage of the lion. Themes of isolation and separation are also examined. Separated from his mother, to whom he has clung for support through the long hours of the bombing, Lenny is even isolated from the other children on the evacuation train, the illustration suggesting his feelings of loneliness among the huge crowd of people. Even when he reaches his billet he is physically separated from the other children – who are all girls – by the presence of a curtain across the huge loft room they share. The illustration shows Lenny alone on his side of the curtain while the text tells how he listens to the girls whispering. His loneliness is further marked by the Nanny's objection that they had asked for a girl. The following morning we have the first overt reference to his religion – the kitchen is as big as the synagogue he attends – and then his sense of isolation is clearly linked to his religion when he refuses to eat the bacon prepared for his breakfast, '"There's good food wasted. I'll not have that!" she scolded. "We don't eat bacon in our house," said Lenny in a low voice. Everyone stopped eating and stared at him.' To a reader versed in evacuee stories the first breakfast at the new home often signals a time of increased acceptance, a feeling of well-being as the evacuee wakes to a new day and eats food that is often unobtainable in their city homes, bacon being usually the height of luxury, where here it becomes a source of even greater misery for Lenny.

Lenny is increasingly isolated after this episode: excluded from the boys' games at school, and not Nanny's favourite at home, he is teased by the children and scolded by Nanny for his bedwetting, but he begins to develop strategies for dealing with his loneliness. The text overtly recalls other stories, suggesting further possibilities of at least mental escape: 'He remembered hearing somewhere about a secret garden that was locked up for years and years and nobody ever went in.' Like Mary Lennox, another lonely child far away from home, Lenny draws strength from the garden whose unicorn statue becomes a symbol for another kind of courage. In the garden Lenny meets a young man whom he takes to be an assistant to the gardener. The young man has lost his leg in the fighting in France but Lenny makes no connection between this ordinary person and the pictures of the brave family members on Lady de Vere's walls, even though he knows that her son is a war hero. The young man, Mick, tells Lenny how scared he was on the battlefield, comforting him by telling him that he too wet the bed, not only as a child but also as an adult after he had been wounded. When Lenny learns that this young man is in fact the revered family war hero he begins to realize that fear affects everyone. His isolation is lessened and this, combined with some practical help from one of the domestic servants who has befriended him, puts an end to Lenny's bedwetting and to his fear of the other children. However, it is not until Lenny, trying to run away in search of his mother whose letters have stopped coming, encounters the stone unicorn which has magically come to life in the middle of the night, that he really understands what Mick has meant when he talked about 'different kinds of courage'. Lenny's courage is compared with that of a unicorn while the girls who bully him are 'a load of mean, mangy old cats', a reminder perhaps of the unicorn's opponent. The illustrations set up an antithesis between lion and unicorn, the beneficent figure of the stone unicorn found in the garden in contrast to the menacing statue of the lion whose shadow looms over the bedroom wall in the middle of the night.

There is an underlying sense in the book that *en masse* the British are as cruel and – by implication – racist as the Germans they fight. Mick is adamant in his distinction between fighting Nazism and fighting the German people, ' "I never wanted to fight Germans or anyone else … It's cruelty, bullying and oppression we're fighting against." ' Cruelty, bullying and oppression are the three things that Lenny has encountered in his relationship with both the local children and his fellow evacuees and there seems little to differentiate them from the Germans Mick fought. Emphasis is placed throughout on the value of individual morality and courage, which are in direct opposition to collective violence. The final double-page spread shows Lenny passing the stone lion, now diminished in stature though still ferocious, as he walks confidently up to the entrance of the stately home, hand in hand with his mother.

A Homecoming for Kezzie

Theresa Breslin's novel A Homecoming for Kezzie (1995) describes the treatment received by an Italian family living in Scotland. Ricardo and his family own a café in Glasgow, usually a busy thriving place in which customers are known by name. But after the declaration of war a mob attacks the café, wrecking it almost completely. This action is clearly attributable not to the war itself, but to the government's bringing in of the Aliens Order, under which all Italian nationals have to register with the authorities. Ricardo makes an explicit link, ' "Since the Aliens Order came into force … we have been a focus of hatred and fear. We are seen as the enemy." ' The family know many of their attackers, some of whom have been customers, but the destructive action of the mob is shown to reflect not their feelings as individuals, but their behaviour as part of a pack: ' "I couldn't reason with them," Ricardo tells Kezzie. "Some of them had been drinking, It was very ugly." ' Kezzie herself, the teenage heroine, is Scottish by birth but has recently been living in Canada, her experience distancing her from the overt 'nationalism' of her compatriots who attack the café. Here the antithesis of collective violence is seen not as individual courage, but as united strength. With Ricardo and his family ready to give up, Kezzie places in the café window a photo of Signor Casella in his British army uniform from the First World War, adorning it with his medals and leaving it in the window overnight in an attempt to shame the perpetrators of violence. Where words have failed with the mob she makes a visible statement of the Britishness of Ricardo's family which is reinforced with a course of action reminiscent of the so-called 'spirit of the blitz' in its determination not to be ground down by events. Leaving the evidence of the wreckage very visible in the café, she and Richard open the sandwich bar, being determinedly jovial all day and announcing loudly that ' "no person [Ricardo] knows, or that he has ever met, or who buys food in his café, would ever do something so horrible to his family" '. Their cheerfulness shames the local community who make good the damage they have caused and the episode ends with relationships repaired, and animosity supposedly forgotten. The moral here is unusually explicit for a book published in the 1990s. Kezzie 'went home that evening with a comforting warm feeling inside her. Her trust in others and human goodness had won through today.'

Afterwards . . .

Bat 6

Bat 6 (1998) by the acclaimed author Virginia Euwer Wolff is set in America in 1949, four years after the end of the Second World War, but its events are closely concerned with the war and with Americans' view of foreign nationals. Its central action concerns the annual softball competition played between the sixth-grade girls of two neighbouring small towns, Bear Creek Ridge and Barlow Road. The game is an event of enormous significance to the entire community, uniting old and young and providing the basis for an annual celebration. Established by the women of the town as a way of getting the men to end their long-standing feud, the game has been played annually for the last 49 years. This is to be the fiftieth Bat 6 and the girls who are to play in it feel they have spent their whole lives preparing for the day. The sense of impending excitement is exacerbated for each team by the discovery of a new and talented player in their midst. In Bear Creek Aki has returned after many years absence, time in which she and her Japanese family have been interned after President Roosevelt's 1942 Executive Order which ordered the evacuation and internment of all those of Japanese ancestry living in the Western United Sates after the bombing of Pearl Harbour. In

Barlow Road the new player, Shazam, has come to stay with her grandmother while her mother 'gets on her feet' again, following her father's death in the Pearl Harbour bombing. On the day of the game itself, with emotions running high in both communities, Shazam attacks Aki, leaving her seriously injured and bed-ridden for several weeks.

The narrative structure of the novel is complex, with each of the girls in the two teams telling part of the story 'now that it's over'. The structure emphasizes the tension surrounding the game, its fragmented nature hinting at the events of the day without disclosing them, drawing readers closer and teasing them with hints of what happened. With more than twenty narrative voices, the variety of both tone and viewpoint allows the expression of a whole range of thoughts and feelings about both the events of the war and its aftermath in the local community. Almost all the girls believe in the need to forgive Shazam, agreeing about the importance of understanding and of compassion. Shazam (her real name is Shirley but she prefers the nickname taken from a Captain Marvel comic and used by her dead father) is revealed in her parts of the narrative as a child barely literate, plagued by nightmares, and subjected to the anti-Japanese sentiments expressed by her mother. However, the narratives of other girls show Shazam's parents in a very different light. They endorse a far more rigid view of morality, are horrified to learn that Shazam's mother was not married when she was born – so horrified that they even shy away from the writing of such things. Although they act kindly towards Shazam and are grateful for her softball skills, their retrospective narratives take up a stance whereby they see friendship towards Shazam as part of their Christian duty.

In the course of the novel the girls collectively pass from innocence into experience. They are at first viewed as too young to know that Shazam was illegitimate. Ila Mae writes:

> 'I said to all the other girls of the town to ask their moms, but nobody's mom told anything clear. They just said like my mom, That must be Floy's girl, poor little thing, she's 11 already? Like that. Brita Marie's mom said Shazam's mother needed to get on her feet and she must of sent Shazam here to live. She would not say no more about it.'

By the end of the narrative the girls know and accept the facts of Shazam's birth and of her parentage and take active steps to heal the rift between Shazam and Aki. Their narratives also report the adults' view that Shazam's father was a thief. One even reports that Shazam is better off with him dead.

While the narrative told by the girls from the Barlow Road school deals with their attitude towards Shazam and the various moral questions involved in both her behaviour and their response to it, that of the Bear Creek girls deals with the return of Aki and, by inference and implication, the morality of ordinary Americans during the war. Set in the final term of their last year at grade school, the events of the year mark a time when the girls turn from children to adults. The events on the day of Bat 6 signal that transition. Like many rites-of-passage books this one examines questions of youth and age and, like many late-twentieth-century novels, it examines questions of guilt and innocence among children as well as among adults. With a number of high-profile cases of brutal acts perpetrated by and towards children making newspaper headlines in the 1990s, several children's writers have examined child cruelty. In Britain, Anne Fine's *The Tulip Touch* (1996) was written partly in response to the Jamie Bulger murder case. The author of *Bat 6* consciously links the theme of her novel to instances of violence perpetrated by children. 'Our daily news is filled with children doing horrific things,' she writes, 'and I'm fascinated by the question: what is it we notice about these kids but decide not to acknowledge?'

The book portrays a series of divisions: the historical feuding between the two towns, the present rivalry over the Bat 6 game, the passionate disagreements about the war. A further division, which runs implicitly through the novel, is that between women and men. The Bat 6 game, the focus of all the surrounding events, was established by the women of the two towns in 1899 as a way of bringing the men together; the link between the legacy of war and the founding of the annual game is made explicit. Shadean writes:

> 'And the men of the different towns went on not talking to each other. They didn't even ride their horses down there to trade or anything. So the ladies decided enough was enough, they wanted peace between the two towns. After a bad winter they arranged a ball game in the spring ... They thought, Well the men can't watch us playing our game for the whole afternoon and not say *anything* to one another can they? And they arranged to take along baskets of food too. See they were forcing the men to have a social. Guess what, they were right ... Not all at once in that afternoon, but slowly the men became friendly. By having their game all the ladies caused peace to break out.'

The story told by the girls of Bear Creek includes a variety of views on the war, including that of Aki herself. Like the other girls who tell the story, Aki portrays herself as too young to understand the full implications of what happened to her and her family. Wolff's introductory note makes clear the critical authorial stance, telling readers that, in 1987, the United Nations Supreme Court declared the internment of Japanese-Americans unconstitutional, calling it 'one of the worst violations of civil liberties in American history'. The other girls have remained in ignorance of what has happened to Aki: 'We were so little nobody explained it to us . . . We went through our grades from first up to nearly the beginning of sixth, without knowing she even existed.' Within the book there are various polarities that relate to war, even before the arrival of Shazam and Aki. The most manifest of these is between Lorelei's father – a conscientious objector – and his community. The views held by the community are expressed at their most extreme by Daisy's father. While Lorelei and Daisy remain friends, Daisy's father will not speak to Lorelei's. The two girls' versions of events suggest a degree of authorial support for the views held by Lorelei's father, a sympathetic character whose house is filled with books and who helps the girls with their homework. His daughter's account is a literate piece of writing, while Daisy's father continues to hold his beliefs even after the war is over, his views expressed by his daughter in a voice clearly less articulate than that of her friend:

> 'My father said no man who wouldn't fight for his country is a friend of his. He said you might as well be a traitor to your country if you wouldn't do your manly duty overseas.'

In a book which places value on education and rational thought, Daisy's father is shown as a bigot, unsupported by his daughter despite her love for him. For Lorelei and her family the aftermath of her father's refusal to fight continues. Their crops are in a worse state than their neighbour's because no one will work on their land. Lorelei has to miss school to help at home since pickers will still not work for her father. More significantly, during much of her childhood Lorelei has been isolated from the other girls in her class by her father's beliefs, left without a friend for her whole first grade until Susannah's mother takes a stand and invites Lorelei to her daughter's birthday party. The sheep-like behaviour of the townsfolk to some extent validates Shazam's unquestioning following of her mother's attitude towards the Japanese. The subsequent helpfulness of the neighbours, however, also foreshadows the bringing together of the girls of the two communities after the Bat 6 game.

At the town council meeting the role of the adults is again brought into question. Lorelei's father makes clear his view that Shazam has been following an adult example. Her crime is not what she has done but when she has done it; it lies in failing to recognize the adult signs that relations are changing:

> 'Every town in America would have cheered this child in 1943. In 1944. In 1945. America has told her what to be and suddenly we are completely modern in 1949 and now we revile her.'

One question runs implicitly through the novel; where does innocence end and guilt begin? Is it a factor of age and experience? Is it to do with the degree to which one recognizes the signs of potential trouble? Is it to do with national beliefs and not a reflection of one's own intention? While the different narrative perspectives explore all these possibilities, the common thread running through the novel is of the destructive power of over-zealous patriotism, even in wartime.

The File on Fräulein Berg

Joan Lingard's novel, *The File on Fräulein Berg* (1980), like *Bat 6*, examines children's capacity for evil as they emulate the wartime behaviour of adults. Set in Belfast in 1944, it tells the story of three teenage girls who convince themselves that their German teacher is a spy and make her life miserable with their misplaced patriotism. In Belfast in the 1940s the girls fail even to consider the possibility that their teacher might be a Jewish refugee; their world is split into the familiar oppositions of Protestant against Catholic – a division which by implication they extend to encompass the whole of the war. For them, Northern Ireland stands firmly aligned with England, while Eire (by virtue of its neutrality) is viewed almost as an enemy. The novel encompasses a movement from innocence to experience similar to that depicted in *Bat 6*. At the opening of the novel Kate, the narrator, tries to distance herself from the war and the spying game, preferring instead to immerse herself in L. M. Montgomery's *Anne of Green Gables* set on Prince Edward Island which, she comments, 'was pretty remote in spirit and place from Belfast and thoughts of German spies'. However, we see her surrounded by patriotic and religious fervour. Juxtaposed with the account of her escapist reading matter we learn of Sally's father who is a staunch Protestant and a member of the local Orange lodge:

> He walked on the Twelfth of July, bowler-hatted and sashed, in the parade to celebrate the Battle of the Boyne in 1689. Mention the Pope in his house and he'd choke on his fried steak.

This final sentence acts as a reminder that Sally's father, for all his religious loyalty, is living a life of black-market financed luxury in wartime. Meanwhile the girls attend a school which appears to place little value on absolute morality; its main concern lies with keeping up appearances:

> Looking back, I only recall the headmistress haranguing us over trifles, never over matters of idealism or the intellect. The only time idealism came to the fore was on Empire Day when the Union Jack was placed at the head of the hall and we all had to file past and salute it.

The three girls are taught an empty patriotism, devoid of morality and filled with nostalgia for the glories of past British rule. They are taught history by the same headmistress who views the independence of India as 'a backward step'. Lessons in school are repeatedly shown as chaotic affairs of little educational value, in which a great deal of misbehaviour is permitted. Emphasis is on outward appearances rather than inner being and this value system is accepted by the girls when they first encounter Fräulein Berg, failing to discover her true identity as a Jewish refugee. The themes of appearance and reality, of looking without really seeing, recur throughout the novel, the adult world forming a corrupt backdrop to the girls' thoughtless activities as they take on the spying role of which they accuse Fräulein Berg. With Kate's reading matter now encompassing titles like *School Versus Spy* and *Schoolgirls in Peril* they lurk on street corners, assiduously writing down every detail of Fräulein Berg's life in a notebook bought specially for the purpose.

On a trip to Dublin we see how the adults themselves have also become distanced from an absolute morality, concerned primarily with keeping up appearances rather than observing the spirit of the law. Sally's mother is making the trip across the border expressly for the purpose of smuggling back rationed goods to sell on the black market. The whole party is caught when the girls invite the customs officials to search Fräulein Berg who shares their railway carriage. Shamed, they return home, the two adult women in the party dressed only in their skirts and tops to preserve decency, even their shoes and stockings removed by the customs officials. What upsets Sally's mother and Harriet's father, however, is not the thought that they have committed a crime, but the knowledge that they have been caught and publicly embarrassed. Harriet's mother herself smuggles contraband articles across the border but, Harriet says:

> 'That was different . . . well they hadn't been taken and searched, had they? That was what had been so ghastly about our trip, and that was what they were objecting to.'

Even Kate's mother – presented as a respectable woman 'down on her luck', as Harriet's parents put it – is not beyond wanting zips to be smuggled across the border for her sewing work.

The book, like *Carrie's War*, is told by an adult narrator looking back over a distance of more than 30 years at her wartime childhood, the tale prompted by her meeting with Sally and Sally's account of a reunion with Fräulein Berg. Only at the very end of the novel do readers learn that Fräulein Berg had in fact been a Jewish refugee, that all her family had perished in the concentration camps. Only now that she has told her story does the knowledge that Fräulein Berg has children and a new life of her own bring Kate a degree of freedom, the final closing of the file.

Pacifism

Going Back

Penelope Lively's novel *Going Back* (1975), is a first person narrative told after an adult woman's return to her wartime childhood home, perhaps 30 years on. The book explores themes of time and memory, of inner and outer space. Medleycott, a Somerset house, was Jane's childhood home, and when she revisits it after her father's death she recalls the war years, and the childhood of herself and her brother Edward. The picture painted is a self-consciously nostalgic one, combining images of childhood innocence with the appeal of the pastoral idyll. Most of the story is set in the house and gardens which demonstrate a prelapsarian quality. The children themselves see the house and garden as the world, the house belonging to the adults and the garden their special territory. The house exudes comfortable domesticity, the red tiles and flour-smelling kitchen an image of home comfort through the years:

> We lived in the playroom and in Betty's red-tiled, flour-smelling kitchen and in Betty's sitting room with the brown wireless crackling to itself on the mantelpiece.

The garden belongs to the children, the world beyond it having the forbidden quality associated with the world beyond the Garden of Eden:

> The garden was our territory – the space within which we knew the arrangement of every leaf and stone and branch. Beyond the garden was an undefined and forbidden world.

Although the world outside becomes more accessible as the children grow older, the garden remains the children's prime concern. Their activities within it are part of the archetypal vision of childhood games fused with happy domesticity:

> And so, through those years of being five, and six, and seven, we were in the garden, making camps in the spinney and fishing for tadpoles in the pond, and trailing round the kitchen garden after Sandy, the gardener, while Sandy earthed up potatoes and hoed the onion beds and pruned the cordon apples.

With the coming of war, however, the pastoral idyll is threatened. Immediately after this description of the children's happy life in the garden, the scene switches to the drawing-room, everyone gathered around the wireless, the presence of the servants in the room signalling that this is a momentous occasion. As readers with a knowledge of the past we know that this moment must signify the outbreak of war, but this is not stated overtly, the adult narrator recollecting not the words about war, but the benediction, 'May God bless you all' and the singing of God Save the King. From pastoral idyll we are transported to wild woods, as Jane hears inexplicably in her head the words from the nursery song, 'If you go down to the woods today, you're in for a big surprise.' When she asks Betty if the war will come to Medleycott, her question is met with silence.

War does bring immediate changes, but for the children these are at first beneficial, removing their disliked father and bringing the landgirls, a novel source of both entertainment and company. The children enjoy the preparations for war, appreciating the 'gloriously inky mush' that will dye the blackout curtains and not understanding the grown-up conversations about evacuees and rationing and the war effort. For the children war is at first, as in so many wartime stories, both a game and something which allows them to feel self-important as they take on adult tasks as their war work. It does not appear to threaten their lives directly.

Although nostalgic for an idyllic period of childhood, the narrator is not nostalgic about the war itself, not least because war is seen as an adult preoccupation, one which, for much of the novel, remains distant from the children's world of house and garden. Any ramifications of the war continue to be pleasant as far as the children are concerned. The arrival of Mike, a Quaker and conscientious objector, gives them their first real food for thought over the war. Conscientious objection is a subject rarely covered in children's books, perhaps because the prevailing ethos of children's literature, particularly British literature of the Second World War, still veers towards a version of history which gives the Allied troops the moral highground, and which ignores the civilian deaths and terrible damage inflicted by the British forces. Through the character of Mike, sent to work on the local farm, the narrative explores questions of internal courage: the conflict between expected behaviour – or duty, as the children's father perceives it – and personal integrity. To the children Mike is at first a novelty. He is clearly presented not as a coward but as a man of mental courage and sensitivity, a stark contrast to the children's own father who demonstrates a chilling preoccupation with rules, regulations and duty. While their father remains a distant figure, Mike, a 20-year-old man, almost but not quite grown up in the children's eyes, is regarded with instant sympathy:

> That curious response, which must be physical in some way or maybe mysteriously spiritual, because it can come even before speech, which tells you a person is sympathetic, someone you will like. And so, even without conversation, we knew that this young man whom we had never seen before, buying his twenty cigarettes from Annie Simpson, was on our side, was a potential friend.

The children, and Betty their housekeeper, sympathize with Mike's stance, quickly dismissing Sandy's view that 'they should have to join up ... if everyone felt like that' with the tart response, 'There'd be no more wars would there'.

This alliance of children, Betty and Mike, in contrast to the harsh disciplinarian father, promotes an overt and sympathetic explanation of the conscientious objector's viewpoint usually absent in children's fiction. Betty's broad-minded tolerance ('It's not how I'd see things ... not with Hitler. But everyone's entitled to their opinions') reflects her open-hearted, informal attitude to the bringing up of the children, an attitude their father later condemns, but one which the children respect and appreciate. The ethos of the novel, like that of Michael Morpurgo's *Friend or Foe*, is one of individual freedom, setting a value on personal beliefs and relative morality rather than on national duty and absolute right and wrong. The narrative places the father and Mike in direct opposition to one another, both in their embodiment of particular values about the war and in their attitude to the children. It is an opposition of which the children are implicitly aware, as we learn from their conversation:

'I think Mike's brave.'
  'Brave?'

'It's brave doing something different from what everyone thinks you ought to do. He doesn't like it when they call him conchie – he pretends he doesn't mind, but he does.'

'He sits by himself when they have their sandwiches. He sits by another bit of the hedge.'

'I know. It's a different kind of brave from soldiers.'

'Betty says father's got leave for Christmas.'

'I know.'

The themes of bravery and cowardice, and the isolation brought by moral rather than physical bravery are reworked when two new boys, merciless bullies, join Edward's school. While Jane has been able to stand up to their father, Edward is intimidated by him, and while Jane is largely ignored by the bullies, they force Edward to join their gang. He cannot stand the cruelty of the gang's behaviour and eventually plucks up the courage to tell the gang that he will not be a part of it. In the ensuing fight not only is he hurt, he also takes all the blame although, as his sister reminds him, it was the others who started it. Edward is, more or less, left to get on with his own life, a reminder of Mike sitting alone to eat his sandwiches. Edward's fight, an episode with a clearly defined set of moral values, acts as a metaphor for Mike's struggles, suggesting narrative sympathy for Mike's viewpoint.

When the children's father insists on sending Edward away to boarding school the father's position and Mike's are diametrically opposed. The father views boarding school as an inevitable part of growing up, unable – or unwilling perhaps – to remember his own misery there and convinced that it is what young men of a certain class must do. Mike, however, when he learns of the decision, reacts with reference to Edward as an individual:

'That was a bad move. That was really a very poor move indeed. . . . If there was one person it wouldn't do to pack off like that, it would be old Edward.'

Edward returns home for half term unable to bear the prospect of returning and together he and Jane run away from their father's rules, heading for Mike – now working on a new farm – who has promised them help should they ever need it. Like Edward's decision about the gang and Mike's about the war, their running away might appear cowardly, but requires mental bravery to carry out. They walk over 20 miles to get to Mike, sleeping in a tumbledown building and facing the unknown together, unable to ask for help or even directions for fear of being discovered. Having reached Mike's they are peremptorily dispatched back to Medleycott, but in running away they feel they have achieved a small victory. Edward does not have to return to school that year, and when the next year comes the return is not such an ordeal. Mike, however, has meanwhile joined up. He and Edward face one another comparing their experiences, linked but different, each a reminder of the difficulties of sticking to one's beliefs in complex situations:

'You're going to be a soldier,' said Edward in a small, stunned voice.
'Yes.'
'But you're a CO. You can't.'
'That's what I thought,' said Mike, 'but I stopped being quite so sure. People do, you know. It sounds muddled, I know. It is. Things are.'
After a moment Edward said, 'You'd have to kill people.'
'Yes,' said Mike. 'I've thought about that.'
'I thought about running away,' said Edward. 'All night. I know it's not the same,' he added.
'You would have done,' said Mike, 'and it is, in the end. Having to choose. Poor old son. It's not fun, is it?'

Mike's decision ends all contact with the children, who never see him again – neither we nor they know what has become of him. His decision to conform to accepted values perhaps fulfils the expectations of readers brought up on more patriotic texts, but leaves a gap for the children who are used to making their own decisions and acting independently.

The Shouting Wind
Linda Newbery's The Shouting Wind (1995) is also consciously determined to present a pacifist view and to question British actions taken during the Second World War. The novel describes the life of a young woman, no longer a child, during the war, telling the story of Kay, daughter of Alice (heroine of the Some Other War trilogy (see pp67–73)). This central narrative is in turn prefaced by an account of a trip by Kay's granddaughter to the RAF station where her grandmother spent much of the war. The major theme of the novel, which links with that of Newbery's First World War trilogy, is of the changing role and position of women in the twentieth century. As well as examining the role played by the war in women's emancipation it also, like Some Other War before it, looks at the human implications of war.

When the story begins Kay has just joined the WAAF. Her mother, who has seen at first hand the horrors of the First World War, is unhappy with her decision, suggesting that when Kay is conscripted she might work instead as a landgirl. Kay however resists Alice's pacifist beliefs, certain that they do not apply in this war:

> Being a pacifist was all very well, but what use was it in the present situation? What were you supposed to do – sit back on your principles while Hitler invaded? Surely working at a fighter base was more useful? She tried not to think of the possibility that she might not end up at a fighter base. That was what she had joined up for.

The rhetorical question perhaps suggests, even at this early stage, a degree of doubt in Kay's mind. However, knowing that she may well not end up on a fighter base as she intends, she nevertheless joins the WAAF and is posted as a telephone operator to a bomber base, a decision which she knows will upset her pacifist mother since many of the planes going out from the bomber bases are targeted on civilian towns and cities.

The account of Alice's First World War nursing work contained in *Some Other War* showed Alice living in harsh physical conditions and coping with the extreme mental stress of tending to wounded and dying men. Kay's life in the Second World War is contrasted with that of her mother 30 years earlier. The physical conditions Kay faces are far easier, she is to a greater extent distanced from the death and suffering caused by the war, and working on the base brings social pleasures never afforded to Alice. Although Kay rejects many of the social occasions enjoyed by other girls working on the base, she nevertheless finds that being in the WAAF brings entertainment as well as hard work. She meets her first boyfriend and takes part in various dramatic productions, experiencing a completely new world that is shown to bring a considerable degree of enjoyment with little real danger for the women who work on the bases. For much of the time the misery of war is distanced from the base itself, the deaths of the many bomber crews who never return neither witnessed nor described in detail, but seen through their failure to return rather than through the sight of their actual deaths. For most of those working on the base death becomes both distanced and routine, as Kay realizes when, at the beginning of her time on the base, she sees a plane crash that kills the crew:

> Planes failed to return from ops, she knew that. She would have to get used to filling in her log and going off duty and treating it as a normal night's work. There would always be new crews to fill

the gaps; the factories were churning out new Lancasters to replace the burnt fragments being cleared up from runways. This was a war, and people got killed in wars. She could hardly pretend she hadn't known that.

The inference, however, is not only that Kay has been pretending that very thing, but also that she wishes to go on doing so. As she grows more accustomed to the work on the base we are still shown how Kay struggles to come to terms with the deaths that others regard as routine. When plane T-Tare fails to return the narrative shows first the general view of the event:

> No one knew Pilot Officer Wenham or his crew anyway, so no one could feel any personal grief. Tomorrow morning an effects officer would sort through their belongings and clear their sleeping huts for another crew to use. A new Lancaster would be brought in and given the name of T-Tare. It was as if the name on the battle order had an existence quite independent of the plane itself or the men who flew her.

This passage is juxtaposed with the account of Kay's own feelings, a description which again shows her struggling to maintain the emotional distance apparently required on the base:

> Kay filled in her log, trying not to remember the nervous new crews she had seen a few hours earlier, not to think of the seven families who would receive *Missing* telegrams next day. No telephone call came, so the plane was assumed lost. It was nothing out of the ordinary, just a routine night on ops.

Kay never fully grows used to the waste of life, still thinking it 'an amazing squandering of lives, not far removed from the slaughter on the Somme and around Ypres in the last war'.

Kay's doubts – which are shared by her boyfriend David as well as by her mother – increase as the bombing raids on towns grow more frequent. David struggles with the knowledge that his navigational skills can bring life or death for those on the ground below:

> 'I know damn well that any small mathematical error on my part, any slight miscalculation, can decide whether someone under-neath lives or dies ... It seems so cold-blooded, sitting there in the clouds with my gauges and charts, playing God with people's lives.'

Kay and David's discussions about the war echo those held in the earlier novel about the previous war by her mother and her fiancé Edward, but whereas Edward was fully aware of the immoral nature of the war, as well as the bungled military decisions, David is less critical of those in charge and views the desire for revenge as understandable in the light of the German bombing raids. He says of his bomb aimer who is Jewish and has relatives in Poland:

> 'He doesn't know whether they have survived the Luftwaffe raids on Warsaw. Now all he wants to do is kill Germans. I suppose it's understandable to want revenge, especially with all the rumours of what's happening to Jews in Germany.'

For Kay and David the British bombing of the German cities is difficult, if not impossible, to justify:

> 'Mum says it's no different from the Luftwaffe bombing London.'
> 'Well, it isn't,' David said.

The two struggle with the issues involved, discussing them without reference to patriotism or national feelings, but purely on the basis of what is best for Europe and its people as a whole. Where Edward spoke of the futility of the First World War, David is more pragmatic about the situation in which he finds himself:

> 'The question is, I suppose,' he said, 'what can bring about the greatest good for the greatest number – what's that called? Utilitarianism or something? If Hitler can be forced to surrender, and that outcome is better for hundreds of thousands of people in Europe, the Jews and the Poles, can that be set against the lives of civilians in Berlin who are being killed to bring that about?'

Alice herself voices concern at Kay working on a bomber base, guessing that the exciting lifestyle may be a part of Kay's motive in joining the WAAF:

> She had had to hide her dismay when Kay had written to tell her of her posting. She could understand the attraction of the WAAF, the glamour and excitement of working on an operational station. War made it an exciting time to be young, in many ways. But it grieved her to think of all the other wartime occupations Kay could have chosen. Of all things, to have ended up in the one place Alice had most feared, a bomber station.

Alice's view is rarely reproduced in children's books, which tend to follow David's argument in favour of utilitarianism. Kay, meanwhile, ignores her doubts and does nothing about applying for a transfer until she personally is hit by tragedy when David is killed on a bombing raid. Kay is borne along by inertia, fuelled partly by uncertainty over what to do next, and partly by loyalty to her colleagues. Although she has some understanding of the horrors inflicted on German cities she is unwilling to act until she herself has experienced loss. Theoretical knowledge alone is not sufficient to make her act, only personal experience brings about change:

> She spent a long time pondering her motives and the courses open to her. It wouldn't be much of a gesture, whatever she did; no one would be any more interested in her reasons than they were in Guy Weldon's. She could not leave the WAAF since she was now eighteen and old enough to be conscripted, and she could not suddenly become a Conscientious Objector since she did not in principle object to the waging of war against Nazi Germany. And she knew that transferring to a non-operational unit was in effect not much different from working on a bomber station; it was simply moving herself a stage back from the front line. But she did not know what else to do.

Like her mother in the First World War, Kay sympathizes with the pacifist cause at the beginning of the war but, as for Mike in *Going Back*, personal experience leads her to take action which supports her beliefs. After David has been killed she applies to leave the bomber base and be transferred to a training station. While for most of those working on the base the bombing raids become routine, Kay has begun to understand her mother's views on the bombing. Her changing views are juxtaposed with occasional accounts of her mother's life in London, first recalling Alice's own experience of the First World War with her fiancé who was killed, and later considering Alice's role in this war. Determined not to do anything that will support the bombing of civilians, Alice concentrates her efforts on helping those whose lives are affected by the Blitz. Alice remains in London despite heavy bombing, although she could escape and go to her brother's home in Ireland. On one occasion when Kay is visiting her mother the area takes a direct hit and Kay believes that her mother could have been killed. Alice, meanwhile, ignores her own injuries until everyone around her has been attended to. Her courage, tenacity and her determination to play an active role which will relieve people's suffering exemplify those qualities shown by the heroes and heroines throughout late-twentieth-century novels about the Second World War.

In all the books considered in this chapter the protagonists are, like Kay and Alice, presented with complex choices, difficult decisions which test their moral strength and loyalty to the limit. While late-twentieth-century novels are almost unanimous in their portrayal of the First World War as tragic and senseless, depictions of the Second World War are more complex, and the decision-making by the heroes and heroines becomes inevitably more difficult. For children – both readers and protagonists – there can perhaps be only limited understanding of the issues involved, yet with mass evacuation and widespread bombing the war had an effect on young lives far greater than that experienced by children during the First World War. Throughout the books we see children who are courageous, thoughtful, caring and determined, who are anxious not to be viewed as children but who, in the main, wish to play a responsible role in the war, and who are often more successful at doing so than the adults they seek to emulate.

CHAPTER 4

The Second World War: Mainland Europe

Through the barbed wire, hollow, shadowed eyes stare out at the reader from the double-page image at the centre of Roberto Innocenti's *Rose Blanche* (1985). Hunched, emaciated figures wear the striped clothing of the death camps. We see what Rose Blanche sees, as the young girl stumbles upon the camp in a forest clearing near her small German town. The bleak greys, browns and mud green of the huts and the puddled earth are broken only by the yellow Stars of David on the prisoners' left breasts.

> Dozens of silent, motionless children stared out at her from behind a barbed wire fence. They hardly seemed to breathe. Their eyes were large and full of sorrow. They stood like ghosts, watching as she came close.

Fearful eyes, this time in a picture composed in relentlessly sombre sepia tones, confront the reader in a second picture book, *Passage to Freedom* (1997) written by Ken Mochizuki based on the experiences of Hiroki Sugihara. We share the viewpoint of the storyteller, the young son of a Japanese diplomat in Lithuania in 1940. Now the barriers between us and the imploring eyes are the iron railings of the Japanese Embassy. Outside stand crowds of desperate Polish Jews, begging the diplomat for visas to take them through Russia away from the advancing German armies.

These disturbing images from *Rose Blanche* and *Passage to Freedom* serve to introduce the perspectives and dilemmas which inform almost all of the books, mainly drawn from the last three decades of the twentieth century, discussed in this chapter. Most of these texts focus upon children: some are conscripted as forced labour in factories; others are refugees, wandering across a dangerous European mainland, searching for lost loved ones; some are locked up for days in the dark stench of cattle trucks; almost all endure acute hunger and sickness; and many are Jews, incarcerated within ghettoes or concentration camps. In only a few of these books are children actively engaged on the fighting front itself – some find themselves on the beaches of Dunkirk, for example; and only in Geoffrey Trease's *The Arpino Assignment* are the central characters young adults old enough to fight. As the century came to an end, publishers and authors seem to have implicitly agreed that what children should be told about the Second World War must concentrate on the suffering war brought to people all over Europe, rather than upon the daring or fighting prowess of the combatants.

These texts provide an international view of the conflict. They are set in Russia, Austria, Italy, Denmark, France, Hungary, Spain, Lithuania, the Netherlands, Germany itself and, inevitably, Poland. Almost half of them reach English readers in translation, an unusual proportion in the United Kingdom where fewer than two per cent of children's books currently in print are translated from other European languages.

Young admirers of Biggles and his fictional comrades-in-arms during and immediately after the war knew where they stood, whether they came from Britain, the Empire, the United States, Scandinavia, or continental Europe (for Biggles was much translated). Right was on their side, the German soldiers were brutal and often stupid, Hitler was Evil incarnate – although somewhat ridiculous at the same time; and, as Frank Richards' Bob Cherry observed, ' "One British pilot's as good as three Huns." '

Readers of the novels, autobiographical accounts and picture books considered in this chapter are offered a more ambivalent experience of the war, usually from the standpoint of victims. Distinctions are made between the conscripted German soldiers and those in the SS, and the suffering of German civilians as the tide of war turns against their country is made clear. Battles fought by land, sea and air provide a distant context for the experiences of individuals, but we are rarely drawn into the actual fighting portrayed in stories written during or immediately after the war itself, where sentries were 'silenced' by a commando's knife or another Luftwaffe Dornier plummeted into the drink.

Claude Gutman's *The Empty House* (1991) tells the story of 15-year-old David, a Jewish boy on the run in occupied France. Before the narrative, Gutman sets the words of the French novelist Joseph Kessel:

> Events on the grand scale, mass sufferings, catch the imagination and arouse compassion only incompletely and in an abstract way. We need a specific example to arouse our love or fear. We are so made that the face of a weeping child touches us more than hearing that a whole province has died of starvation.

The faces of the individual children we meet in the texts discussed in this chapter – and they will often be weeping – are sometimes those of the authors themselves, half a century ago, or of people the writers knew personally. In this regard, the narratives have a unique intensity. This writer *needs* to tell this story. Perhaps they must tell it now, 40 or 50 years after the events, while they can; possibly the writing is itself an attempt to bring resolution to an uncontainable experience. More often, however, there is a powerful sense that writers believe these are stories children need to hear. Stirrings of nationalism or fascism in, for example, Germany, France, Austria or Britain – whether among politicians or football hooligans – evoke the insistent protest that 'this must never be allowed to happen again'. Young people should know, writers argue, of the cruelty human beings are capable of inflicting upon each other; and how, time and again, barbarism was met with courage and endurance which, from our own usually peaceful perspectives, we can barely envisage.

Some of these writers themselves survived the death camps or fled their homes as refugees, and have given much of their lives to speaking to children about their experiences. Their books are testimony to their suffering. Hiroki Sugihara, for example, whose family's story is told in *Passage to Freedom*, adds an afterword to the story of how his father sat through days and nights, hand-writing visas for some 10,000 Jews to pass through Russia to safety, despite the instructions of his masters, the Japanese government. His actions cost him his job as a diplomat and subsequently led to 18 months of imprisonment in a Soviet internment camp. Some thirty years later, Sugihara's father was invited to Israel to be honoured at the Holocaust Memorial, Yad Vashem. In 1985, he became the first Asian to receive the 'Righteous Among Nations' award, and six years after his death, in 1992, a monument was erected to him in Japan. The book itself concentrates on the father's quiet bravery during that critical month in Lithuania, knowing of the consequences of his actions for his family and himself. Sugihara's tone is optimistic, drawing upon an ideal of selfless care for others lived out in practice:

The story of what my father and my family experienced in 1940 is an important one for young people today. It is a story that I believe will inspire you to care for all people and to respect life. It is a story that proves that one person can make a difference.

Making a difference, especially through confronting difficulties and confirming your sense of self when you do so, are common enough themes in children's literature in other genres – consider, for example, the fantasies of J. R. R. Tolkien and Ursula Le Guin. In the case of war literature, however, the trials which face the protagonists are extreme; no questing hobbit or mage ever faced a situation more horrifying, and less relieved by the excitements of high adventure, than the gas chambers of Auschwitz. For a child, few experiences could be more terrifying than the arbitrary removal of parents: their sudden and absolute humiliation, as they are stripped of their dignity and bundled into the abyss of captivity in the middle of the night, never to be seen again. No word of farewell. Such is the stuff of children's nightmares. The reader's knowledge that these stories are based on historical fact – at a time which their grandparents lived through – gives a unique dimension to the exploration of the human spirit under extreme duress which these books offer.

The Camps

Hiroko Sugihara's belief that his father's story is one which needs to be told to present-day children is echoed in prefaces and afterwords by several of the writers in our selection. It is worth quoting one of them at length to stand for all, since Livia Bitton-Jackson's words state the convictions which seem to drive many of this group of authors to write, and express their hopes for the impact of their books:

> My hope is that learning about past evils will help us to avoid them in the future. My hope is that, learning what horrors can result from prejudice and intolerance, we can cultivate a commitment to fight prejudice and intolerance.
>
> It is for this reason that I wrote my recollections of the horror. Only one who was there can truly tell the tale. And I was there. For you, the third generation, the Holocaust has slipped into the realm of history, or legend. Or, into the realm of sensational subjects on the silver screen. As you read my personal account I believe you will feel – you will know – that the Holocaust was neither a legend nor Hollywood fiction but a lesson for the future. A lesson to help future generations prevent the causes of the

twentieth-century catastrophe from being transmitted into the twenty-first.

My stories are of gas chambers, shootings, electrified fences, torture, scorching sun, mental abuse, and constant threat of death.

But they are also stories of faith, hope, triumph and love. They are stories of perseverance, loyalty, courage in the face of overwhelming odds and of never giving up.

My story is my message. Never give up.

Adult readers may find the tone of this passage itself a little melodramatic, even sensationalist. Such scepticism would be misplaced, for Livia Bitton-Jackson's memories are indeed of appalling horrors. *I Have Lived a Thousand Years* (1999), her autobiographical account of her experiences during the war, including her survival of Auschwitz, is an eloquent and shocking complement to her Foreword.

In 1944, the 13-year-old narrator was living in a small farming town in a region of present-day Slovakia, then a part of Hungary. She is just awakening to womanhood, to intellectual ideas, to poetry. As the occupation of Hungary intensifies, her Jewish family is repeatedly harried by the Hungarian military police (the thud of boots in the middle of the night, the humiliation of her father, the callous theft of personal valuables). Then, as the Germans occupy Budapest, the Jews are shipped off, family by family, in freight trains to unknown destinations. The narrative is told through diary entries – written with hindsight and with no pretence of being written at the time. The device is effective, for even though we know the author survived, the diary format gives a sense of an ominously uncertain future – diaries can suddenly end, as Anne Frank's readers know. By the end of the first entry in her notebook, Elli (Livia's family name) writes: 'Budapest, the city of my dreams, has become the anteroom to Auschwitz' and the inevitability of the route leading to the death camp is established: 'We are lost and helpless. Like lifeless matter we are carried along on a powerful conveyor belt towards an unknown fate.'

After four days and nights in the waggons, the doors are finally opened to reveal the station's name: Auschwitz. Her much-loved brother, Bubi, is literally kicked into a different group and disappears; months later, in another camp, he is reunited with Elli and her mother – her father has already been taken from them; but Bubi is so damaged in mind and body that for a while he inhabits a kind of life-in-death. As Livia reaches the SS officer selecting prisoners into different groups, she is directed to a separate line, because she has 'goldenes haar'. Later, she learns that the officer who made the selection, for the purposes of his experiments upon the prisoners, was the notorious Dr Joseph Mengele; ironically, he has saved her life. Her mother is thrust alongside her, but her fragile Aunt Serena is herded along with the larger crowd by the snarling Alsatian dogs and the SS guards:

> Wild fear floods her hazel eyes. She stretches out her arms to reach me. An SS soldier gives her a brutal thrust, hurling her into the line marching to the left. She turns again, mute dread lending her added fragility. She moves on.
> I never saw Aunt Serena again.

The detail of camp life makes painful reading: the hysterical, giggling girls after their hair has been shaved off; the food, sometimes heaving with worms, which must still be eaten if the prisoners are to survive; the slaughter of a batch of newly arrived prisoners after their interrogation ('One SS man does the shooting, like target practice, he fells the civilians, one by one.'). One day, Elli writes, 'a new dimension has been added to our identity. A number freshly tattooed on our left arms. I am no longer anonymous. I have a name. It is A-17360.' As punishment for talking to her desperately sick mother through the wall of the camp hospital, Livia is forced to kneel on the gravel in front of the command block for 24 hours without food or drink.

Throughout her torment, all of Elli's energies are channelled into the survival of her mother and herself. Life is stripped to that one purpose. No humiliation, no cruelty, physical or psychological, can finally reach the core of her being. She and her mother are sent briefly to a factory, where they meet some kindness from German civilians, then to Dachau. With cruel irony, the railway trucks she and her mother are travelling in are strafed by American planes. Eventually, as they are liberated, she is approached by a middle-aged German woman:

> 'We didn't know anything. We had no idea. You must believe me. Did you have to work hard also?'
> 'Yes,' I whisper.
> 'At your age, it must've been difficult.'
> At my age. What does she mean? 'We didn't get enough to eat. Because of starvation. Not because of my age.'
> 'I meant, it must have been harder for the older people.'
> For older people? 'How old do you think I am?'
> She looks at me uncertainly. 'Sixty? Sixty-two?'
> 'Sixty? I am fourteen. Fourteen years old.'

The events of Livia Bitton-Jackson's life make the Holocaust experience horrifyingly accessible to an adolescent reader – and to an adult, for that matter. The use of the dramatic present throughout has an intimacy which every oral storyteller knows. The effect is almost physical – as if the writer is leaning forward, drawing readers forward themselves in fascinated response.

This book examines its reader. So relentless is the account of life in the camp that, to allow yourself to read on in the narrative, you must steel yourself into detachedness from the horror of the text. Throughout, the detail of the descriptions confirms for the reader that this writer was, as her Foreword emphasizes, 'really there': the whiteness of the writhing worms in the putrefied stew, the line of blood left by a crawling victim as a soldier pumps bullets into him and then kicks the corpse with manic savagery. And, against all that, there is Elli's spirit.

It seems presumptuous to demur from the opinion of a Holocaust survivor, but Livia Bitton-Jackson's claim that 'only one who was there can truly tell the tale' is not confirmed by the evidence. Gudrun Pausewang's *The Final Journey* (1996) is a claustrophobic and wholly convincing account of a journey to the death camp, first published (in Germany) in 1992. In the previous decade, Gudrun Pausewang had published her *Rosinka* trilogy, addressed to juvenile readers, in which she records her own experiences towards the end of the Second World War. Aged seventeen, she and her German family were forced to leave their home in Czechoslovakia as the Red Army came closer. Her father had died fighting on the Russian Front. Pausewang herself was an admirer of National Socialism and of Hitler, and her immediate grief for the Führer's death surpassed her sense of loss for her father (though a fuller mourning for him came later). Her father, she explains, had died in the service of his country, a death which did not therefore seem to be in vain, even to his daughter. Now, with Hitler's death, Pausewang remembers crying inconsolably. 'For he had directed our existence for years, everything depended upon him. Without him, the last spark of hope was extinguished.'[1] The trilogy seems to be a coming-to-terms with the past for herself and for her generation, with the perspective of experience. If these books are an act of atonement, *The Final Journey* must surely be an intensification of an attempt to deal with the sense of guilt which her generation in Germany can perhaps never wholly resolve. For her, and for many of the mainland European authors considered in this chapter, the sharp detail of their work may well spring in part from a source which British and North

American writers cannot draw upon. It all happened *here*, on the avenues of Berlin, or Budapest, or Warsaw, or Leningrad, in rural Poland or the vineyards of Italy. In my lifetime, or my parents' lifetime, on my street, in my village. Fifty or so years ago, the railway track which now takes commuters to work carried cattle trucks crammed with doomed prisoners.

The Final Journey begins, 'The sliding-door of the railway truck closed with a deafening clang.' And for all but a dozen of the book's 154 pages, the truck doors barely open; the characters remain confined, and there is no relief for the reader other than passages in which the central character, Alice, recalls her home and the events leading up to her deportation. Those memories of the past only serve to intensify the pain of the present. Restricting the action of the novel to a cattle truck allows the reader no escape, especially as, unlike the occupants, the reader knows the journey's end will be the gas chamber. Throughout her childhood, 11-year-old Alice has been shielded within a cultured, close, genteel Jewish family. She has been kept by her parents and grandparents in hiding in the basement of their house for two years. One morning she wakes to find her parents' beds are empty; her grandparents tell her that her mother and father have gone to 'a dental clinic ... a long, long way to the east' to deal with her mother's persistent toothache. After her parents have been deported, Alice's grandparents even maintain the pretence, composing cheerful letters which they say have arrived from her parents.

So Alice goes trustingly with her grandparents when they are hauled out of bed in the middle of the night and taken to a waiting hall *en route* to the station, almost relishing the fresh air after her months hidden in the basement. Here, a policeman chases the occupants out of the stalls of a lavatory:

> 'Pack of swine!' he had roared.
> Alice was scared to death. Why was the policeman so nasty?
> 'He is overworked,' Grandfather explained.

On the platform, they are separated from Grandmother. They never see her again. Alice and her grandfather are loaded into a cattle truck.

The journey is a peculiarly terrible rite of passage. The reader is positioned close to Alice's innocent perspective; the viewpoint is skilfully chosen, since the reader's lack of detailed knowledge about the treatment of the Jews may well parallel Alice's naivety. Day by day, her innocence is violated – first in small matters which conflict with her upbringing, then through brutal experiences which devastate all that she has known and loved. Some of the children in the truck are very different from herself – they call their mother by her first name, they argue, squabble, make up; a woman suckles her baby; the behaviour of a mentally damaged boy, Ernstl, inevitably imposes upon the other occupants of the truck. A man fondles his girlfriend's breasts. A woman gives birth. All the while, the stinking pile of excrement in the corner of the truck grows, mosquitoes and horseflies are a constant torment, there is no water, diarrhoea attacks many of the occupants. And the train rumbles on eastwards. As she gradually learns the truth – mostly from the other children in the waggon – that they are being transported to the camps and their deaths, and that her parents have almost certainly taken this journey before her, Alice's fury that her trusted Grandfather has lied to her increases. Finally, she confronts him. As she shouts her accusations of betrayal at the bowed, defeated head, the broken man dies, crumpled on the floor of the waggon.

There are moments of kindly awakening too. There is warmth from the mother of the three children, who tells Alice stories and draws her into her own family after her grandfather's death. There is a good-looking young man, Paul, who lifts her up to a knothole to glimpse the countryside or to show her the evening sky:

> For a moment, Paul pressed his cheek tenderly to her temple.
> 'You will get over it, Alice,' he said quietly. 'You will see how much a human being can bear.'

Paul is shot in an attempted escape and his corpse, eyes staring, lies in the truck alongside Alice and the body of her grandfather.

As each slow day goes by, the mound of excrement grows, spreading throughout the truck, despite attempts to dam the flow with suitcases and bags.

The ending is told swiftly: arrival at the camp, uniformed men with dogs, 'striped men' directing the newcomers to the showers, the crazed Ernstl screaming as he is forcibly separated from his sisters. There is a quick undressing, a first glimpse for Alice of naked bodies. A lady, an opera singer, who has struggled to preserve some vestige of her elegance throughout the journey, dabs scent between her breasts ('You feel less naked with it on') and gives some to Alice ('Here, you cover yourself in lilac too'); and then the women and children are herded into the shower room.

> Alice glanced up at the ceiling. There really were not many nozzles – not nearly enough for so many people. But perhaps they squirted in all directions and sprayed over a wide area? ...
> Suddenly Alice felt something wet running down the inside of

her thigh. She bent forward and turned her leg outward. It was blood.

As her first period arrives, the shower room door opens and a crowd of naked men and boys is thrust in to join them. Alice notices that a young boy she had admired in their truck is among them: 'Aaron was beautiful – Paul would certainly have been more beautiful'. As the heavy iron door of the shower room slams shut, Alice looks longingly upward anticipating the refreshing 'water of life'. The book closes with 'She raised her arms and opened out her hands'.

Roberto, the central character of Donna Jo Napoli's *Stones in Water* (1999), and Tania, the heroine of *Hostage to War* (1994), are not Jewish. But both find themselves virtually enslaved in work camps where the regimes are almost as harsh and life valued almost as cheaply as in the death camps. For Roberto, a Venetian boy, the desperate irony is that his country is allied with Germany. This has not prevented the Nazis loading the entire youthful Italian audience at a cinema matinée into a train and sending them off to forced labour camps, first in Germany and then in the Ukraine. If the cold efficiency of the removal of the boys from the cinema is terrifying in its arbitrariness, the growing realization that they will probably never see their homes or families again has a numb finality that may evoke a connecting empathy in a young reader. The captives' fears are confirmed as the train reaches the border with Austria and they watch three older boys who have simply decided that they will go no further. The three defy the guards, arguing that it is against the law to cross borders without papers. The boys stand on the platform confronting a soldier:

> [The soldier] shouted in German, fast and harsh. Then he held out his pistol and shot one of the boys in the head. Red spray fanned out in front of the boy as he fell forward. People screamed. One of the other two boys broke away and ran. The soldier shot him in the back. Then he shot the third boy in the head. They fell dead on the platform.
>   Pools of blood widened around their bodies.

The red spray and the pools of blood intensify the bleak efficiency of the murder. The starkness of the prose reflects the lack of feeling in the executioner and the numbed responses of the watchers on the train.
    Roberto's friend Samuele is Jewish, and the boys know that if his race is discovered, that will mean almost certain death. Samuele adopts the name Enzo to conceal his Jewishness but daily events inevitably

bring the possibility of discovery. A refreshing swim in a lake – a moment of leniency from the guards – after a day's labour allows Enzo's circumcision to be noticed by another boy who callously blackmails him each mealtime into surrendering his rations.

Stones in Water is not autobiographical, but it is based ('loosely, very loosely') upon the life of one who survived such harshness. The unrelenting oppression of *I Have Lived a Thousand Years* or *The Final Journey* is here relieved by a sense of excitement and adventure more familiar to young readers, though the context is always genuinely dangerous. The boys are required to build a barbed wire pen which is filled with Jewish prisoners. Roberto decides that he will find food for one particular girl and her young sister. The escapades of Roberto and Enzo in stealing eggs and hoodwinking the guards have a comic dimension, and the guards themselves are not uniformly inhumane. It is this nameless girl who gives Roberto a stone – all she can find – which becomes a talisman for him in his determination to survive.

The courage of the two boys and their different senses of who they are grow through adversity. Enzo is strengthened in his Jewishness through the danger he is in, and the narrator recognizes how important his Venetian roots are to him. One of the recurring motifs of the novel is a belief in the power of story to help you to retain a sense of identity, a sense of your origins. Enzo is a storyteller, and each night he shares a story with Roberto – sometimes biblical, sometimes improvised as he goes along. Enzo has been a reader, especially about the natural world:

> Enzo wove these bits of their surroundings into the bedtime stories he still told every night. And he wove in their mothers and their fathers and Sergio and Memo and the canal near the big wooden bridge of the Accademia under the midnight moon and the winding staircase called the Bovolo that looked like a snail shell and oh so many things of Venice that made Roberto's heart want to keep pumping against all odds.

Enzo does not survive. In the middle of a freezing Ukrainian night, other boys attempt to steal their boots. After the ensuing fight, the weakened Enzo dies in Roberto's arms, urging him to ' "Speak Venetian all the time. Remember who you are." '

Roberto's escape, which occupies the rest of the novel, would stretch credulity were it not for the fact that it is a matter of history that young people did cover huge distances in wartime Europe. Roberto simply decides he is going home, and his adventures along the way are exciting reading. He encounters a starving wolf and convoys of soldiers, and his life is saved by a young boy, the sole survivor of a village devastated by a raiding army. At last, Roberto reaches the Black Sea and with Maurizio, an Italian deserter, he sets off in a small boat to sail to his homeland. Through his friendship with Maurizio, Roberto determines to join the *partigiani*, the partisans, to become a saboteur, to help in the rescue of Jews and to build a different Italy.

In some ways, Roberto's experiences in the camps have made him wiser than the older Maurizio. One day he shows his companion the stone given to him by the Polish girl:

> 'All you need is stones, Maurizio. If you have enough stones and the water is shallow enough, you can build a city up through the waves. Like Venice ... I'm going to be a stone ... I'll be part of the new city.'

Taken out of context, such an aspiration may seem lightweight in tone compared with the bleak content of the texts discussed earlier in this chapter. However, it is an expression of feeling which will be readily grasped by young readers – the image of building a new world with the stones of humanity and care is complex enough for readers coming to understand how metaphor works. And Roberto faces enough racism and brutality to transmute the conventional excitements of an adventure story into something more substantial in its impact.

Like Roberto, the 16-year-old heroine of Tatiana Vassilieva's *Hostage to War* (1996) finds herself as a foreigner working for the German war effort in camps and factories. The author was born in Leningrad in 1928 and worked for the Germans as a captive labourer from 1942 to 1945, first on a farm, then for a printer and then in a munitions factory. This is another autobiographical account and it shares the oppressive bleakness which marks Livia Bitton-Jackson's story. The book's own journey is noteworthy in itself. It was published in Leningrad in 1990, and then in Germany in 1994 – presumably it could not have found a publisher before the Wall was torn down, since it is, in its final chapters, bitterly critical of the Soviet regime. Admirably translated into English by Anna Trenter in 1996, it is now an increasingly popular text in an educational edition in British schools. The author's decision – or that of her publisher – to direct this book to adolescent readers is well founded. Tania's story has much of the appeal of *Anne Frank's Diary* in that the central character is, like her readers, awakening to new experiences and ideas. The harshness of her circumstances is obviously quite unlike that of her adolescent readers; but there may well be a sense of constriction, a will to break free, a wish to be more than circumstances allow, which at a psychological level readers, male as well as female, will readily recognize.

The narrative begins in Wyritza, some 60 kilometres from Leningrad, where Tania's family has rented a dacha. Tania is not strong and her doctor believes it would be good for her to live away from the city for a year. Ironically, Tania's physical strength is soon tested to its extreme. Within months, the Germans have arrived, the dacha is burned, and the family is subsisting on gruel made from grated birch wood. Her father dying, her younger sister desperately ill, her mother helpless and broken, Tania sets off through the snow, dragging a sledge, to find food further south in the corn-growing villages. The hazards of that journey – five days in each direction, meeting hostile soldiers, peasants starving like herself, corpses by the roadside, a community dying of typhus – are themselves powerful and moving, but they serve merely as a prelude to Tania's transportation to Germany to work a 12-hour day in the fields. Soon too exhausted to eat or drink the meagre rations, she is sent to a factory in a town.

Like Livia Bitton-Jackson, Tatiana Vassilieva adopts a diary format. Again, the tense used is the dramatic present. Clearly, the notion that a girl in a constant state of exhaustion and hunger would spend her evenings writing up her diary would be a literary device too far, but the author's solution is neatly plausible. Before the Panzer tanks roll down the Siwersker Highway outside the dacha, Tania buys a notebook which she calls her 'Diary of Happy Days' in which she plans 'to record every good thing that ever happens to me'. That resolution soon proves impossible, and the 'entries' Tania makes after her transportation are written to her mother in her imagination – a means of keeping alive the hope of reunion, and allowing us a dual focus upon her thoughts alongside the daily events she endures. The structure gives a sense of day-to-day engagement and an uncertainty about what tomorrow may bring.

Tania's life as a conscripted labourer is often lived alongside German civilians, some of whom show genuine kindness to her, putting themselves at risk. There are few glimpses of the stereotypical German soldier. Civilians are themselves close to starvation; a couple with sons on the Russian front at Leningrad feel a particular closeness to Tania, especially when one boy is killed and the other wounded; and the Allied bombs destroy much of the town. Here, friends among her fellow conscripts – including a first love – are made and lost as they are moved about by the authorities; the coincidences and reunions of fiction are not available to the writer of autobiography.

Tania's experience of war on the Eastern front may provide new insights for Western readers more familiar with stories of the war as it impinged upon their own countries. Such readers may also be surprised by the section of the book which follows Tania's liberation by American forces. She is adrift in a devastated Germany, with no one to feed her, no one to give her the means to make the long journey home. With the impulsive courage she has shown throughout the narrative, she decides to leap aboard a train, not knowing where it is going, rather than remain where she is. That train actually heads west, away from her home, to Belgium, where she is treated warmly and urged to stay by the family who take her in. But her home, and the possibility of finding her own family, are in the East. She sets off but is held for almost a year in a bureaucratic web in East Germany. When she finally reaches Wyritza, she finds her mother living in a tiny hut, her sister barely alive. As Tania tries to pick up a life, determined to make a living to provide for her mother and sister, she finds that returned captive labourers are not welcome; a friend who has also survived experiences similar to her own in the labour camps tells her:

> Most of us who were taken to Germany as slave labour were taken away again after we had returned home. We weren't even allowed to see our relatives. But this time we were transported to a Soviet camp, for tree-felling. Even prisoners-of-war had to go there, and they had already suffered enough torment in German captivity. Do you know what they call us now? 'Traitors.' Can you imagine that? 'Traitors!'

With characteristic persistence and a dash of sheer impertinence, Tania makes her way through the hostile officialdom of the communist regime to teacher training college and ultimate qualification.

So intense is the suffering which permeates the four texts so far discussed in this section that it seems improbable that the camps should have featured in a format usually associated with younger children, the picture book. *Let the Celebrations Begin!* (1991) (text by Margaret Wild, illustrations by Julie Vivas) was first published in Australia, and evidently grew from a sentence in Gwen White's *Antique Toys and Their Background* (1971):

> A small collection of stuffed toys has been preserved which were made by Polish women in Belsen for the first children's party held after the liberation.

As in *Rose Blanche* and *Passage to Freedom*, the illustrator offers us a memorable image in which the wide eyes of a group of prisoners in the camp gaze out at us. Now, however, there are no barriers between us and them, for our perspective is that of the unseen liberating soldiers. The figures here are thin rather than skeletal, the faces are rounded rather than gaunt, the clothes are in contrasting gentle pastels. The hair may be cropped to a fuzzy halo, as they look at their deliverers and at us, but there are tentative smiles and these eyes are daring to be hopeful.

The story is told by Miriam, who may be 10 or 12 years old, for she remembers her home before the war, and she and the women in the hut are

> planning a party, a very special party ... when the soldiers come to set us free – and they are coming soon, everyone says so! – they will open the gates. And for dinner we will cook chickens – chickens for everyone! – and each child in the hut will get a toy. A toy of their own.

Wild and Vivas tell the story of the making of the toys with gentle humour. The hunger and death which were inescapably present in Bitton-Jackson's account are mentioned but held at a distance. Against the objection that such omissions are bound to distort could be levelled the view that for young children, with whom this book could readily be shared, it is necessary to make choices of emphasis in the realities which are offered. Some would suggest, even in this extreme case, that children need to celebrate the human spirit's will to nurture and to create which can survive and even thrive under the most extreme pressures. The text and images leave enough space for the questions a child might choose to ask of the sharing adult: why were these people imprisoned? who are they? and, what do *these* words mean?

> David peeps at the soldiers through his mama's old black shawl, and the soldiers stare back at us, oh, so strangely, making soft noises in their throats. They seem afraid to touch us – it's as if they think we might break.

Julie Vivas' huts, on the first page of this intriguing and ambitious picture book, stand neatly side by side upon an almost lawn-like surface, their pleasantly shaded wooden walls in good condition, much like elongated garden sheds. Figures move around them in what could be sociable groups, and we see the camp as from a bird's-eye view – over the top of the wire.

The huts which Roberto Innocenti's Rose Blanche discovers in the forest a little way outside her town are altogether more forbidding – uniform and threatening in muddy browns and greens, with corrugated iron roofs, broken glass or wire mesh in the frames, and in the background some windowless blocks with ominous chimneys.

Rose Blanche is an extraordinary book by any criteria. In their valuable bibliographical resource *War and Peace in Children's Books* (2000) Carol Fox and her colleagues describe the book as a 'picture storybook for older children' and suggest a readership age of 10 plus. They would probably agree that the 'plus' could include adults of any age (the book stuns groups of undergraduates, for example) much like Raymond Briggs' *The Tin Pot Foreign General and The Old Iron Woman* (1984) and *When the Wind Blows* (1982).

The illustrations have accompanied two different texts. The original story by Christophe Gallaz was written in Italian and used as the basis for the award-winning American translation. In this text, Rose Blanche tells her own story until the moment of her death, when an impersonal narrator takes over. A third person narrative voice is employed throughout Ian McEwan's expanded British version.

The story opens with the arrival of German troops *en route* to the Eastern front, welcomed by the residents of a small town. Children wave, the fresh-faced soldiers smile, a bandsman with a brass instrument greets the passing troops, the mayor beams across the bustling sunlit square and Rose Blanche stands with her mother, a small swastika flag in her hand. Only the red of the flags contrasts with the dull greens and greys of uniforms and military vehicles. Against this festive mood, McEwan's text begins:

> When wars begin people often cheer. The sadness comes later . . .
> Rose Blanche was shivering with excitement. But her mother said
> it was cold. Winter was coming.

The words confirm what the cover of the book has already foreshadowed. Here, a thin-faced, anxious Rose draws aside a tattered net curtain to peer out of a window. In its reflection, we see exhausted, wounded German soldiers slumped across a gun carriage, splashes of blood on their bandaged heads. The intense blue of Rose Blanche's eyes as she stares out at the scene – and perhaps beyond with her mind's eye – is emphasized against the dull, weary colours of the rest of the illustration.

Greys, greens and browns predominate throughout the book as Rose's life is jolted out of the secure rhythms of her home in the little town. One day, a closed lorry – one of many trundling through the cobbled streets – breaks down as Rose Blanche is close at hand on her way home from school. ('Some said they were going to a place just outside the town.') A small boy escapes from the lorry, is recaptured at gun-point and thrown back among the pale-faced figures crouched inside. Rose follows the lorry through a town already showing signs of wartime disrepair. Finally, climbing 'under fences and barriers in places she wasn't meant to go' she finds herself in a clearing, confronting the image of the caged Jewish prisoners with which we began this chapter.

Day by day, despite the deprivations the war inflicts upon her family and the town, Rose Blanche takes food to the prisoners. The defeated soldiers return, the townspeople flee the oncoming Soviet Army, but Rose will not go – she still takes whatever food she can find out to the camp. As the story nears its end, she stands in the fog-shrouded clearing where the trees are laid waste and the caterpillar tracks of a tank show how the wire of the concentration camp has been smashed through:

> Behind her were figures moving through the fog. Tired and fearful soldiers saw danger everywhere.

A flame knifes through the mist towards Rose from the gun of a soldier – is he retreating German or advancing Russian? A final double-page spread returns us to the scene of Rose Blanche's death. It is a clear, bright day, with blue skies and trees in leaf. Creepers in bloom wind among the barbed wire, and splashes of red poppies spread across the meadows, marking the deaths of those who were enslaved here. A blue flower Rose Blanche had been holding in her hand remains, long dead and caught on the wire. The concluding words of the text are 'Spring had triumphed'; but the image of the flower on the rusting wire is repeated as an isolated detail on the final wordless page of the book, now with winter tears of water, or even ice, on the leaf tips and the barbs, standing as an epitaph to the girl.

There is an element of autobiography in this book too, for Innocenti notes on the back cover:

> I wanted to illustrate how a child experiences war without really understanding it. I was a little child when the war passed in front of my door [near Florence] ... My father did not want to answer my questions, but I knew that something terrible was happening ... In this book, fascism is a day-to-day reality. Only the victims and the little girl have known its real face.

Rose Blanche's clear-sighted logic and sense of compassion may provide points of entry for the young reader of this seemingly overwhelming book. In illustration after illustration, Rose Blanche's bright colours – the red of her ribbon and her dress, the transparent purity of her skin, the blue of her eyes – isolate her against the sombre uniforms of the soldiers, the decaying town and the bleak concentration camp. Innocenti named his heroine 'Rose Blanche' which might suggest a mingling of blood and innocence; but Innocenti tells us that his heroine was so named to honour the group of young Germans who, to their cost, protested against the war. Only as we re-read might we wonder whether the red of her ribbon and the flags anticipated the death we never see on the page.

In Hiding

Anne Frank's Diary, first published in Holland in 1947 and in an English translation in 1952 (*The Diary of a Young Girl*), must be the best-known account in Western schools of experiences of the war on the European mainland. Anne's description of her family's life in hiding in the upper floors of an old building in Amsterdam is so well known as to need no retelling here. Teachers of English, history and social studies have all judged that the diary provides a poignant introduction to the sufferings of the Jews in the Holocaust, and indeed there are many elements which account for the powerful impact the diary has made on young readers for almost 50 years, most of which stem from Anne's personality as much as from her predicament.

Anne's ambition was to become a writer and even in her teenage years, she captures the tensions between herself, her family, the irritable Van Daans and the fussy middle-aged Mr Dussel, with whom Anne has to share a room. Above all, however, adolescent readers may be drawn by the acute self-awareness with which Anne examines her own feelings and behaviour:

> I have one outstanding character trait that must be obvious to anyone who's known me for any length of time: I have a great deal of self-knowledge. In everything I do, I can watch myself as if I were a stranger. I can stand across from the everyday Anne and, without being biased or making excuses, watch what she's doing, both the good and the bad. This self-awareness never leaves me, and every time I open my mouth, I think, 'You should have said that differently,' or 'That's fine the way it is.'[2]

Anne knows she is, by turns, a wilful, innocent, even ignorant girl and an attractive, intelligent, emerging woman. She longs for the love and admiration of her parents while protesting that they cannot understand her. She is powerfully drawn to the awkward Peter Van Daan, three years older than herself, even while she coolly recognizes the limitations of his mind, a coarseness in the grain.

Her perceptions and feelings must have seemed familiar enough to many of the diary's teenage readers in the 1950s and 1960s, as they still seem to be in the present day, though today's adolescent would be reading 'the Definitive Edition' of the diary published in 1991 (English translation 1995), edited by Anne's father Otto and Mirjam Pressler. This version is more explicit than the 1952 edition about Anne's sense of her developing sexuality and her feelings for Peter Van Daan, and it also preserves more of Anne's critical comments on some of those who shared the cramped annexe with her, including her own mother. Anne receives her diary for her 13th birthday in June 1942, before the family has gone into hiding. She confides to her diary that she intends to make frequent entries, for reasons her readers will recognize:

> I want to write, but more than that, I want to bring out all the kinds of things that lie buried deep in my heart … And now I come to the root of the matter, the reason for my starting a diary; it is that I have no real friend.

She tries to clarify her sense of being alone. She knows her parents love her, that she loves them, she has aunts and uncles, a good home. She knows boys find her attractive but

> I can never bring myself to talk of anything outside the common round. We don't seem to be able to get any closer, that is the root of the trouble. Perhaps I lack confidence, but anyway, there it is, a stubborn fact and I don't seem to be able to do anything about it.

Anne's instinctive and writerly decision is to claim her diary as her friend. She even gives her new confidante a name, so that each entry begins, 'Dear Kitty … ', a practice she continues through to the last entry, for Tuesday, 1 August 1944. Three days later, armed German Security Police and Dutch Nazis raided the building and all the occupants of the 'Secret Annexe' began their journeys to the death camps. The diary was found among a pile of old newspapers by two of the Dutch women who had helped the Franks to survive in the annexe, and was eventually given, unread, to Anne's father Otto, the sole survivor of those who had hidden in the annexe. Anne herself died in Bergen-Belsen in March 1945.

The diary chronicles the daily lives of the hidden families but their confinement inevitably means that few events occur to interest either Anne or indeed her readers. The fascination of the book lies in Anne's inner life, her sense of awakening, her perceptions of the others confined to the annexe, her realization of her own growth and power as a woman and as a writer, even in these circumstances (or possibly because of them). She understands her own writing processes without inhibiting them:

> I am the best and sharpest critic of my own work. I know myself what is and what is not well written. Anyone who doesn't write doesn't know how wonderful it is ...

As far as the diary is concerned, given its intimacy, it would seem she was its *only* critic. Her teachers were the adored father who wrote himself and loved to talk about literature and ideas, and the supply of books which Dutch friends smuggled into the annexe.

Her relationship with her mother was far more ambivalent, partly because she was honest enough to admit that her love for her father was unqualified, while she could not help but notice her mother's 'untidiness, her sarcasm, and her lack of sweetness'; though at other times her mother, sister and Anne combine in opposition to the selfish and even devious Mr and Mrs Van Daan. A year after the family has gone into hiding, the 14-year-old Anne feels her love for her mother has died; and a year later she writes, with clear-sighted self-confidence:

> I am becoming still more independent of my parents, young as I am, I face life with more courage than Mummy; my feeling for justice is immovable, and truer than hers. I know what I want, I have a goal, an opinion, I have a religion and love [for Peter Van Daan]. Let me be myself and then I am satisfied. I know that I'm a woman, a woman with inward strength and plenty of courage.

The appeal of the book for young readers mainly lies, then, in the development into maturity of an exceptional girl – her growth as a woman and as a writer, her honest, almost merciless observation of individuals and their interactions, only occasionally tempered by humour and possibly heightened through the narrow focus brought about by her incarceration in the Secret Annexe; and, tragically, the poignancy lent to all of this by the knowledge, which many readers will have before they open the book, that such talent was cut brutally short in Bergen-Belsen.

Anne Frank's Diary is the favourite book of Jacob Todd, the central character of Aidan Chambers' *Postcards from No Man's Land* (1999). It is easy to see why, for Jacob – in his late teens – is also acutely aware, responsive to people, to places and to situations; and since we see much of the narrative from Jacob's perspective, our reading of events is filtered through his perceptions. *Postcards from No Man's Land* is not a war novel in any conventional sense. In fact, it breaks several different kinds of convention and was an adventurous but wholly justifiable choice as the Carnegie Medal winner in 2000.

At a structural level, it shares something with the novels of Rachel Anderson, Robert Westall and Bernard Ashley discussed in Chapter 1 (see pp. 49–52). As in those novels, there are dual, interplaying narratives – one set in a warzone, the other in a peacetime city. What happened in the context of war shapes what develops in the other part of the narrative. Here, however, there is the extra dimension of time, for what happens to Jacob Todd in the ill-conceived Arnhem offensive of 1944 influences the experiences of his grandson and namesake in present-day Amsterdam.

The younger Jacob has come to Holland to visit his grandfather's grave in the battle cemetery at Oosterbeek, where the annual memorial service is being held. His days in Amsterdam are crowded with incident; a meeting with a girl he fancies who turns out to be male, a mugging, an encounter with a calm, wise older woman, a visit to Anne Frank's house – and, at the service, he meets a girl to whom, for the first time, he 'could open his secret self'. He also meets the dying Geertrui, who is the link between the two narratives for she nursed and fell in love with the wounded paratrooper who was Jacob's grandfather.

The significance of the war lies not so much in the historical events of Arnhem, but in what kinds of behaviour and thinking the circumstance of war liberated. For the older Jacob and Geertrui, this was a time out of time, where past and future seemed irrelevant and conventions and other commitments lost their hold. It was a time when people gave themselves to each other in an assertion of love against the danger and senselessness around them.

Geertrui tells the narrative of 1944 in the first person – in what, we realize, is an account she has written for the younger Jacob, for there are revelations to be told and decisions to be made about what to do with new information. All of the younger Jacob's heightened experiences in Amsterdam, and what he learns from Geertrui's life and her imminent death, work upon him – for he is in a situation which holds parallels to that of his grandfather. He is in an enclosed capsule of time, in a foreign country, a different culture, in a city whose openness is at once risky and exciting, meeting experiences he has never met before. As with his grandfather, circumstances allow him to become more than the self he knew in England.

Chambers is a wonderfully inventive, exploratory writer, and has been so for more than a quarter of a century. *Postcards from No Man's Land* is the fifth in a series of novels, often employing postmodern techniques, which catch adolescent characters at points where they are discovering something important about themselves. They are demanding, and absolutely uncondescending towards their readers:

> I will not compromise on language or content. At 15 people can handle the same language as me, they're just as complicated as me, and are very interested in thinking about important questions for the first time.[3]

This is a substantial book in every sense. Here the reader must handle the narratives, told over 336 pages, from different perspectives and in different registers, encounter different genres (for excerpts of writing by Arnhem veterans are inserted between the dual narratives), manage a vocabulary which is occasionally perverse in its difficulty, and live alongside the younger Jacob's anxiety and confusion. The reader also needs to be sensitive to a number of literary allusions, including a Ben Jonson poem whose ideas are central to the plot. Finally, readers may need to ask, with Jacob, how much of what he has learned of his grandfather's life should he share when he gets home – especially with the grandmother whom he loves more than any other relative. So, is the truth sometimes better left unsaid, even if that leaves a burden to be carried? What happens when the old conventions of young Jacob's life resume on his return home? And, for that matter, if Ben Jonson is right that 'in short measures life may perfect be', where does that leave the rest of Jacob's life when he gets back from Amsterdam? And perhaps, by extension, what questions does that ask of the reader's life?

Aidan Chambers says he receives letters from teenagers telling him of their relief at finding a book where characters of their age are shown thinking intensely. Somehow, Chambers still has access to the painful edge of adolescent restlessness and the unique excitement of those years around 14 to 17.

The Ghetto

For all its strengths, as a means of introducing the experience of the Holocaust and its repercussions across Europe *Anne Frank's Diary* offers a less illuminating account than the texts discussed earlier in this chapter. As a study in the resilience of a child in virtual captivity, it is matched by Uri Orlev's *The Island on Bird Street* (1984) and Christa Laird's *Shadow of the Wall* (1989).

The Island on Bird Street was translated from the Hebrew by Hillel Halkin, and published in the USA two years after its appearance in Israel in 1981; the first British edition was in 1984. Orlev himself was a child of the Warsaw ghetto. He chooses to set his story in an 'imaginary city' in Poland, perhaps to give more freedom to his plot, but his introduction makes it clear that the experiences of his hero Alex are informed by his own childhood:

> And I can remember how once on my way to 'school', which was really only a little room with three students and one teacher, a man snatched a sandwich bag right out of my hands and swallowed the paper and the string together with the sandwich. It baffled me how he managed to get down the string – the paper was one thing, but *string*? And then two well-dressed men came along and gave him a beating because he had stolen food from a well-dressed child . . . And there were birthdays and toy shops and a bakery that belonged to an aunt of mine who gave me a pastry every day. There was a boy who lay for a long time on the pavement outside her shop until he died.

The child-like perspective implied by the chapter titles reminds us that Alex is still very young: 'The Pistol Really Shoots', 'The Nicest Day' or 'I'm Hungry, But So Are They'. The register of the language throughout may be that of a child in its simplicity, but the content is harsh.

Orlev remembers also the decision to send large groups of the inhabitants of the ghetto 'far away'. At the time, those remaining had no certain knowledge of the nature of the destinations. A sense of threat is established in the first chapter as Alex is trained to use his father's Beretta pistol; his mother, visiting a friend in another ghetto across the city, has never returned. Within another two chapters, the Germans and the Polish Jewish policemen sweep through the houses, and Alex, his father and their friend Old Boruch are caught and herded towards the railway for a 'selection'.

His father is taken, but Old Boruch engineers Alex's escape, at the cost of his own life. As Alex makes a run for a ruined house and the refuge of a secret cellar, Boruch gives him a knapsack containing the pistol, and tells Alex that he must wait for his father at an abandoned house in Bird Street, on the edge of the ghetto.

Where Anne Frank grew rapidly to intellectual and emotional maturity through confinement, Alex quickly becomes streetwise through the daily need to survive on his own resources. At several points during the narrative Alex recognizes that he has become a man, despite the absence of a beard and his unbroken voice. His growth is brought about through exciting incidents and dangerous encounters which should make easier reading for many readers than the self-discoveries of *Anne Frank's Diary*. Alex's need for secrecy means that

Orlev can allow him only occasional contact and conversation with others, though his pet mouse Snow does provide company and, occasionally, a silent audience. Those people he meets are on the run themselves, and it is in saving two of the resistance fighters after an unsuccessful ghetto uprising that Alex shoots his father's pistol. A German soldier laughs sadistically as he is about to kill the wounded escapees. Alex fires at him:

> He still had a look of surprise on his face when he spun around and fell. The rifle dropped slowly from his hands. He dropped to the ground slowly too, like a rag doll. His body shuddered slightly once or twice, as though trying to finish its laugh.

Alex takes the men with him to his lofty hideout, accessible only by an ingenious arrangement of rope ladders which Alex has devised. By this stage, in his resilience and ability to survive, Alex is the equal of the adult partisans.

From his eyrie high in a ruined house, Alex can look out at the street beyond the ghetto, much as on a play set. He comes to know the characters in the street below as they go about their relatively normal lives outside the ghetto walls – a perspective which heightens the reader's understanding of the painful juxtaposition of deprivation and civilization the ghettoes created. Eventually, with a recklessness born of familiarity, Alex makes regular forays beyond the ghetto, plays football with boys in the park, has an encounter with a street bully, and enjoys a friendship with a first girlfriend, Stashya, whom he has watched daily doing her homework across the street from his window in Bird Street. To his astonishment, it emerges that she too is Jewish. Even more dangerously, Alex fetches a doctor from outside the ghetto to extract a bullet from the chest of his wounded partisan friend, Henryk.

Throughout, Alex resists the attempts of others to persuade him to leave his hiding-place and, perhaps, to join the partisans operating from the forests outside the city. His faith is finally justified for his father does return. Having escaped the Germans and joined the partisans himself, Alex's father comes back to Bird Street to visit what he thinks must be the site of his son's death. Only then – when he actually sees his father – does Alex realize that he had ceased to believe that his father would ever come, though he had never allowed the doubt to come to the surface of his mind.

The notion of creating your own small space, of making do with very little, of escaping detection or threat, of managing without adult support, is of basic appeal to young readers, but there is little romance about Orlev's story, for all its excitement. Christa Laird's *Shadow of the Wall* is also set in Poland, but this time in the Warsaw Ghetto itself, and many of its characters are drawn from real life. The book's central narrative focuses upon Doctor Janusz Korczak, 'a teacher, scientist, writer of classic children's stories and plays, fund-raiser, commentator on social welfare, physician, educational theorist and, in the 1930s, a much loved radio broadcaster on matters relating to children'. Born in 1878, Korczak initially worked as a paediatrician, but from 1911 he took over his first orphanage and dedicated himself to working with homeless and destitute children, regardless of race. Jewish himself, the home he is running at the outset of *Shadow of the Wall* is in the ghetto; the rules he devised for its management share something of the practical idealism of A. S. Neill's Summerhill, or the work of the Steiner schools in the favellas of Sao Paolo. A Children's Court sat to maintain justice within the orphanage, and no member of staff ever struck a child. Life for these destitute children included the performance of their own plays and concerts, and the publication of the weekly *Orphanage Gazette*.

Korczak was selfless in his attempts to feed, clothe and educate his children and, as the novel makes clear, he had the gift of the rare teacher who saw far below the surface behaviour of the orphaned boys and girls of the ghetto to the pain and sense of betrayal beneath. On 6 August 1942, the Nazis marched Korczak and his children out of the ghetto to the compound by the railway sidings, the Umschlagplatz, prior to their transfer to the death camps – the same route taken by Wladyslaw Szpilman and his family in *The Pianist* (1999) which able readers will find makes interesting parallel reading to this novel and *The Island on Bird Street*. Realizing that Korczak might become a martyr and a focus for resistance, the Germans offered him a letter of last-minute reprieve. Not for the first time Korczak refused the offer, and led his children into the waggons. Details of his death are not known, but it seems certain that he and his young charges were among the 10,000 people exterminated in Treblinka on the day of their deportation.

The life of 'Mister Doctor' and the orphanage is seen from the perspective of Misha, a 13-year-old whom Korczak has accepted into the orphans' home with his sister, since their mother is too ill to care for them. Like Uri Orlev's Alex, Misha learns how to work the ghetto streets, risking his life to find food for his mother and the orphanage.

Misha is something of a writer, and hence we are able to see one of Mister Doctor's institutions in action, the weekly gazette. Misha is also elected to the panel of the Children's Court, convened on one occasion to pass judgement on Musik who had been charged with bullying. The belligerent Musik had been abandoned by his terrified mother, and after discussion, Musik is not condemned but ordered by the court to find an older child to be his supervisor during a probationary period. A Postscript to the novel notes that, like many of the other child characters, Musik is drawn from life – in this case, a boy abandoned by his destitute mother who worked in a brothel for German officers.

There are violent scenes in this short novel. It opens with a shooting and Misha eventually joins the underground, but its interest lies more in Misha's tenderness towards his dying mother, in the daily life of the orphans' home, and the character and fate of Doctor Korczak. To a degree, there is a sense that the author's research constrains the flow of the narrative, since she is determined to provide a full picture of life in the orphanage. But the historical facts do yield the unforgettably courageous moment as the children, Misha's sister among them, march out to their transports led by the 64-year-old doctor, with Musik defiantly carrying the orphanage flag, the blue and white Star of David. Misha, who has moved out of the home to work with the resistance, 'simply watched as all that was dear and familiar to him quite literally marched out of his life for ever'.

Dunkirk

As Winston Churchill said to the House on 4 June 1940, 'Wars are not won by evacuations'; but the rescue of some 340,000 men from the Dunkirk beaches played a crucial part in the Allies' capacity to continue the war and in stiffening the sinews of a nation. 'Operation Dynamo' had begun on 26 May and Churchill's speech marked its completion.

John Masefield, the Poet Laureate, wrote:

> Through the long time the story will be told,
>   Long centuries of praise on English lips,
>   Of courage godlike and of hearts of gold
> Off Dunquerque beaches in the little ships.
>
> (from *To the Seaman*, 1940)

A recent retelling of the Dunkirk evacuation includes this verse on its dedication page. The picture book, *The Little Ships* (1997, text by Louise Borden, illustrations by Michael Foreman) recounts the story through the words of the young girl whose father is a Deal fisherman; her own brother, John, is trapped 45 miles away on the French beaches. Louise Borden's text avoids the declamation of Masefield's verse, preferring an understatement more acceptable to our own times. The words are organized in blank verse, maintaining a quiet rhythm which echoes the determination of those engaged in the operation:

> That afternoon we sailed for Dunkirk.
> Dad didn't have much time for talk.
> He kept his words in his hands,
> stowing a rope ladder
> and checking the engine gears.
> And he kept his words in his eyes,
> reading the Channel charts and maps,
> scanning the sky, thick with clouds.
> My father wasn't famous,
> but he knew about the sea and the tides and the currents
> and how to steer clear of the Goodwin Sands.

The pauses dictated by the patterning of the lines and the measured rhythms of the language suggest that this event is out of the ordinary, and that it deserves a uniqueness in the telling. The line length varies to reflect its content:

> I listened to the low throb
> of the *Lucy*'s engine.
> Hour after hour.
> Mile after mile.
> Steady engine.
> Steady friend.

The words are printed against a sand-brown background or, when the illustrations extend to fill both landscape pages, are superimposed upon Foreman's muted watercolours. The misty tones of the morning light contrast with the violence and danger which we know lies across the Channel as the civilians – a postman, a locksmith, a teacher – sign up to join the operation. Foreman takes our vantage point down among the spray and the waves as the fishing smack *Lucy* sets out with the narrator crewing for her father. They pass a returning warship, a khaki line of soldiers crowding its decks, its shadowy bulk filling almost all of the landscape illustration:

> They made a silent parade.
> Not grand.
> Just uniform brown
> and battleship grey.

When the *Lucy* arrives off the French beaches, the illustration extends across the double page, emphasizing the length of the winding lines of soldiers leading to the chains of small vessels ferrying troops out to the larger transports lying off shore. On the next pages, again filling the double landscape pages, young readers hunting among the detail of the illustrations will find panic-stricken horses racing along the beach, medical orderlies tending wounded soldiers, corpses slumped by craters, diving Stukas, exploding ships and burned-out aircraft. Later, from a closer viewpoint, an exhausted man is hauled on board clutching a wild-eyed dog, while another cradles a caged cockatoo:

> I had to rub the sting from my eyes,
> not from tears, but from the black smoke.
> And I couldn't look for more than a second
> at a soldier who cried for me to give him water,
> who had no bandages,
> just blood all down his front.

In each picture, sometimes foregrounded but sometimes taking her place among the flotilla of small ships, the gallant *Lucy* with her father-and-daughter crew goes about her work.

At one level the clear intent of the book is to inform, even to educate; here again, as with the Holocaust, is a story which must be told to every generation. The text is preceded by a note from a veteran skipper who took the author with him on one of the 'pilgrimages' made every five years by surviving boats from the Dunkirk evacuation. The story is followed by brief factual information and an extract from Churchill's speech. This is memorable history teaching – a great event re-experienced through a child's narrative, extended by Foreman's haunting images. The final illustration brings us right alongside the *Lucy*, close enough to see the bullet holes punched through her name on the bows and her wooden gunwhales. The narrator's shadowed, exhausted eyes stare off the page to our right into a future she cannot know, though we do; the rescued dog she holds in her arms looks out directly at us; the rounded bullet holes are echoed in the shapes of the dog's alert brown eyes, its tongue out so that we can almost hear it panting, tired out yet somehow *ready for more*. Behind them arches a pale rainbow.

The Little Ships would tell its story readily enough to quite young children sharing the book with an adult, but it would also make its impact through the crafting of word and image, and the power of its content, upon much older readers. In practice, secondary students are more likely to encounter two prose fictions which find their climaxes in the Dunkirk evacuations: both have been classroom favourites for many years. Paul Gallico's *The Snow Goose* has been in print for more than 50 years, and Jill Paton Walsh's *The Dolphin Crossing*, first published in 1967, is still in print.

The Snow Goose was published in both the USA and Great Britain in 1941, the first major work of its American author who lived and worked in England during the late 1930s. It may well be that Gallico's book played its part in alerting his countrymen to Britain's beleaguered situation, as well as giving heart to British readers, for it rapidly became a best seller.

The novel is usually ignored by children's books critics – it appears on publishers' adult lists – but teachers have long known of its impact in the classroom. It is barely 40 pages long, and 'reads aloud' to adolescent groups quite superbly; the calm pacing of the prose draws together the growing love between two vulnerable people, the almost mystical bird of the title, and the story of Dunkirk. Gallico's opening sentences evoke a sense of the timeless:

> The Great Marsh lies on the Essex coast between the village of Chelmbury and the ancient Saxon oyster-fishing hamlet of Wickaeldroth. It is one of the last of the wild places of England, a low, far-reaching expanse of grass and reeds and half-submerged meadowlands ending in the great saltings and mud flats and tidal pools near the restless sea.

Gallico served in the US Navy in the First World War, and the shifting sea itself is one of the major players in this drama. Apart from a chorus of soldiers' voices after the evacuation, only two human characters populate his expansive stage: the girl Frith and the mis-shapen Philip Rhayader, 'a painter of birds and of nature, who, for reasons, had withdrawn from all human society'. Rhayader, in this elemental setting, and in Gallico's pared-down narrative, assumes a stature we might expect of a folk-tale hero:

> Physical deformity often breeds hatred of humanity in men. Rhayader did not hate; he loved very greatly, man, the animal kingdom, and all nature. His heart was filled with pity and understanding.

Young readers may well know, with Rhayader, that a love for animals does not expose the giver to rejection or ridicule, and often wins unconditional love in response. They may also empathize with the perspective of Gallico's other principal character who, at the outset of the story is no more than twelve, slender, dirty, nervous and timid as a bird, but beneath the grime as eerily beautiful as a marsh faery. She was pure Saxon, large-boned, fair, with a head to which her body was yet to grow, and deep-set, violet-coloured eyes.

Frith's idiom, with its roots deep in rural Britain, gives a sense that she is a part of this remote landscape. Given its brevity, its setting and the lean nature of its prose, *The Snow Goose* has indeed the feel of an old tale, an echo perhaps of *Beauty and the Beast*. The affection between Rhayader and Frith grows almost unnoticed as the man cares for the wounded goose which the girl brings to him. The healed bird flies off to its northern home as winter approaches and then returns, year by year, to Rhayader's lonely cottage on the marshes. Some seven years later, however, the bird chooses to spend the winter season in the enclosure, and Frith, by now nineteen, realizes that

> The spell the bird had girt about her was broken, [she] was suddenly conscious of the fact that she was frightened, and the things that frightened her were in Rhayader's eyes – the longing and the loneliness and the deep, welling, unspoken things that lay in and behind them as he turned them upon her …

Children's book publishers in recent years might well be unwilling to allow deformity to be central to the plot, and they might even be anxious about the power of the attraction described in the passage above. Such timidity would surely be misplaced. The love between Rhayader and Frith grows from a shared feeling for life itself, the bird, the marshes – and the men on the beaches, when their enclosed world is invaded by news from Dunkirk. Rhayader speaks of the men, 'huddled on the beaches like hunted birds, Frith, like the wounded and hunted birds we used to find and bring to sanctuary'. Frith, 'young, primitive, inarticulate' begs him not to go, or to take her with him, for she sees for the first time 'that he was no longer ugly or mis-shapen or grotesque, but very beautiful'. A place in the boat for her would mean one less for a soldier, though, and he will not take her. As Rhayader sets sail, the great snow goose rises and beats out to sea above the boat.

Rhayader does not come back, though returning soldiers testify to his bravery as he made trip after trip, ferrying troops to larger vessels off shore. He dies, machine-gunned, in his boat. The goose stays with the boat for a while, and legends swiftly gather about the bird (' "If you saw it, you were eventually saved. That sort of thing," ' say the soldiers.)

Frith waits, sensing Rhayader will not return, until one sunset, she hears the call of the snow goose:

> She came running to the sea wall and turned her eyes, not toward the distant Channel whence a sail might come, but in the sky from whose flaming arches plummeted the snow goose. Then the sight, the sound, and the solitude surrounding broke the dam within her and released the surging, overwhelming truth of her love, let it well forth in tears.

As the snow goose skims low, then spirals upwards for the last time, Frith sees only 'the soul of Rhayader taking farewell of her before departing for ever'. The story is of its time in its account of a transcendant love which remains untold and unfulfilled. Adult taste might find the book naively romantic or even melodramatic; but young readers, perhaps *because* it stands in contrast to much of contemporary culture, may well find in the tale an appealing idealism in the relationship between Frith and Rhayader, and a poignancy in the way in which war severs the temporal link between them, though their love seems finally beyond destruction.

Dunkirk provided the climax for at least three children's novels in the late 1960s and early 1970s: Hester Burton's *In Spite of All Terror* (1968) and Philip Turner's *Dunkirk Summer* (1973) and, more impressively, Jill Paton Walsh's *The Dolphin Crossing* (1967) which proved to be a consistent favourite in schools and is still in print.

The present-day reader has, in effect, a kind of double telescope through which to view events. Jill Paton Walsh's late 1960s perspective is imposed upon events of almost 30 years earlier. Her two main characters, John Aston and Pat Riley, would not normally have met in pre-war Britain. John comes from a secure middle-class family and would have been at boarding school but for the war. His father, a figure of distant authority, is away at sea in command of a tanker. Pat has been evacuated from the East End, and is living in a derelict railway carriage close to the Kent coast with a woman he thinks of as his mother, though she is not in fact a blood relative.

Both John and Pat are therefore outsiders to the local village boys. John is articulate and strong-principled, but ill-equipped to deal with the raucous lads who mock him about his conscientious objector brother. He is appalled by the conditions Pat and his mother are living in and offers them accommodation in a disused stable at his own home.

As John and Pat carry out the hard physical labour needed to make the stable habitable, they are drawn together in mutual respect, not least because Pat is far more practical than John; the dynamic of this unlikely friendship remains one of the sources of energy which drives the book, for the boys will have to depend upon one another in extreme circumstances. Working-class characters were still uncommon in children's fiction of the late sixties, though John Rowe Townsend, in both his criticism and his novels, pointed to the fact that the middle-class ambience of children's novels assumed a similar social grouping among readers. Thirty or more years after the publication of *The Dolphin Crossing*, Pat's sparky, honest Cockney resilience, John's condescending treatment of a boatman who has lost his nerve and dabbles in the black market, and the plucky resourcefulness of John's mother in the absence of her husband may seem close to stereotype. But the behaviour of the 1940s, especially during wartime, did conform to expected norms and in this sense the book provides readers with an interesting window on their grandparents' world.

The war casts a daily shadow over John's life. He studies for his university entrance exams with a tutor, but wishes he were old enough to fight; he follows the fortunes of the army closely through the newspapers and the wireless, plotting troop movements with flags on a map of Europe. Keeping track of events allows him to give Pat, and the reader, a clear account of the plight of the hard-pressed army. He and his mother listen eagerly to Churchill's great speech of defiance, offering nothing 'but blood, toil, tears and sweat' (' "Things will go better now," said Mrs Aston. "Your father thinks highly of Winston Churchill: he said he is a great man." '). Suddenly John's opportunity comes.

As the British Expeditionary Force is driven back towards the beaches, John sees the little boats gathering off the English coast. He needs Pat to help him take *Dolphin*, the family's small boat, across the Channel:

> 'But look, Pat, I can't let you in for this without warning you. We might get killed. In fact we'll probably get killed. Nobody will be defending us. It couldn't be a more dangerous thing to do. But England isn't short of boys like us; she is short of trained soldiers.'

John's tight-lipped courage is counterpointed by Pat's chirpy determination. Once the boys set off, the novel gathers pace. They join the fleet and make the crossing, though it takes a while for Pat to find his sea-legs. There is a painterly description of the orderly evacuation of the Dunkirk beaches, shattered by the swooping descent of 'a great swarm of black planes'. The description of the Stuka attacks is uncompromising:

> A line of fountain-like upward spurts of sand ran along the beach,

among the groups of helpless men. From the heart of each jet of
sand came a flash of fire, and clouds of thick black smoke. A man
with his body stiffly spreadeagled was thrown high in the air, and
shot backwards twenty yards from one of them.

Both boys are terrified among the flames and the screams of wounded
men, and the floating bodies which 'stained the froth on the waves
with faintly visible red streaks'. As John vomits over the side, 'the body
of a man with no face floated by, smelling of charred flesh'. Somehow,
the boys help each other through their terror and, mechanically at first,
make repeated trips to the beaches, bringing eight men at a time out to
the destroyer *Wakeful*. There is no great celebration of British grit or
affirmation of moral rectitude. As John's anger mounts against the
German pilots bombing and machine-gunning their helpless victims,
'he realised that our own pilots would do the same, if the positions of
the two armies were reversed'. In that moment, he can make sense for
the first time of his brother's stand as a conscientious objector.

Since Jill Paton Walsh was looking back to Dunkirk over more than
20 years, there is no propagandist need to strengthen the resolve of the
readers, to caricature the Satanic evil of the enemy. There is courage,
but no glamour, in the actions of the two boys and the soldiers they
attempt to rescue. Men are afraid, even cowardly; a private soldier has
to remind an officer that he has no right to a place in the boat until all
his men are on board first, but in this firestorm there is no shame in
fear. John is wounded when the *Dolphin* strikes a mine, though she is
not sunk, and Pat is able to remove a jagged piece of metal from John's
arm and dress the wound. A rabble of hysterical soldiers desperately
tries to board the little boat, almost capsizing her, so that Pat has to
beat the knuckles of the raiders until they let go. There are spats of
anger between the boys as Pat becomes obsessed with taking more and
more troops, regardless of the seaworthiness of the *Dolphin*.

As they are on their way home, they pass the hull of the *Wakeful*,
broken in two by a torpedo, taking with her the men the boys had
rescued. John's despair and frustration turn to fantasies of vicious
revenge towards the U-boat crew who have sunk the destroyer, but
even in his hatred he remembers his brother's words: '"You can only
kill a man if you hate him first. And it is always wicked to hate."' The
impossibility of the dilemma leaves John miserable in his confusion.

There are no resolutions to his thoughts, and there is no optimistic
conclusion to the novel itself. John and Pat get back safely, and John's
father, home on leave, is among those who welcome the boys. John is
deeply content to earn the respect of his father, to be treated as a man:

'You're a rascal, John,' said Captain Aston, pouring a [whisky] for John too, and handing it to him as though it were the most natural thing in the world … 'Who'd have a son?' he asked happily.

In the euphoria of the homecoming, however, Pat slips away and, inexperienced sailor though he is, he takes *Dolphin* out on his own, back to Dunkirk. John wonders if Pat believes his own father could still be stranded on the beaches – certainly he was consumed by the vision of the lines of waiting, desperate men. Ironically, Pat's father has been brought safely home on a warship but Pat fails to return.

Captain Aston mouths the conventional wisdom, but that is not enough for John. He is left with the anguish of loss as the book closes:

'You know,' [Captain Aston] said gravely, 'in a war there are always people who lose friends, or family. That's what war is like. But you have saved something too. Think of the men you saved.'

But John didn't even hear him; his thoughts were drowned, he couldn't think of saved men now.

Of the books discussed in this chapter, *The Dolphin Crossing* gives perhaps the most graphic account of the confusion and ruthlessness of war in its description of the action at Dunkirk. The contrast with popular literature – especially the comic books – produced during and ever since the war is self-evident. Those who are killed are not simply snuffed out like extras in a Hollywood epic; those who are wounded, suffer; and those who survive look forward to lives that are forever scarred. The *Wakeful* was sunk; and Pat's reckless sacrifice may well have been pointless.

Refugees

Ian Serraillier's *The Silver Sword* (1956) is an account, based on factual evidence, of the fortunes of a family of Polish children, Ruth, Edek and Bronia, who have survived the last years of the war on the Warsaw streets; their mother has disappeared and their father has been taken off to a concentration camp. Edek is caught by the Germans smuggling food and is taken to a labour camp in Germany. When the girls learn that their father has escaped and may have made his way to Switzerland, they determine to join him. As the fighting comes to an end, they set out on their dangerous journey across war-torn Europe, and are joined by Jan, a streetwise orphan whose resourcefulness helps the other children through a number of perilous encounters. They are fortuitously reunited with Edek, whose treatment by the Nazis leaves him weakened with tuberculosis, though, usefully, he has learned to speak German. Eventually the children are reunited with both their parents in Switzerland and Jan, much changed through his experiences, is adopted by the family.

Parents in the 1980s and 1990s may well have been surprised to find their children bringing home a class reader they had read in school themselves. Almost 50 years on from its publication, the novel's language, characterization and authorial stance seem dated in their self-conscious awareness of their audience. Serraillier's careful balancing of personalities in his little band of refugees might be compared with Ransome's composition of the Walker family in the *Swallows and Amazons* series or even Blyton's characterization of the Famous Five. Ruth, who is 17 when they set out, is 'brave, resourceful and unselfish' at all times, no matter how testing the circumstance. In the ruins of Warsaw, she manages to run a small school where she proves to be 'a born teacher'. She provides a mothering security for the others, including the wayward Jan. Only in the last pages of the book, when reunited with her parents and her role as surrogate mother has been played out, does her self-control waver. Her younger sister Bronia (only four when the story begins) is a dreamer – a talented artist, who drifts through the arduous journey without a tantrum, resting in Ruth's security. Edek is described by a British officer, writing home to his wife, as 'brave and intelligent and looks as if he had suffered a lot – he spent nearly two years slaving for the Nazis. You can see it in his face – a lad's face oughtn't to be creased and pinched like his.' (The letter serves as a handy device to give us an outsider's perspective on the family.) Edek's usefulness to Serraillier is partly to provide a contrast with Jan, an Artful Dodger of the Warsaw streets. He is a pickpocket, a shifty trickster, who entrusts his affection only to animals, such as a pet cockerel and a chimpanzee.

The children's adventures are never allowed the genuine edge of danger which Tania experienced, for example, as she searches for food for her family in the opening of *Hostage to War*. They are closer to the excitements and optimism of the family adventure story popular at the time Serraillier was writing. Much of the continuing appeal of the story depends upon Jan, for he is the source of many of the excitements and much of the humour of the plot. Through the escapades, and especially through Ruth's steadfast patience with him, Jan finally learns that humans may offer richer relationships than animals. At one point, he is torn between jumping into a boat with Ruth and Bronia, or running after Ludwig, a dog he has befriended. Ruth, as close to losing her patience as she ever becomes, tells him to run after the dog, since she and Bronia can manage on their own:

> It was a bitter moment for Jan. More than anything in the world
> he wanted to go after Ludwig. But Ruth's words had hurt him.
> They had stirred something deep down in his heart, and he
> hesitated. With a great effort of will he shed Ludwig from his
> mind and turned to his friends. In Ruth's face he saw what he had
> hardly noticed though they had long been there – courage, self-
> sacrifice and greatness of heart. He hesitated no longer. He had
> lost Ludwig, but he had not lost Ruth.

He jumps into the boat and 'in that moment of decision, Jan began to
grow up'. Where a present-day writer for young readers would embed
the notion of growing up in dialogue or action, Serraillier offers a direct
comment. For young readers of the 1950s, psychological insights were
made explicit.

Hardly surprisingly, the language of the book has dated also: 'all day
long the sun smiled down upon them; upon toilers in the fields where
the fresh crops were springing … '; or, 'a suspicion of a smile stole
across his face'. The children's high spirits are quickly restored, no
matter what adversities they have faced. With 750 miles to go to
Switzerland, with no resources and no realistic certainty of finding their
father, 'off they went, singing a gay song, with their heads in the air';
or, 'they all laughed so much that they nearly spilt the coffee'. The
dialogue sometimes lacks the idiom of actual speech: ' "We were on a
raft, floating downstream between wooded peaks" '. And an avuncular
authorial voice occasionally intervenes: 'And what of Jan, that
charming bundle of good intentions and atrocious deeds?'

However, critics at the time praised the book's 'fine, free, colloquial
prose with plenty of spirit and even gaiety', its 'restraint and economy'.
The Junior Bookshelf noted 'It is sometimes said that children should be
shielded from the harsh realities of life – a book like *The Silver Sword* is
sufficient refutation of such a doctrine' while the *Daily Telegraph*
reviewer was 'glad to find a happy ending to one of the most exciting
books I've read for a long while'.

For the adult reader today, the book's chief interest may lie in the
insights it provides into the conventions of a period when writers and
publishers were rather more certain about what children should be told
and how they should be told it. If it had been possible to conceive of an
adolescent culture of drugs and sexual relationships in 1956, it would
certainly *not* have been conceivable that a novel such as Melvyn
Burgess' *Junk*, which explores such a culture, would be rewarded by the
Carnegie Medal. (In 1956, the year of *The Silver Sword*'s publication,

the award was given to C. S. Lewis' *The Last Battle*, a novel which some present-day critics might find unacceptably harsh in its moral judgements.) *The Silver Sword*, however, has continued to be a popular class reader, and while teachers may be conservative in their choices, they do not go on using texts which are dismissed by their classes with hostility or apathy. The continuing popularity of apparently dated family adventure series, and even the traditional boarding school settings of the Harry Potter books, suggest that young readers are still attracted by the notion of closely-knit groups of children depending upon each other, without adult support. When those children have clearly delineated, predictable characteristics, readers find it easier to impose themselves upon – or empathize with – such characters, to see themselves behaving as they do. More complex, unique characters may not evoke the engaged empathy which is the hallmark of engrossed reading in childhood. The archaisms of the language may concern young readers less than they trouble the adults reading over their shoulders; and what Serraillier's novel did, and possibly still does, is to make the suffering of refugees accessible to readers when filtered through the literary restraints of the time.

By contrast, Michael Morpurgo's central characters in *Waiting for Anya*, published 35 years later in 1990, are caught up directly in the senseless cruelties of war. His drama is played out among the mountains of the High Pyrenees by reluctant participants. The German soldiers in Lescun are there to guard the frontiers, to prevent escaping Allied servicemen and Jewish refugees from crossing into Spain. In the barn of the Widow Horcada – the last stop for escaping travellers on an underground railway through France – a party of Jewish children has gathered, waiting for the moment when they can slip across the border to Spain. They are cared for by Benjamin, the Widow's Jewish son-in-law, who has already taken many Jewish children over the mountains to safety by the smugglers' paths. Benjamin waits at the farm for his own child, Anya, from whom he was separated when German planes strafed a column of refugees heading south near Poitiers; Anya's mother had died in giving birth to her. The story's central character, 12-year-old Jo, stumbles across Benjamin and his secret work when the two share an encounter with a bear cub in the forest.

Most of the Germans posted to Lescun are older men, no longer fit for the fighting front; they are sharply distinguished from the black-uniformed SS who execute two men from a neighbouring village. Some are veterans of World War I. Almost against his will, Jo develops a friendship with a German corporal, Wilhelm, a mountain man himself from Bavaria. Both are bird lovers, and as they rest on a trip to watch a pair of eagles, their conversation turns to the futility of war. The German has recently learned that his grown-up daughter has been killed in an Allied bombing raid on Berlin; tentatively, Jo tells him how sorry all the villagers were to hear of the death:

> 'If there has to be a war,' [Wilhelm] said, 'then it should be fought between soldiers, that I can understand. I do not like it, but I can understand it. At Verdun it was one soldier in a uniform against another soldier in another uniform. What have women and children to do with the fighting of wars, tell me that? Every day since I hear about my daughter, every day I ask myself many questions and I try to answer them. It is not so easy. What are we doing here, Wilhelm, I ask myself? Answer: I'm guarding the Frontier. Question: why? Answer: to stop people escaping. Question: why do they want to escape? Answer: because they are in fear of their lives. Question: who are these people? Answer: Frenchmen who do not want to be taken to work in Germany, maybe a few prisoners-of-war escaping, and Jews. Question: who is it that threatens the lives of Jews? Answer: we do. Question: why? Answer: there is no answer. Question: and when they are captured, what happens? Answer: concentration camp. Question: and then? Answer: no answer, not because there is no answer, Jo, but because we are frightened to know the answer.'

The Pyrenean landscape is populated by wild boar, eagles, vultures and a few bears; and by shepherds who spend the summer months high in the pastures tending and milking their flocks and herds, making their cheeses. The rhythms of the natural world, and the affinity with those rhythms of the mountain people, contrast sharply with the cruelties and triviality of the German regime in which the soldiers themselves are unwilling pawns.

Morpurgo's war has its casualties. Jo's father is sent home from prisoner-of-war camp, wounded in spirit as well as in body. Not all the Jews make their escape. Leah, a Polish girl, refuses to be parted from Benjamin at the border, and they are captured by a German patrol as they return. They are despatched to Auschwitz. And there is the engaging Hubert, who 'had the mind of a child and could only speak a few recognisable words'; even as the Germans leave Lescun as the war turns against them, Hubert is shot.

The cruel futility of this corner of the war is epitomized by these three deaths. In time, Jo leaves school and becomes a shepherd himself. One summer Sunday afternoon, high in the mountains where he is caring for his herd, his family bring a stranger up with them to visit him in his hut. It is Anya.

Many of the book's considerable satisfactions lie in its dangerous excitement, for in this story readers sense that characters may well not make it to the last page. The strand of adventure involving the escape of the Jewish children draws increasingly taut, and the annual transhumance provides a fine set-piece climax to the novel as the villagers drive the animals up to the summer meadows. As a means of getting them out of the village and into the mountains undetected by the German garrison, the Jewish children mingle among the locals. There is a particularly tense episode when Wilhelm is sent on duty to the area where the Jewish children are in hiding in a shepherd's hut. As a mountain man himself, Wilhelm knows that women and children would not normally be needed to drive the animals up to their summer grazing and he suspects that there may well be escapees in the hut. Faced with the conflicting demands of duty and humanity, Wilhelm chooses the latter.

The characterization of the villagers confirms some widespread British perceptions of the French, without descending to stereotypes. Children's books too rarely employ adult characters who are thoroughly alive, open to excitement, to fear, who are capable of change. Here there is an independence of spirit about the people of the village, especially Jo's Grandpère, whose fierce hatred for war derives from his own experience in the Great War; now, through the events of this story, Grandpère decides that 40 years ago he really ought to have married the woman who has become Widow Horcada, and puts his mistake right before the end of the book. There is Monsieur Audap, the austere schoolmaster, whose care for his children is balanced by his love of scholarship; Father Lasalle, the village priest who organizes an interminable organ recital so that the Jewish children can make their way out of hiding (the polite Germans are a captive audience – the priest is playing Bach); and Armand Jollet, the entrepreneurial grocer who believes he ought to be compensated for loss of earnings when he closes his shop on the day of the transhumance. Above all, however, lies the enduring quality of the life of a Pyrenean mountain village contrasted with the ephemeral, but lethal, triviality of warfare.

Lois Lowry's *Number the Stars* (1989) also tells a story of Jews fleeing the German invaders. This time the setting is Denmark. The book's origins lie in the stories told the author by a friend who was herself a child in Copenhagen during the German occupation, and episodes are drawn directly from those stories. King Christian rides his horse alone through his occupied capital each morning, greeting his people. A rabbi, secretly warned by a high-ranking German official, tells his congregation that German plans to 'relocate' the Jews are about to be implemented. Almost the entire Jewish population of Denmark – some seven thousand people – was smuggled in small boats across the sea to Sweden by Danish fishermen. German tracker dogs were thrown off the scent of the hidden Jews by handkerchiefs impregnated with a powder concocted by Swedish scientists and given to Danish skippers – and such a handkerchief is central to the plot of *Number the Stars*. The escape by fishing-boat of a party of Jews provides the climax to this novel.

Lois Lowry's impulse for this book, like so many of those discussed in this chapter, is to inform and also to inspire her readers. In an Afterword, she writes, 'Surely . . . the gift of a world of human decency is the one that all countries hunger for still. I hope that this story of Denmark, and its people, will remind us all that such a world is possible.'

The novel won the Newbery Medal in 1990. It has been much translated and reprinted. It is short (137 pages) and language, characterization and plot structure present few complexities. Ten-year-old Annemarie lives with her parents and her sister Kirsti in the city. Her older sister Lise has died in an accident two weeks before her wedding; her fiancé, Peter, still calls frequently on the parents. Annemarie's best friend, Ellen Rosen, is Jewish and Annemarie's parents take Ellen in, at great danger to themselves, when Ellen's parents flee before the Germans implement their relocation programme. The escape of the Rosen family, along with other Jews, is engineered by Peter and Annemarie's Uncle Henrik, captain of a small fishing boat. Annemarie plays a crucial part in the escape, as she carries the all-important impregnated handkerchief through a patrol of German soldiers to her uncle.

Although the brave Peter dies (he and Lise were members of the Resistance and Lise's death had been no accident), his capture and execution are merely reported in a concluding chapter which is not integral to the plot. The novel certainly tells a story of heroism, though it has few of the harsh edges of other novels discussed in this chapter describing the plight of the Jews. In part, the lack of tension springs from the historical success of the Danish rescue operation. But there may also be a sense that the research and the stories told to the author have dictated the plot, limiting the freedoms of fiction.

The book's strengths are that it tells a little-known story of bravery and some excitement in terms quite young readers will grasp. The narrative viewpoint remains consistently close to Annemarie's perspective, making the story particularly accessible to the younger reader, and its moral stance is clear-cut and simply expressed. After the episode of the handkerchief and the German patrol, Uncle Henrik praises Annemarie for her bravery, despite her protest that she didn't really stop to consider the risks:

> 'That's all that *brave* means – not thinking about the dangers. Just thinking about what you must do.'

On Active Service

Geoffrey Trease's *The Arpino Assignment* appeared in 1988, some 54 years and more than 100 books after he published *Bows Against the Barons* (1934). The novel, set behind enemy lines in Italy, carries several of the characteristic hallmarks of a novelist whose work remained sensitive to changing mores without losing its integrity. Whether he was writing about Shakespeare's theatre, classical Athens or the fall of Ceauşescu in Bucharest, Trease's work was always closely but unobtrusively researched; and although he was keen to inform, he never fell into didacticism. Well into his nineties, Trease remained insatiably curious and his curiosity was infectious. Here it was the activities of Churchill's Special Operations Executive (SOE) and particularly their equipment, which intrigued him:

> The more I learnt about it, the more enchanted I became by its inventiveness and ingenuity: the fountain pens that spurted tear gas in emergencies, the tiny compasses concealed in fly buttons, the plastic explosives that looked like horse-droppings when scattered on the mountain road in the path of the pursuing enemy.

In fact this novel did not have an entirely untroubled birth; Trease's meticulous concern for accuracy is reflected in an anecdote recorded in *Farewell the Hills* (1998), the privately printed final volume of his autobiography:

> In the first fifty years of my professional career I had known only the minimum of editorial interference. Now I found myself in a world where editors felt it was their role to polish and improve the raw material of the author's manuscript. Things must seem right to them. I had armed my British parachutists with 'pistols'. To [my editor], the word suggested only highwaymen of long ago. I explained that 'pistol' was the official word for the weapon of these SOE agents. My regular army major would not say 'gun',

because that would suggest a piece of heavy artillery. Trivial? To an author his choice of words is not trivial.

Trease was an intrepid traveller in Europe, where all his novels are set. He resolved never to set a novel in a country he had not visited, and with his wife and young daughter he explored European byways long before the tourist industry distanced the traveller from the events and customs of the local population. His favourite destination was Italy, and Rick Weston, the hero of *The Arpino Assignment*, shares with his author a detailed knowledge of a region of that country.

Rick's mother, who died just before the war, was Italian. His father was an Oxford University lecturer in ancient history who had spent a series of summers, with his family, excavating a Roman villa near the hill village of Sant'Arpino. It is now 1943, and Rick is old enough to be doing his basic training in the Army. He is suddenly summoned from square-bashing to London. His local knowledge and fluent Italian are needed by the SOE.

Within 20 pages, Trease has parachuted Rick into the Italian countryside, along with the taciturn but experienced SOE officer, Major Blair, and their Welsh wireless operator. The resistance story which unfolds is consistently exciting – trains are blown up, prisoners-of-war liberated, and for once in recent children's literature there is actual combat:

> The Sten jerked and trembled in [Rick's] hands, spitting vicious death. The guards went down, whether hit or taking cover he could not tell.

The cruelty of the occupying Germans is balanced by the ruthlessness of the tough guerrilla communist leader, Rossi, a veteran of the Spanish Civil War. (Trease gave a more human face to Oberleutnant Fischer in *Tomorrow Is a Stranger* [1987] set in occupied Guernsey.) Here, there is also torture and humiliation. The victim is Lina, the 15-year-old village girl with whom Rick falls in love, despite regulations forbidding entanglements with the locals. Trease's heroines, no matter in what era, have been of a type. They are active, independent and witty; courageous and reliable in adventures, without sacrificing their femininity. Rick glimpses Lina with her 'long dark hair swinging across her shoulders' and within a couple of pages Rick (and the wireless operator) cannot help but notice her 'mischievous eyes', 'what good legs she had' and how 'lightly and confidently she moved' on her bare feet. Lina is tied to a chair for many hours, bitterly ashamed that she cannot prevent her need to urinate, though she remains silent and undaunted by the Gestapo's interrogation. Trease makes sure her torturers are duly punished as she is rescued by Rick and the Italian resistance:

> The door crashed open. She could not see who stood there. She saw only the absurd amazement on the pink face of the Gestapo man and then, as some automatic weapon sputtered over her shoulder, the spreading gush of blood, like the flowering of some ghastly crimson orchid across his chest.

Although Trease does not flinch from such detail, he once observed that 'It's not the splitting of skulls with battle axes that inspires me, it's the opening of minds in a gentler sense.'[4] There is plenty of action and excitement in the story, and Trease, as he always does, hurries his readers along to the next adventure, alongside a continuing interest in character. Rick's encounter with Lina is a revelation to him, but at the same time he is learning about the nature of war and the duty it requires of him. There is courage, coolness under fire, a deepening respect between comrades-in-arms of differing backgrounds and beliefs. But there is none of the jingoism or the assumption of British superiority of *Greenmantle* or *Biggles Defies the Swastika* (two other stories set behind enemy lines).

Trease is like both Buchan and W. E. Johns, however, in using adults on active service as his main characters. In our selections for this chapter, this is the only novel where this is so. The belief, conscious or otherwise, among authors and publishers that young readers want to read exclusively about young central characters is surely fallacious. Their appetite for comic books, adult novels and films about, for example, SAS men in the Gulf War or the invasion of the Normandy beaches, demonstrates this. Many young readers *are* fascinated by active combat, whether adults like it or not. *The Arpino Assignment* shows how violent conflict can be managed without indulgence, and it seems unfortunate that more novelists writing for children have not explored the war through adult characters.

Notes

1. *The Impossible Legacy* (1999), p. 161, Gillian Lathey's excellent discussion of autobiographical children's literature set in the Third Reich and the Second World War.
2. This quotation is taken from the expanded edition of the book, *The Diary of a Young Girl: The Definitive Edition* (1995). All other quotations from the diary are taken from the 1947 edition, translated into English in 1952 (see Bibliography).
3. In 'Reading habits for real lives' by Nicholas Tucker in *The Independent*, 8 July 2000, marking the award of the Carnegie Medal.
4. From 'The historical novelist at work', p. 41 in *Writers, Critics, and Children* (ed. Geoff Fox *et al.*) (1976).

Afterword

A sustained period of reading literature for children about war has been, for us, a powerful experience in itself. Wilfred Owen famously wrote, 'My subject is War, and the pity of War. The Poetry is in the pity ... All a poet can do today is warn. That is why the true Poets must be truthful.' Very many of the authors whose work has moved us as we have prepared this book would undoubtedly echo his words, and extend them to include their own forms of writing or illustration. They share a passionate belief that children must be made aware of the evils of the past and the courage with which that evil has often been met; and also that young readers need narratives which explore the nature and experience of war if they are to make sense of the world they have inherited and the future they confront.

A story from the former Yugoslavia illustrates the commitment of those concerned with children, books and war. Even during the fighting, publishing houses in Bosnia and Croatia managed to produce stories for children in comics and paperbacks, and many of the stories were about the war that was going on around their readers. One such publisher, Muhamed Sarajlic, saw his offices in Sarajevo razed to the ground by Milosevic's soldiers. As the invading army left the city, one of their last acts was to torch the publisher's warehouse, burning all the firm's stock of children's books. Such was the belief of Sarajlic and his colleagues in their business and in children's need for stories, that they rebuilt their offices and warehouse with their own hands. Within two years of the departure of the Serbs, and with some help from publishers in other countries, Sarajlic's list for Bosnian children included more than 20 new titles.

Bibliography

Anderson, R. (1984) *The War Orphan*. Oxford: Oxford University Press.

Anon (1943) *Boo-Boo the Barrage Balloon*. London: Raphael Tuck.

Anon (1961) *Battler Britton*. London: Fleetway Publications.

Anon (n.d.) *I Flew with Braddock*. Dundee: D. C. Thomson.

Ashley, B. (1999) *Little Soldier*. London: Orchard Books.

Auer, M. (1992) *The Blue Boy*. Illustrated by S. Klages. London: Gollancz.

Barker, P. (1991) *Regeneration*. London: Viking.

Bawden, N. (1973) *Carrie's War*. London: Gollancz.

Bell, E. M. (1944) *Chippity Cuckoo*. London: Lutterworth Press.

Bennett, R. (ed.) (1939) *The First War-Time Christmas Book*. London: London University Press.

Bitton-Jackson, L. (1999) *I Have Lived a Thousand Years*. London: Simon & Schuster.

Borden, L. (1997) *The Little Ships*. Illustrated by M. Foreman. London: Pavilion.

Brent-Dyer, E. (1940) *The Chalet School in Exile*. Edinburgh: W. & R. Chambers.

Brent-Dyer, E. (1941) *The Chalet School Goes to It*. Edinburgh: W. & R. Chambers.

Brereton, F. S. (n.d.) *At Grips with the Turk*. London: Blackie.

Breslin, T. (1995) *A Homecoming for Kezzie*. London: Methuen.

Briggs, R. (1980) *Gentleman Jim*. London: Hamish Hamilton.

Briggs, R. (1982) *When the Wind Blows*. London: Hamish Hamilton.

Briggs, R. (1984) *The Tin-Pot Foreign General and the Old Iron Woman*. London: Hamish Hamilton.

Briggs, R. (1998) *Ethel and Ernest*. London: Jonathan Cape.

Bruce, D. F. (1943) *Toby at Tibbs Cross*. London: Oxford University Press.

Buchan, J. (1915) *The Thirty Nine Steps*. London: Nelson.

Buchan, J. (1916) *Greenmantle*. London: Nelson.

Burgess, M. (1996) *Junk*. London: Andersen Press.

Burroughs, D. (n.d.) *Teddy, The Little Refugee Mouse*. London: Hutchinson.

Burton, H. (1968) *In Spite of all Terror*. London: Oxford University Press.

Cadogan, M. and Craig, P. (1978) *Women and Children First: The Fiction of Two World Wars*. London: Gollancz.

Cadogan, M. (1988) *Frank Richards: The Chap Behind the Chums*. London: Viking.

Cadogan, M. (1990) *The William Companion*. London: Macmillan.

Chambers, A. (1999) *Postcards from No Man's Land*. London: Bodley Head.

Childers, E. (1903) *The Riddle of the Sands*. London: Dent.

Conlon-McKenna, M. (1995) *Safe Harbour*. Dublin: O'Brien Press.

Crompton, R. (1938) *William the Dictator*. London: Newnes.

Crompton, R. (1939) *William and A.R.P.* London: Newnes.

Cullingford, C. (1998) *Children's Literature and its Effects*. London: Cassell.

Custer, C. (1914) 'The human shields', in *The Dreadnought and War Pictorial* (10 December). London: Fleetway.

Darke, M. (1990) *A Rose from Blighty*. London: Collins.

De Jong, M. (1956) *The House of Sixty Fathers*. London: Lutterworth Press.

de Groen, E. (1997) *No Roof in Bosnia*. Barnstaple: Spindlewood.

Dickinson, P. (1990) *AK*. London: Gollancz.

Dronfield, J. (ed.) (2000) *Burning Blue*. London: Headline Feature.

Dyer, W. A. (1915) *Pierrot, Dog of Belgium*. London: Duckworth.

Eco, U. and Carmi, C. (1989) *The Bomb and the General*. London: Secker & Warburg.

Edwards, O. D. (2000) 'The Battle of Britain and children's literature', in J. Dronfield (ed.) *Burning Blue*. London: Headline Feature.

Eldridge, J. (1999) *Tank Attack*. London: Puffin.

Eve, M. (2000) 'From better little books to Baby Puffins', in *Children's Literature in Education* Vol. 31, No. 2. New York: Kluwer Academic.

Faulks, S. (1993) *Birdsong*. London: Hutchinson.

Filipovic, Z. (1994) *Zlata's Diary*. London: Viking.

Fine, A. (1996) *The Tulip Touch*. London: Hamish Hamilton.

Fisher, M. (1986) *The Bright Face of Danger: An Exploration of the Adventure Story*. London: Hodder & Stoughton.

Foreman, M. (1967) *The Two Giants*. Leicester: Brockhampton.

Foreman, M. (1974) *War and Peas*. London: Hamish Hamilton.

Foreman, M. (1989) *War Boy*. London: Pavilion.

Foreman, M. (1989) *War Game*. London: Pavilion.

Fox, C. et al. (2000) *War and Peace in Children's Books*. Brighton: Brighton University.

Fox, G. et al. (eds) (1976) *Writers, Critics and Children*. London: Heinemann Educational.

Frank, A. (1952) *The Diary of a Young Girl*. London: Vallentine, Mitchell.

Frank, A. (1995) *The Diary of a Young Girl: The Definitive Edition*. O. H. Frank and M. Pressler (eds). New York: Doubleday.

Frank, R. (1931; English translation 1986) *No Hero for the Kaiser*. New York: Lothrop, Lee & Shepard.

Gallico, P. (1941) *The Snow Goose*. London: Michael Joseph.

Gifford, D. (1988) *Comics at War*. London: Hawk Books.

Gilson, G. (n.d.) *A Motor Scout in Flanders*. London: Blackie.

Grahame-White, C. and Harper, H. (1915) *Heroes of the Flying Corps*. London: Oxford University Press.

Granfield, L. and Wilson, J. (1995) *In Flanders Field: The Story of the Poem by John McCrae*. London: Gollancz.

Green, M. (1980) *Deeds of Adventure, Deeds of Empire*. London: Routledge & Kegan Paul.

Greene, B. (1973) *Summer of My German Soldier*. New York: Dial.

Gutman, C. (1991) *The Empty House*. Stroud: Turton and Chambers.

Harris, R. E. (1987) *The Beckoning Hills*. London: Julia MacRae Books.

Harris, R. E. (1986) *The Silent Shore*. London: Julia MacRae Books.

Harris, R. E. (1989) *The Dividing Sea*. London: Julia MacRae Books.

Harris, R. E. (1994) *Beyond the Orchid House*. London: Julia MacRae Books.

Hart, F. (n.d.) *Animals at War*. London: Blackie.

Hasek, J. (1921; English translation 1939) *The Good Soldier Schweik*. Harmondsworth: Penguin.

Hazard, P. (1944) *Books, Children and Men*. Boston: Horn Book.

Holm, A. (1965) *I Am David*. London: Methuen.

Hughes, S. (1998) *The Lion and the Unicorn*. London: Bodley Head.

Hunt, P. (1995) *Children's Literature: An Illustrated History*. Oxford: Oxford University Press.

Innocenti, R. (1985) *Rose Blanche*. London: Jonathan Cape.

Johns, W. E. (1932) 'Affaire de Coeur', in *The Camels Are Coming*. London: John Hamilton.

Johns, W. E. (1935) *Biggles Learns to Fly*. London: Boys' Friend Library.

Johns, W. E. (1941) *Biggles Defies the Swastika*. London: Oxford University Press.

Johns, W. E. (1941) *Worrals of the W.A.A.F.* London: Lutterworth Press.

Johns, W. E. (1945) *Worrals of the Islands*. London: Hodder & Stoughton.

Johns, W. E. (n.d.) *Biggles of the Camel Squadron*. London: Dean & Son.

Johns, W. E. (1960) *Biggles Looks Back*. London: Hodder & Stoughton.

Johns, W. E. (1995) *Worrals z W.A.A.F.* Brno: Nakladatelstvi Navrat.

Johns, W. E. (2000) *Biggles A Tajmeny Vetrelec*. Prague: T & M.

Laird, C. (1989) *Shadow of the Wall*. London: Julia MacRae Books.

Lathey, G. (1999) *The Impossible Legacy*. Bern: Peter Lang.

Le Queux, W. (1906) *The Invasion of 1910*. London: The Daily Mail.

Lea, J. (1918) *Brave Boys and Girls in Wartime*. London: Blackie.

Lepman, J. (1969) *A Bridge of Children's Books*. London: Brockhampton.

Lewis, C. S. (1956) *The Last Battle*. London: Bodley Head.

Lingard, J. (1980) *The File on Fräulein Berg*. London: Julia MacRae Books.

Lively, P. (1975) *Going Back*. London: Heinemann.

Lofts, W. O. G. and Adley, D. J. (1970) *The Men behind Boys' Fiction*. London: Howard Baker.

Lowry, L. (1989) *Number the Stars*. Boston: Houghton Mifflin.

Magorian, M. (1988) *Goodnight, Mister Tom*. London: Kestrel Books.

Magorian, M. (1991) *A Little Love Song*. London: Methuen.

Maruki, T. (1983) *The Hiroshima Story*. London: A & C Black.

Mochizuki, K. (1997) *Passage to Freedom: The Sugihara Story*. Illustrated by Dom Lee. New York: Lee and Low Books.

Morpurgo, M. (1982) *War Horse*. London: Kaye & Ward.

Morpurgo, M. (1990) *Waiting for Anya*. London: Heinemann.

Morpurgo, M. (1977) *Friend or Foe*. London: Macmillan.

Napoli, D. J. (1999) *Stones in Water*. Oxford: Oxford University Press.

Newbery, L. (1988) *Some Other War*. London: Collins.

Newbery, L. (1991) *The Kind Ghosts*. London: Collins.

Newbery, L. (1992) *The Wearing of the Green*. London: Collins.

Newbery, L. (1995) *The Shouting Wind*. London: Collins.

Newbolt, Sir H. (1893) 'Vitai Lampada', reprinted in M. R. Turner (1967) *Parlour Poetry*. London: Michael Joseph.

Nimmo, J. (1999) *The Rinaldi Ring*. London: Egmont.

O'Brien, R. (1975) *Z for Zachariah*. London: Gollancz.

Orlev, U. (1984) *The Island on Bird Street*. London: Hutchinson.

Orwell, G. (1940) 'Boys' weeklies', in *Critical Essays*. London: Secker and Warburg.

Pardoe, M. (1939) *Four Plus Bunkle*. London: Routledge and Kegan Paul.

Parker, P. (1987) *The Old Lie*. London: Constable.

Paton Walsh, J. (1967) *The Dolphin Crossing*. London: Macmillan.

Paton Walsh, J. (1969) *Fireweed*. London: Macmillan.

Pausewang, G. (1996) *The Final Journey*. London: Viking.

Pearson, K. (1989) *The Sky Is Falling*. Toronto: Penguin Books.

Pearson, K. (1991) *Looking at the Moon*. Toronto: Penguin Books.

Pearson, K. (1993) *The Lights Go On Again*. Toronto: Penguin Books.

Popov, N. (1996) *Why?* New York: North-South Books.

Raymond, E. (1922) *Tell England*. London: Cassell.

Raymond, E. (1968) *The Story of My Days*. London: Cassell.

Rees, D. (1978) *The Exeter Blitz*. London: Hamish Hamilton.

Remarque, E. (1929) *All Quiet on the Western Front*. London: Putnam.

Richards, F. (1940) 'The Nazi spy's secret', in *Magnet* (5 November). London: Amalgamated Press.

Richards, J. (1988) *Happiest Days*. Manchester: Manchester University Press.

Richards, J. (ed.) (1989) *Imperialism and Juvenile Literature*. Manchester: Manchester University Press.

Richter, H. P. (1961, Germany; 1971, UK) *Friedrich*. London: Longman.

Richter, H. P. (1962, Germany; 1973, UK) *I Was There*. London: Longman.

Riordan, J. (1999) *The Prisoner*. Oxford: Oxford University Press.

Roberts, R. (1971) *The Classic Slum*. Manchester: Manchester University Press.

Rochester, G. E. (1933) 'The Poison Train', in *Modern Boy*. London: Amalgamated Press.

Rowe, A. (1990) *Voices of Danger*. London: Methuen.

Serraillier, I. (1956) *The Silver Sword*. London: Jonathan Cape.

Sims, S. and Clare, H. (2000) *The Encyclopaedia of Girls' School Stories*. Aldershot: Ashgate.

Stables, G. (1896) *How Jack Mackenzie Won His Epaulettes*. London: Nelson.

Stables, G. (1909) *From Slum to Quarterdeck*. London: The Religious Tract Society.

Strang, H. (1912) *The Air Scout: A Story of National Defence*. London: Henry Frowde and Hodder & Stoughton.

Swindells, R. (1984) *Brother in the Land*. Oxford: Oxford University Press.

Szpilman, W. (1999) *The Pianist*. London: Gollancz.

Taylor, A. J. P. (1963) *The First World War: An Illustrated History*. London: Hamish Hamilton.

Townsend, J. R. (1990) *Written for Children*. London: Bodley Head.

Tozer, K. (1941) *Mumfie Marches On*. London: John Murray.

Travers, P. L. (1941) *I go by Sea, I go by Land*. London: Peter Davies.

Trease, G. (1934) *Bows against the Barons*. London: Lawrence.

Trease, G. (1987) *Tomorrow Is a Stranger*. London: Heinemann.

Trease, G. (1988) *The Arpino Assignment*. London: Walker Books.

Trease, G. (1998) *Farewell the Hills*. Privately published.

Tregellis, J. (1914) 'The mailed fist', in *The Boys' Friend* (19 September). London: Fleetway Publications.

Turner, P. (1973) *Dunkirk Summer*. London: Hamish Hamilton.

Vachell, H. (1905) *The Hill*. London: John Murray.

Vassilieva, T. (1996) *A Hostage to War*. London: Hamish Hamilton.

Voigt, C. (1988) *Tree by Leaf*. London: Collins.

Walker, R. (n.d.) *Deville McKeene: The Exploits of the Mystery Airman*. London: Partridge.

Walker, R. (n.d.) in *Stories of the Great War*. London: Aldine.

Warner, P. (1978) *The Best of Chums*. London: Cassell.

Watson, J. (1983) *Talking in Whispers*. London: Gollancz.

Watson, J. (1998) *Justice of the Dagger*. London: Puffin.

Westall, R. (1975) *The Machine-Gunners*. London: Macmillan.

Westall, R. (1989) *Blitzcat*. London: Macmillan.

Westall, R. (1990) *The Kingdom by the Sea*. London: Methuen.

Westall, R. (1992) *Gulf*. London: Methuen.

Westall, R. (1994) *Blitz*. London: Collins.

Westall, R. (1994) *Time of Fire*. London: Macmillan.

Westerman, P. (1919) *Winning His Wings: A Story of the R.A.F.* London: Blackie.

White, G. (1971) *Antique Toys and Their Background*. London: Batsford.

Wilcox, B. (1943) *Bunty of the Flying Squad*. London: Oxford University Press.

Wild, M. (1991) *Let the Celebrations Begin*. Illustrated by J. Vivas. London: The Bodley Head.

Wolff, V. E. (1998) *Bat 6*. New York: Scholastic.

Name Index

Subject Index